# BUILDING
# WOODEN
# MACHINES

**Gears** & **Gadgets** for the **Adventurous Woodworker**

**Alan** & **Gill Bridgewater**

### DEDICATION

We would like to dedicate this book to all the men and women of the past—inventors, engineers, clockmakers and the like—who spent countless hours in workshops making little machines and working models in wood. We all know about Leonardo da Vinci and his helicopter, and Stevenson and his loco, but who was it I wonder who made the first working model for, say, the first padlock? Or the first pair of roller skates?

### ACKNOWLEDGMENTS

We would like to thank all the manufacturers who have supplied us with the best of the best:

**Tim Effrem**, President, Wood Carvers Supply, P.O. Box 7500, Englewood, FL 34295-7500
*Wood Carving Tools*

**Jim Brewer**, Research and Marketing Manager, Freud, P.O. Box 7187, 218 Feld Ave., High Point, NC 27264
*Forstner Drill Bits*

**William Nelsen**, President, Foredom Electric, Bethel, CT 06801
*Power Tools*

**John P. Jodkin**, Vice President, Delta International Machinery Corp., 246 Alpha Dr., Pittsburgh, PA 15238-2985
*Band Saw*

**Nick Davidson**, Managing Director, Craft Supplies Ltd UK, The Mill, Millers Dale, Buxton, Derbyshire, SK17 8SN, UK
*Wood for Turning*

**Dawn Fretz**, Marketing Assistant, De-Sta-Co, P.O. Box 2800, Troy, MI 48007
*Clamps*

**Paragon Communications**, Evo-Stick, Common Road, Stafford, ST16 3EH, UK
*PVA Adhesive*

**Frank Cootz**, Public Relations, Ryobi America Corporation, 5201 Pearman Dairy Rd., Suite 1, P.O. Box 1207, Anderson, SC 29622-1207
*Thickness Planer*

Most of all, we would like to thank **Friedrich Wilhelm Emmerich** —E.C. Emmerich Planes, Herderstrabe 7, Remscheid, Germany— for his beautiful wooden planes. They are special! If you are looking to set yourself up with the best of all modern planes, then these are the ones to go for.

# Contents

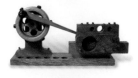

# Introduction

My grandpa used to tell my mother that I was one of those complicated sticky-fingered little boys who needed watching! He always used to say that I was up to tricks and learning. As I remember, all this meant, in effect, was that I was borrowing tools without permission, usually missing at meal times, and generally difficult to track down. It wasn't that I was in any way naughty or up to no good, but rather that I was always "inventing." I made a cross bow that was more a lethal man trap than a weapon, an electric alarm clock that couldn't be touched unless you were wearing rubber gloves, a lever mechanism for the gate that very nearly skinned and quartered the neighbor's cat, and so the list goes on. So you see, it wasn't that I was a horrible little boy bent on mischief, but only that I loved mechanisms and enjoyed working with tools and wood.

I was never so happy as when I was tucked away in the back shed hacking away with knife and saw on one or other of my labour saving inventions.

And of course, now that I am a man and fully grown, one of my chief pleasures is being out in my shed workshop dreaming up new mechanisms. But I'm not alone! The miraculous thing, the thing that makes our marriage so successful, is that my wife Gill is a soul mate, a true kindred spirit. We both get pleasure working with wood. Picture us if you will... out in our workshop, the radio humming away, our two dogs fast asleep in a couple of ancient armchairs, mugs of tea, both of us up to our armpits in a glorious miasma of tools, shavings, beeswax, wood and working drawings. Our shed workshop is a haven! And now that our two sons are out of the nest, it doesn't matter too much if we spend most of the night working. If we are tired but still willing, we simply settle down in the armchairs with a knife and whatever part needs sorting, and drift and dream away the hours. The incredible thing is that at the end of it all—after hour upon hour spent sawing, planing, gouging, turning, whittling and waxing—we get to make the most amazingly intricate machines and mechanisms.

Our ambitions involve sharing with you the pleasures of creating small machines and mechanical prototypes from wood. We want you to share in the fun. The projects are small, so you don't need a vast workshop full of tools or a fortune in wood; all you need is enthusiasm.

With each of the projects, we take you through all the wonderfully satisfying procedures of choosing the wood, setting out the designs, sawing, planing, drilling and all the rest. We give you working drawings and templates to explain how, why and what-with. There are drawings showing details, and there are photographs to explain the various step-by-step stages. We have done our best to describe all the procedures that go into making our working wooden wonders.

Each project draws inspiration from a specific mechanism. There are twenty-eight projects in all—all exciting, all dynamic, all beautiful and all made from wood.

## CONVERSION CHART

| TO CONVERT | TO | MULTIPLY BY |
|---|---|---|
| Inches | Centimeters | 2.54 |
| Centimeters | Inches | 0.4 |
| Feet | Centimeters | 30.5 |
| Centimeters | Feet | 0.03 |
| Yards | Meters | 0.9 |
| Meters | Yards | 1.1 |

**Note**

**All measurements are in inches, and the sizes allow for a generous amount of waste. The dimensions in the cutting lists are given in the order of thickness, width and length. As with any wooden sculpture, the dimensions indicated are starting points only. Modify dimensions, spacers and parts as necessary.**

# Circular Movement Machine

## PROJECT BACKGROUND

This machine is amazingly interesting in that it beautifully illustrates one of the key principles of horology. It shows how, in the context of a traditional grandfather-type clock, a pulley drum, length of cord and weight are able—like a coiled spring—to store up and provide energy.

The movement is handsomely direct and uncomplicated. As the weight falls at a constant rate, so the drum-and-beam flywheel spins at a uniform speed on its pivot. The fascinating thing is that the position of the pill-shaped weights on the beam dramatically alters the speed of spin.

To set the machine into motion, the cord is wound up with the crank handle, the two beam weights are adjusted so they are equidistant from the center of spin, and the bob weight is allowed to descend. If you have a yen to play around with beam weights, crank handles and pulley bob weights, and if you enjoy a good working mix of wood turning, fretting on the scroll saw and drilling, this might well be the project for you.

## PROJECT OVERVIEW

Have a look at the project picture (right), the working drawing (Fig 1-1A) and the templates (Fig 1-1B), and see that we have designed the machine so it can be easily positioned on the edge of a surface. The idea is that the machine can be located on a mantle shelf or the edge of a table in such a way that the bob weight can fall three or four feet lower than the base of the machine.

Although at first sight this project may look almost too simple to be true, I think it fair to warn you that turning the beam boss with its integral pulley wheel and spindle, plus turning, drilling and fitting out the long, sausage-shaped bob weight, are all procedures that call for a deal of patience and expertise. There are several points along the way that require delicate work if you are to avoid mess-ups. For example, the fit of the spindle needs to be just so—not too loose, not too tight. Also, the bob weight hole has to run straight and true. If the drill bit veers a little off-center, you have got a dowel with a gash in the side—not a pretty sight!

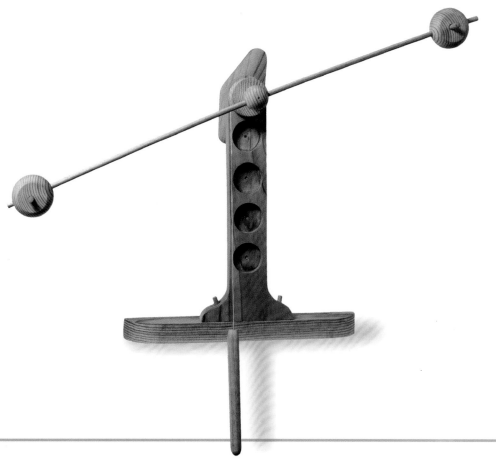

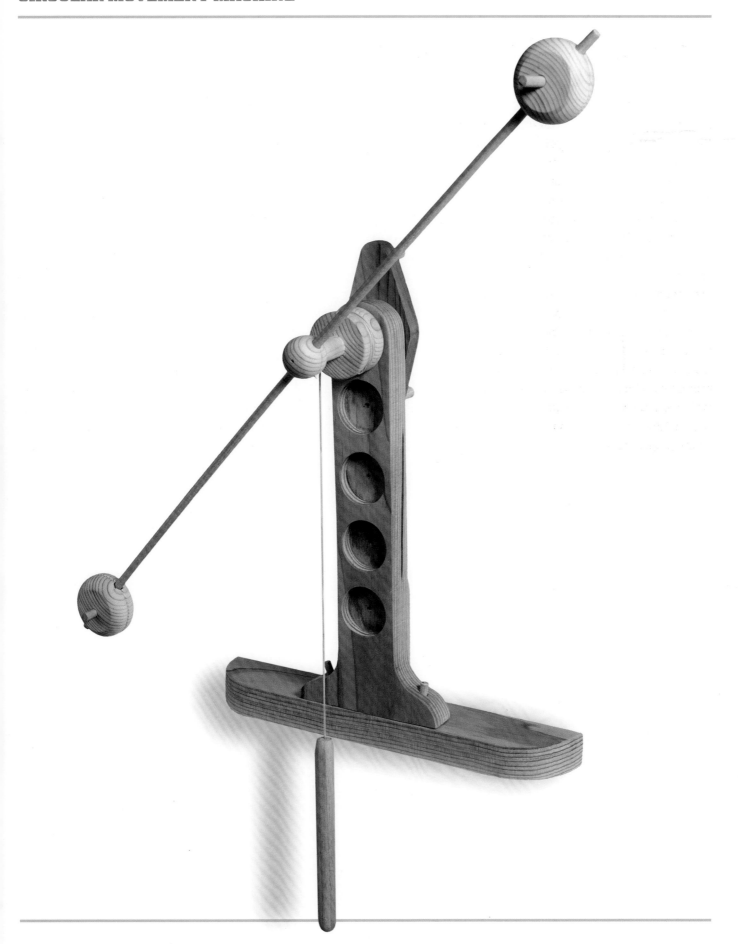

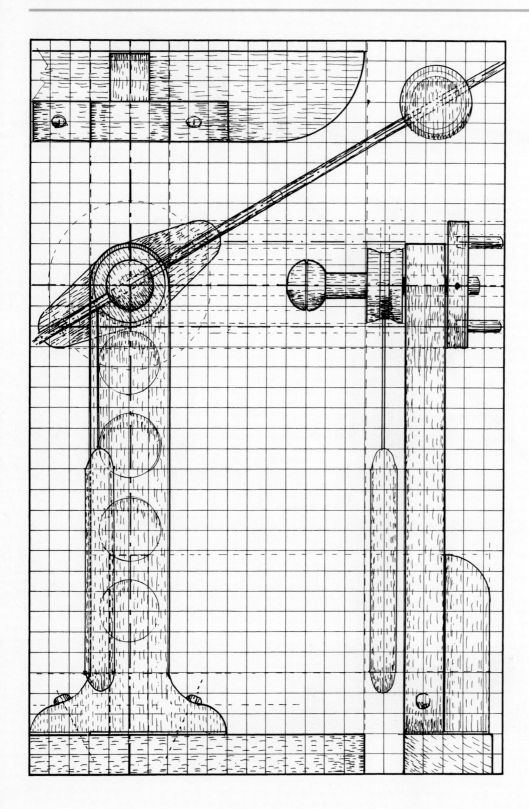

**FIGURE 1-1A**

At a grid scale of two squares to 1", the machine stands about 13" high and a little over 24" wide across the span of the beam rod.

# CIRCULAR MOVEMENT MACHINE TEMPLATES

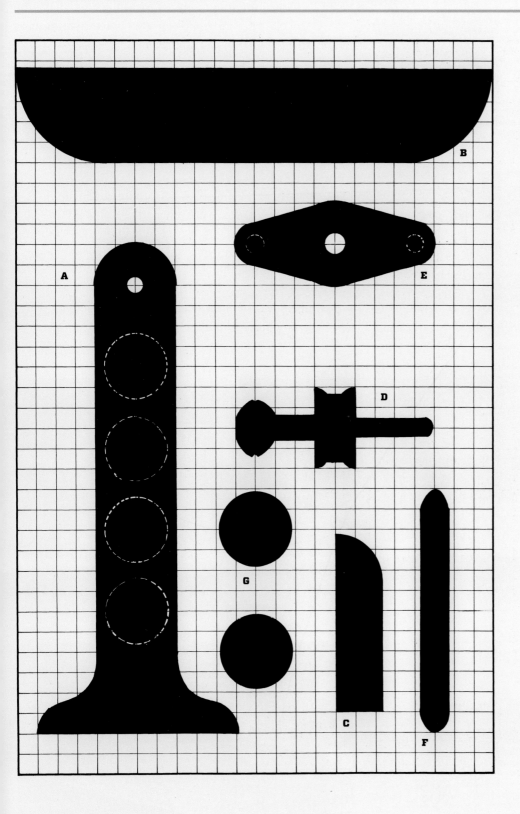

**FIGURE 1-1B**

**The scale is two grid squares to 1".**

**A** Stand.

**B** Base.

**C** Buttress support.

**D** Boss spindle drum, boss and shaft.

**E** Crank handle.

**F** Weight.

**G** Beam weights.

## CUTTING LIST

| | | |
|---|---|---|
| A | Stand | 1 × 5½ × 13½ pitch pine |
| B | Base | 1 × 2¼ × 12 pitch pine |
| C | Buttress support | 1 × 1¼ × 4¼ pitch pine |
| D | Boss spindle drum and flywheel cam disks | 2 × 2 × 12 pitch pine |
| E | Crank handle | 1 × 2 × 6 cedar |
| F | Weight | 6"—¾" pale wood dowel |
| G | Beam weights | 2 × 2 × 8 pine |
| | Beam | 24"—¼" dowel |
| | Handles, fixing pegs | White wood dowel pieces |

## CHOOSING YOUR WOOD

Although we went for pitch pine for the base, stand, buttress support and boss spindle, a length of off-the-shelf pale wood dowel for the weight, and odds and ends of various white wood dowel for the handles and fixing pegs, this is not to say you can't go for almost any wood that takes your fancy. There are two provisos: the bob weight is best made from a heavy, dense wood, while the boss spindle needs to be made from a wood that is straight grained and easy to turn. That said—and mindful that we all ought to be using nature-friendly, sustainable timbers—you could go for a variety like lime, jelutong or perhaps even beech. My overall thinking is that if the wood is easy to work, not too expensive, free from knots, splits, warps and stains, and from a reputable source, it's the right timber for the task.

## MAKING THE BASE, BACKBOARD AND CRANK HANDLE

**1** Study the working drawing (Fig 1-1A) and templates (Fig 1-1B). Draw the profiles to size and make clear tracings.

**2** Set to work carefully cutting out the profiles.

**3** Take the two cutouts—the stand and crank—and make sure the position of all the holes is clearly established with punched center points (Fig 1-1B). You need center points for the ½"-diameter spindle bearing at the top of the stand, the four 1½"-diameter blind holes that decorate the front of the stand, the ½" hole at the center of the crank for the spindle, and the two ⅜"-diameter holes at the ends of the crank for the handle dowels.

**4** With all the center points clearly fixed, drill them out with the appropriate bit size. Warning: for safety's sake, if the bit size is greater than ½", have the workpiece held with a clamp (Figs 1-2 and 1-3).

## TURNING THE BEAM WEIGHTS

**1** Having established the end centers by drawing crossed diagonals, mount the wood on the lathe, draw up the tailstock, set the tool rest at the correct height, and see to it that all your tools are within reach.

**2** Take the large gouge, either square ended or round nosed, and swiftly turn down the 2" × 2" square section of wood to the largest possible diameter. With the wood roughed out, take the skew chisel and bring the wood to a smooth cylinder.

**3** Starting with the two beam disks, or pucks, and working from right to left along the workpiece,

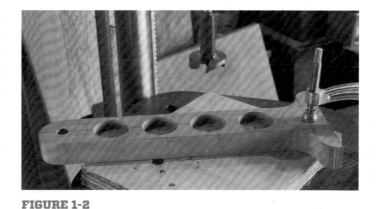

**FIGURE 1-2**

**Clamp the workpiece securely to the worktable, and run the blind holes in to the depth of the head of the Forstner bit.**

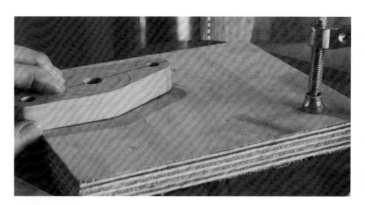

**FIGURE 1-3**

**Have a piece of waste wood under the workpiece—we use a sheet of plywood—so you can drill right through the workpiece without doing damage to the bit. The waster also ensures that the exit hole is crisp and clean edged.**

meaning from the tailstock end, take the dividers and mark all the step-offs that make up the design. Allow about $1/2$" for tailstock waste, 1" for the first disk, $1/4$" for part-off waste, 1" for the second disk, and then a final small amount for part-off waste.

**4** With the two disks carefully marked, take the parting tool and sink the waste areas to a depth of about $1/2$" so you are left with a core diameter of about $1/2$".

**5** Take the skew chisel and use the toe, or point, to swiftly mark in the midlines of each l"-wide disk. Then flip the tool over, and use the heel to turn away the corners of waste. Aim for a nicely rounded profile. I first cleared the parting waste, then trimmed off the sharp corners, and then rounded each of the shoulders (Figs 1-4 and 1-5) and so on, all the while trying to match up the mirror-image forms.

**FIGURE 1-4**

**To turn off the round shoulder, set the skew chisel flat on the workpiece, slowly twist the tool until the back or heel of the blade begins to bite, and then run in a continuous sweep down and round into the valley.**

**FIGURE 1-5**

**Having turned off facing shoulders, take the parting tool and deepen the parting waste to reveal and define the flat face of the disk.**

**6** Finally, when you have what you consider is a well-matched pair of disk-shaped weights, bring them to a smooth finish with the skew chisel and a piece of fine-grade sandpaper, and part off.

## TURNING THE INTEGRAL SPINDLE, CORD DRUM AND BOSS

**1** Check your wood over for faults and mount it securely on the lathe.

**2** Having used the square- or round-nosed gouge to achieve a roughed-out cylinder and the skew chisel to bring the wood to a smooth finish, take your ruler and dividers and mark all the step-offs that make up the design. Working from the tailstock end, allow a small amount for tailstock waste, 2" for the spindle, 1" for the drum, 1" for the length of spindle between the drum and the boss, 1" for the boss itself, and the rest for chuck waste. Mark the 1" drum with a midline.

**3** Take the parting tool and lower the waste between the various step-off points to achieve the required core diameter (Fig 1-6). For example, if we take it that you are starting out with a 2"-diameter cylinder, then you need to lower the spindle by $3/4$" for a $1/2$" core, the drum by about $1/16$" for a $1^7/8$" core, the area of spindle between the boss and the drum by a little over $5/8$" for a $5/8$" core, and the boss by $3/8$" for a $1^1/4$" core (Fig 1-7).

**4** With each of the step-offs lowered to the required depth, take the tool of your choice—I like using a skew chisel—and shape up the various profiles (Fig 1-8). The boss and the drum and the length of spindle in between can be turned to any shape that takes your fancy, but the spindle shaft must be turned down so it is a smooth fit in a $1/2$"-diameter hole. If you can't use a $1/2$" drill bit, turn your spindle shaft to the nearest size.

**FIGURE 1-6**

**Take the parting tool and establish the main core diameters.**

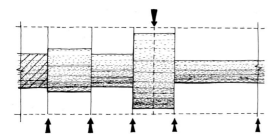

**FIGURE 1-7**

Lower the step-offs until you reach the core diameters of $^1/_2$" for the spindle, $1^7/_8$" for the drum, about $^5/_8$" for the length of spindle between the drum and the boss, and 1" for the boss.

**5** When you have turned the various profiles to size and shape and rubbed them down to a smooth finish with a scrap of sandpaper, carefully ease the tailstock center out of the way, and have a trial fitting of the spindle through the bearing hole at the top of the stand. Be mindful that it needs to be a good, smooth-running fit (Fig 1-9).

**6** To part off, hold and cradle the workpiece in one hand, and carefully nip it off with the toe of the skew chisel (Fig 1-10).

**7** Finally, set the rag-muffled spindle in the jaws of the chuck—the rag being used to protect the spindle from crush damage—and sand the part-off point down to a smooth finish.

## MAKING AND LOADING THE BOB WEIGHT

**1** Before you put tool to wood, have another look at the working drawing (Fig 1-1A) and templates (Fig 1-1B). Note how the weight needs to be long and thin so it can pass between the stand and the spinning beam weights, while at the same time it must be heavy. Consider how we drilled out a length of $^3/_4$"-diameter dowel and loaded it with lengths cut from a 6" nail.

**2** Take your 6" length of $^3/_4$"-diameter dowel and check it over for faults. If it is warped, split, stained, or in any way less than perfect, select another piece.

**3** Make a jig that allows you to stand the dowel on end at right angles to the drilling table and hold the dowel securely in place. If you look at the step-by-step photographs, you will see that we solved the problem by clamping the wood between a couple of heavy, steel V-blocks.

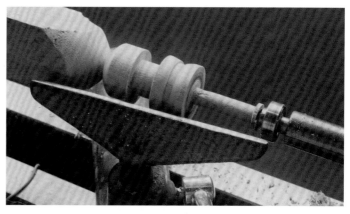

**FIGURE 1-8**

The partially turned workpiece, showing (from left to right) the boss, length of decorative spindle, drum and spindle shaft. Note that, at this stage, we were still undecided as to how we wanted the boss to be finally shaped.

**FIGURE 1-9**

With the workpiece still secure in the jaws of the chuck, draw back the tailstock and have a trial fitting of the spindle shaft through the bearing hole. Be very careful not to jolt the turning off-center.

**FIGURE 1-10**

When you have achieved what you consider is a good, well-finished turning, use the toe of the skew chisel to part off from the lathe. Be careful that the toe of the chisel doesn't slip between the workpiece and tool rest.

**FIGURE 1-11**

**Secure the dowel so it is perfectly aligned with the drill, and run a ³/₈"-diameter hole down to the full depth of the bit. Do this from both ends of the dowel.**

**4** Run a ³/₈"-diameter hole down through the length of the dowel. Bore the hole down into one end—to the full length of the bit—and then turn the wood over and repeat the procedure for the other end (Fig 1-11).

**5** With the holes in place—either right through the dowel or at least a good way into each end—cut one or more lengths from a 6" nail, and load it to within about ³/₈" of the ends.

**6** Push a length of split and glued ³/₈" dowel into the end hole—both ends—tap a shaved wedge into the little stopper, and put it to one side to dry (Fig 1-12 right).

**7** One end at a time, secure the loaded dowel in the jaws of the lathe chuck, and use the skew chisel and the graded sandpapers to turn it down to a round-ended shape—like a torpedo (Fig 1-12 left).

**8** Finally, cut and finish all the secondary components: the buttress at the back of the stand and all the little pins and pegs.

## ASSEMBLY AND FINISHING

**1** With all the component parts meticulously cut and worked (Fig 1-13), and with all unglued surfaces lightly oiled, set the stand on the base so it is flush with the front edge and aligned with the center line, and draw in a couple of discreet alignment marks.

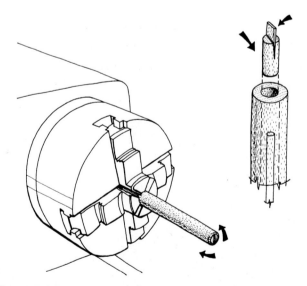

**Figure 1-12**

**(right) Cut a length from a 6" nail, and push it down into the cavity; aim to finish up with a space of about ¹/₂" at the top of the hole. Plug the hole with a short length of wedged dowel.**

**(left) When the glue is dry, set the workpiece in the jaws of the chuck, and carefully turn down the end to a round-nosed finish.**

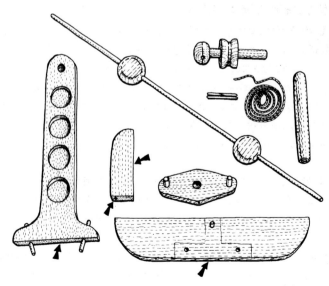

**FIGURE 1-13**

**Note that the areas to be glued, on the base, the underside of the stand, and two sides of the buttress, are not oiled.**

**2** Clamp the stand lightly to the base, and run ¹/₄"-diameter peg-fixing holes down at an angle—through the feet and on into the base. The best procedure is to drill one foot, secure it with a peg, and then repeat the technique for the other side. Be aware that because the feet are short grained, they are relatively fragile. Note: don't glue the pegs at this trial fitting stage .

**3** Take the buttress piece and set it firmly against the back of the stand. When you feel there is good, tight, right-angle coming-together of the three components, fit with a dowel (Fig 1-14).

**4** Take the boss spindle and the beam weights and, one piece at a time, secure them in an appropriate clamp-and-block jig. Drill out the ¹/₄"-diameter holes for the beam rod. Make sure the holes are aligned at right angles to the run of the grain. Drill two ¹/₁₆"-diameter holes—one into the drum for fixing the cord and the other through the side of the crank and into the spindle (Fig 1-15).

**5** When you have fitted the stand to the base and the spindle is sitting comfortably in place at the top of the stand, push fit the ¹/₄" beam dowel through the boss (Figs 1-16, 1-17 and 1-18), set the weights on the beam, fit the length of fine cord and the weight, and then have a trial run.

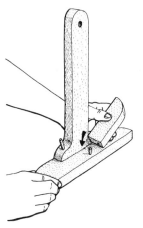

**FIGURE 1-14**

**Fit and fix the stand to the base, and then brace with the buttress.**

**FIGURE 1-15**

**Build clamp-and-block jigs for the difficult-to-hold components that need to be drilled. Minimize the risk of splitting the wood by having the holes set across the run of the grain.**

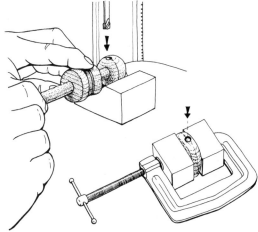

## PROBLEM SOLVING

The whole success of this project hinges on the spindle shaft being a smooth, friction-free fit through the top-of-stand bearing hole. Try waxing the contact surfaces.

**FIGURE 1-16**

**The beam rod needs to be a tight push fit through the boss hole, while at the same time a loose push fit through the disk weights.**

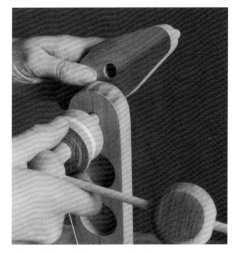

**FIGURE 1-17**

**Pass the shaft through the bearing hole, set the crank on the shaft, and fit and fix with a round toothpick.**

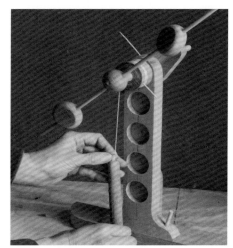

**FIGURE 1-18**

**Fit the weight on the end of the cord, and have a trial run. If need be, reduce the friction by waxing the shaft and all the other moving mating faces.**

# Harmonic Oscillation Punch Machine

## PROJECT BACKGROUND

The oscillation punch machine is a gem to make. With its intriguing movement and attractive structure, it is the sort of machine that is just asking to be set into action!

As to the name of this machine, it is not so easy to come up with a clear-cut definition or meaning. OK, no problem with the term oscillation punch—it simply describes the up-and-down punch action that is created by the oscillating, or side-to-side, movement of the sector weight—but the term harmonic is a bit of a stickler. I reckon it has something to do with symmetrical, harmonic frequency, but I'm not sure. Have you got any ideas?

The best way to operate this machine is to put your forefinger in the sector weight hole and to flick it rapidly from side to side. If everything is right, the swift side-to-side movement should result in the punch joggling up and down.

## PROJECT OVERVIEW

Have a look at the working drawing (Fig 2-1A), the templates (Fig 2-1B) and the various photographs, and you'll see that this project is somewhat complicated in that it is made up of a large number of small moving parts. This is not to say that each component is in itself difficult to cut—far from it—but rather that the sum total of putting all the parts together does require a lot of thinking and a lot of fine adjustment.

Study the working drawing (Fig 2-1A), and consider how the machine is made up of the primary units: a base with a low, glue-fixed backboard, a high, round-topped backboard with a pivot rod location slot and various pivot holes, a plate and spacer to hold the sector, the swinging sector weight itself, the connecting rod, the pivoted crosshead joint and punch, and the bracket.

In action, as the sector weight swings to the side, the connecting rod rises, which in turn lifts the punch in its supporting bracket. And, of course, as the sector comes to rest in the midposition, the punch goes down in its bracket. The best bit about the action, meaning the way the parts move, is the way the loose-fit crosshead joint at the bottom of the connecting rod is kept in place by the pivot pin that passes through the unit and into the backboard slot.

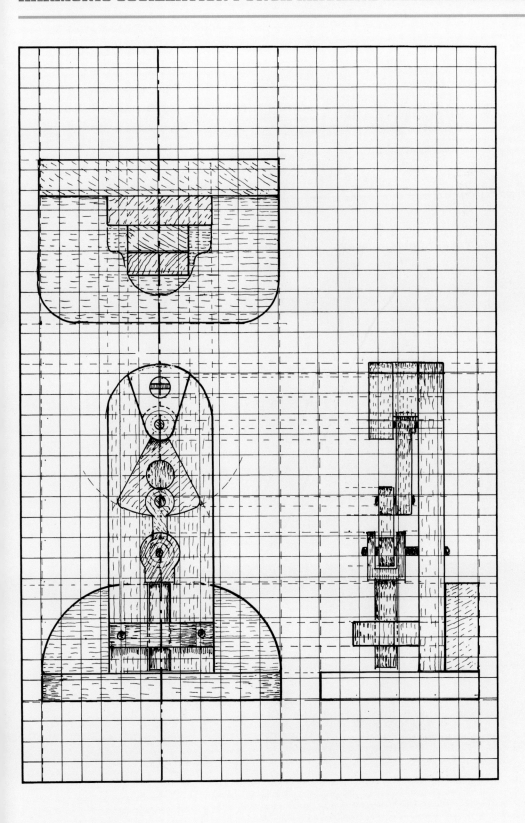

**FIGURE 2-1A**

At a grid scale of two squares to 1", the machine stands about 8$^{1}/_{2}$" high and 6" wide across the span of the base.

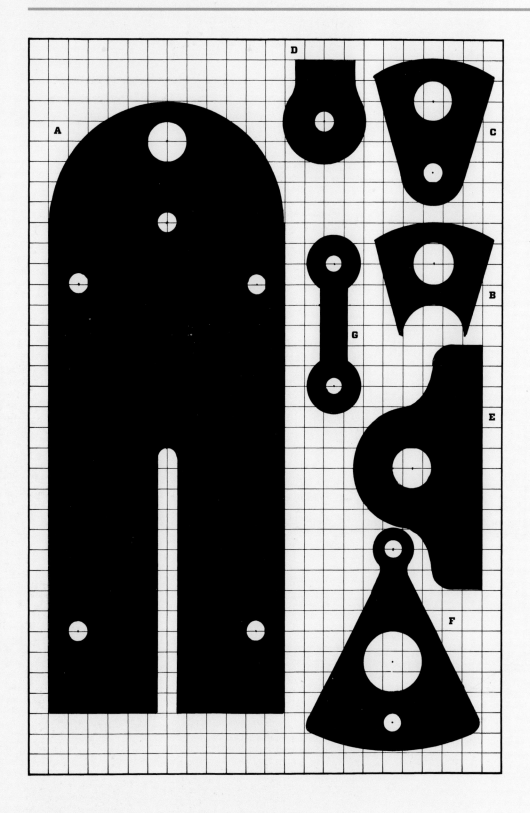

**FIGURE 2-1B**

**The scale is four grid squares to 1". Note that we have only illustrated the difficult-to-visualize components.**

**A** Tall, round-topped backboard.

**B** Spacer.

**C** Front plate.

**D** Crosshead joint.
sides.
center.

**E** Bracket.

**F** Sector weight.

**G** Connecting rod.

## CUTTING LIST

| | | |
|---|---|---|
| A | Tall, round-topped backboard | $5/8 \times 3 \times 7^1/2$ oak |
| B | Spacer | $5/8 \times 1^3/4 \times 2$ oak |
| C | Front plate | $5/8 \times 1^3/4 \times 2$ oak |
| D | Crosshead joint sides | $1/4 \times 1^1/2 \times 2$ oak |
| | center | $1/2 \times 1^1/2 \times 2$ olive |
| E | Bracket | $5/8 \times 2 \times 3$ oak |
| F | Sector weight | $1/4 \times 2^1/2 \times 3$ oak |
| G | Connecting rod | $1/2 \times 1 \times 2^1/2$ olive |
| | Base | $5/8 \times 4 \times 6$ oak |
| | Low, horizontal backboard | $7/8 \times 2^1/4 \times 6$ olive |
| | Pegs and pivots | 18"—$1/4$" dowel |
| | Wedged dowel and punch rod | 8"—$1/2$" dowel |

## CHOOSING YOUR WOOD

We decided to emphasize and draw attention to the various parts by using two strong-grained, fancy woods. We used Spanish olive for the horizontal backboard, the connecting rod, and the middle layer of the laminated crosshead joint, and a piece of uncharacteristic English oak for the rest.

## MAKING THE BASE AND BACK BOARDS

**1** Having carefully studied the working drawing (Fig 2-1A) and templates (Fig 2-1B), take the two 6"-long pieces of wood—the oak at $5/8$" thick and 4" wide, and the olive at $7/8$" thick and $2^1/4$" wide—and the $7^1/2$"-long, 3"-wide board, and use the pencil, ruler, square and compasses to mark all the lines that make up the design.

**2** Spend time carefully marking in the position of the center lines, the main peg and pivot holes, and any other guidelines you think will help you on your way.

**3** When you are sure all the guidelines are well placed, use the tools of your choice to cut the three boards to shape and size.

**4** Peg and glue the low backboard to its base, check with a square, secure with clamps, and put it to one side until the glue is set.

**5** Having cut the tall backboard out on the scroll saw, establish the position of the two top holes—the $1/4$"-diameter pivot hole and the $1/2$"-diameter wedge-peg hole—and drill them on the drill press.

**6** Finally, when you have achieved what you think is a good fit and finish of the three boards, set the tall backboard on the base and draw in a couple of alignment marks (Fig 2-2).

## MAKING AND FITTING THE SECTOR PLATES

**1** Have a good, long look at the working drawing (Fig 2-1A) and photographs, and note how this project is perhaps slightly unusual in that all the small parts are cut out on the scroll saw.

**2** When you have a clear understanding of how the parts fit together, take the two $5/8$"-thick pieces of oak that make up the sector support—the spacer and the front plate—and use the compasses, ruler and soft no. 2 pencil to draw the design on the best-looking piece.

**3** With the two pieces of wood clamped securely together, establish the position of the sector pivot hole, and drill with the $1/4$" drill bit.

**4** Push a length of $1/4$" dowel through the pivot hole to hold the two pieces of wood together, and cut the wedgelike shape out on the scroll saw (Fig 2-3).

**FIGURE 2-2**

**Make sure the backboard is set at right angles and aligned with the center line.**

**5** Have a trial fitting of the two cutouts on the backboard (Fig 2-4). Fix the position of the wedge-peg hole center point, and mark on the spacer plate the area that needs to be cut away .

**6** With the pivot pin still in place, use the ½" drill bit to run the wedge-peg hole through the two pieces of wood. Note: don't forget to back up the workpiece when drilling with a piece of scrap wood to prevent tearout.

**7** Having achieved two identical cutouts, take the one that is to be sandwiched between the front plate and the backboard and cut away the waste, the whole ³/₄"-diameter circle with the ¼"-diameter pivot hole.

**8** Cut a piece of ½" dowel to length—so it passes through the sector plate, the spacer and the backboard—saw a slot about ½" down into the end of the dowel, and knife cut a shaving of waste to fit.

**9** Align the dowel so the wedge slot runs across the grain, and have a trial fitting just to see if the wedge holds the tenon in place in its hole (Fig 2-5).

## CUTTING AND LAMINATING THE CROSSHEAD JOINT

**1** Take the three pieces of wood that make up the crosshead joint—the two pieces of oak at about ¼" thick and the piece of olive at about ½" thick—and sandwich them together so the olive is the filling and the grain runs vertically up and down. Mark the three layers "top," "middle" and "bottom."

**2** Draw the design on the top board, fix the position of the center point, and then tap a pin through the waste area to link all three layers.

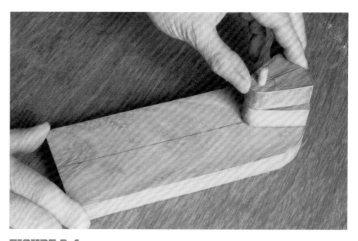

**FIGURE 2-4**

**Set the cutouts in place on the backboard, make sure the arrangement is symmetrical, and then draw a couple of registration marks.**

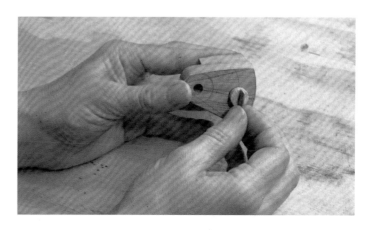

**FIGURE 2-5**

**Align the slot so it runs at right angles to the grain, and have a trial fitting of the wedge. If all is correct, a push fit should be enough to hold the tenon firm.**

**FIGURE 2-6**

**Saw through the three-layered stack to achieve three identical cutouts. Note how my heavy-handed nail fixing very nearly resulted in a complete mess-up—with a split running along the grain.**

**FIGURE 2-3**

**Saw through both layers so as to achieve two identical cutouts.**

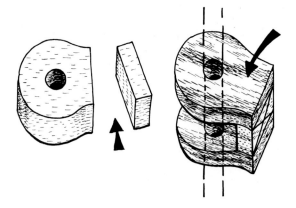

**FIGURE 2-7**

**Cut away the top half of the middle layer so you are left with a
¹/₄" slice.**

**3** Run the ¹/₄"-diameter pivot hole through all three
layers, and push home a generous length of ¹/₄"
dowel (Fig 2-6).

**4** With all three layers of wood held secure by both the
pin and the dowel, fret out the shape on the scroll saw.

**5** When you have achieved the cutout and carefully
removed the dowel so you have three layers, mark
on the middle layer the area that needs to be cut away
(Fig 2-7).

**FIGURE 2-8**

**Smear glue on mating faces, align the holes with the pivot dowel,
and then carefully clamp up.**

**6** Cut away the waste, replace the dowel, and then
glue and clamp the three layers to make up the unit
(Fig 2-8). When the glue is dry, run a ¹/₂"-diameter hole
through the base of the component, and have a trial fitting
of the punch rod.

## MAKING THE BRACKET AND SECTOR

**1** Have a look at the working drawing (Fig 2-1A) and
templates (Fig 2-1B), and see how the two
components—the bracket and the sector—are simple
flatwood profiles that are cut out on the scroll saw.

**2** Take the ⁵/₈"-thick piece of wood you've set aside for
the bracket and use the pencil, ruler and compasses
to mark all the lines that make up the design.

**3** Establish the position of the punch rod hole, and run
it through with the ¹/₂"-diameter drill bit. Note: be
mindful that the precise position of the bracket hole,
meaning its distance from the backboard, will relate to the
finished thicknesses of the sector, the connecting rod and
the crosshead joint. If you are at all unsure as to the
finished sizes, you can make the bracket at a later stage,
or you can allow extra depth to the bracket, and then trim
back to fit.

**4** When you have double-checked that all is correct,
cut out the bracket on the scroll saw.

**5** Take the piece of wood for the sector weight—all
marked out and measured and with a clear center
line—and give it another look-over, just to make sure the
three holes are well placed. No problem with the ³/₄"
diameter finger hole—it can be just about anywhere on
the center line—but the two ¹/₄" pivot holes need careful
positioning. The top pivot hole must be at the center of
swing, meaning at the center of the ¹/₂"-diameter circle of
wood, while the connecting rod pivot hole must be
centered about ³/₈" up from the bottom of the arc.

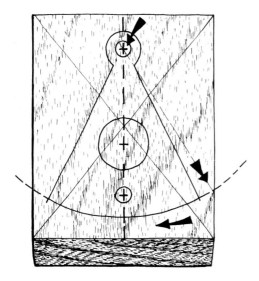

**FIGURE 2-9**

**Avoid weak, short-grained areas by having the design arranged and centered so it is set symmetrically with the run of the grain.**

**6** With all the lines and center points in place, and having carefully checked for accuracy, drill the three holes on the drill press—$1/4$" diameter for the two pivot holes and $3/4$" diameter for the finger hole (Fig 2-9). Lastly, cut out the profile on the scroll saw.

## MAKING THE CONNECTING ROD

**1** Take the $1/2$"-thick piece of olive you've put aside for the connecting rod and mark it with a center line that runs in the direction of the grain. Mark the line with two center points that are $1^1/2$" apart, and draw in all the lines that make up the design—the two $3/4$" circles and the $3/8$" width to the rod.

**2** Run the two center points through with a $1/4$"-diameter drill bit, and then have a trial fitting to link up the sector and the crosshead joint (Fig 2-10). If need be, reduce the thickness and diameter of the bottom end of the rod so it is a good, loose fit between the ears of the crosshead (Fig 2-11).

**3** Having cut the profile out on the scroll saw, take a small, sharp knife and set to work whittling the straight part of the rod to a roundish section. The best technique is to set the circle line in with a stop-cut—on both sides of the wood and at both ends—and then to carefully slice the blade into the stop-cut so the waste falls away. If you work with a careful, thumb-braced paring cut, you won't have any problems with the knife slipping (Fig 2-12).

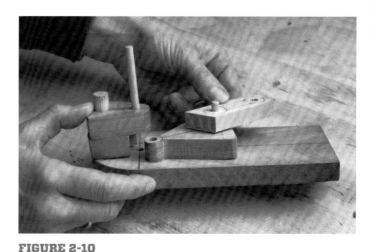

**FIGURE 2-10**

**Have a trial fitting of both the sector weight and the partially worked connecting rod. Adjust the various thicknesses so the movement is smooth and easy.**

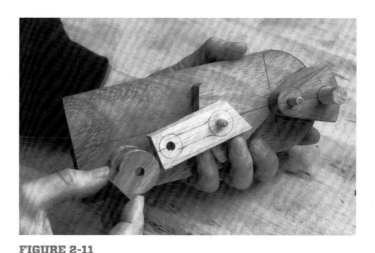

**FIGURE 2-11**

**To minimize friction, adjust the thickness of the wood at the end of the rod and inside the ears of the joint. Use a twist of sandpaper to ensure that the end-of-rod hole is a loose fit on the $1/4$"-diameter dowel.**

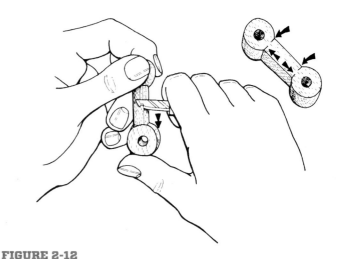

**FIGURE 2-12**

**Use a tight, thumb-braced paring cut to whittle the rod to a round section. Work from the center through to the stop-cut.**

**4** When you have rounded and slightly lowered the round section so the flat faces of the end circles stand slightly in relief, take a scrap of sandpaper and rub down the knife-worked area to a smooth finish.

**5** Take the tall, round-topped backboard and mark, drill and cut the various holes and the crosshead pivot runner slot.

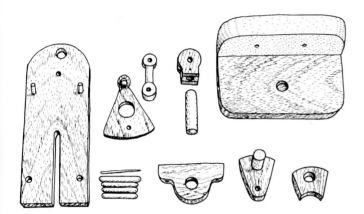

**FIGURE 2-13**

**Check the parts over for flaws and blemishes. Turn a damaged face away so the flaw is hidden from view.**

## ASSEMBLY AND FINISHING

**1** When you have completed all the component parts that make up the project (Fig 2-13), then comes the fun of trying to get everything together so it works!

**2** When you are happy with the overall finish, glue and peg the low backboard to the base so it's at right angles. It's important that everything is square.

**3** Set the backboard in place on the base, establish the position of the bracket, and fix the whole works together with a couple of ¼"-diameter dowel pegs (Fig 2-14). Have the pegs running through all three layers of wood. While the ¼"-diameter dowel is at hand, fit the two pegs that limit the swing of the sector weight.

**4** Slide the end of the connecting rod into the crosshead joint, push the dowel pivot in place, and check for a smooth, easy fit (Fig 2-15). If need be, reduce the wood—on the rod end, in the rod hole or in the joint— so the movement is smooth running.

**FIGURE 2-14**

**The bracket dowels need to run through all three components: the bracket and the two backboards. Note that—as an afterthought— we drilled a ½"-diameter blind hole in the base for the punch rod.**

**FIGURE 2-15**

**Set the connecting rod and joint unit in place on the punch rod, and locate the dowel in the guide slot.**

**FIGURE 2-16**

**Set the joint in place on top of the punch rod, and hold the two together with a round toothpick dowel.**

**5** Push the punch dowel into place in the bottom of the joint, and drill and fit with a round toothpick that runs through the whole width of the unit (Fig 2-16).

**6** Take the sector and lower the wood at the back by about $^1/_{16}$" so the circle of wood around the pivot stands out in relief—like an integral washer. Fit the sector on its pivot, and spend time easing and sanding until it swings with the minimum of friction (Fig 2-17).

**7** Use a dowel to link the top end of the connecting rod to the sector (Fig 2-18) so the dowel is a tight fit in the sector hole and a loose easy fit in the rod end.

**8** Push the spacer and plate in place over the sector pivot, and test for fit and function (Fig 2-19). If all is well, you should be able to tickle the sector from side to side in such a way that the punch rod joggles up and down in its bracket.

**9** When you are pleased with the fit, finish and function, glue the whole works in place, rub down all the surfaces with a sheet of fine-grade sandpaper, wipe the dust, and give the project a wipe with the teak oil.

## PROBLEM SOLVING

• If you like the idea of this project but want to change the design, it's important you realize that the relationship between the swing of the sector weight and the length of the connecting rod is critical.

• If you decide to modify the design and are at all unsure about the feasibility of the design, it's best to make a working model.

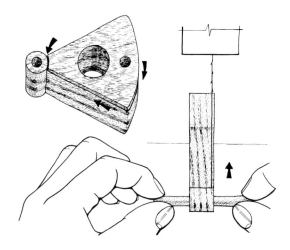

**FIGURE 2-17**

**(top left) Reduce the total thickness of the back face by about $^1/_{16}$". Run a guideline around the edge, and run a saw cut down into the face—between the pivot circle and the sector face so the pivot area will be left to act as a washer or distance piece. (right) If you decide to clear the $^1/_{16}$" slice of waste on the band saw, then run a dowel through the pivot hole so you have a safe handhold. Having run a $^1/_{16}$" hole through the sector and the dowel pivot and followed through with a round toothpick, set the dowel pivot in place in the backboard hole.**

**FIGURE 2-18**

**Link the connecting rod and the sector weight with a short length of dowel so the dowel is a tight push fit in the sector and a loose easy fit in the rod.**

**FIGURE 2-19**

**Set the plate and spacer in place on the sector weight pivot, and adjust for an easy movement.**

# Cam and Fork Machine

## PROJECT BACKGROUND

This machine is a joy to make and a joy to watch.

Our dictionary describes a cam as being "a rotating cylinder with an irregular profile attached to a revolving shaft to give a reciprocating motion to a part connected to it." With our machine, the off-center, or eccentrically mounted, disk is the cam, while the fork is the in-contact connection that gives reciprocating motion.

When the crank handle is turned—clockwise or counterclockwise—the cam revolves eccentrically on its fixed bearing, with the effect that the fork and control rod oscillate on the pillar bearings. The fork is fixed on the rod, while the rod is free to slide from side to side through the bearings.

## PROJECT OVERVIEW

Have a look at the project picture (right), the working drawing (Fig 3-1A) and the templates (Fig 3-1B), and note that the disk cam is pin fixed to a shaft in such a way that its movement is off-center. Consider carefully how, when the contained off-center disk cam turns, the fork has no option but to track and follow the cam profile.

Although the design is pretty flexible—inasmuch as there is no reason you can't chop and change various wood thicknesses and dowel sizes to suit your needs—the size of the disk cam, the distance between the fork prongs, and the distance between the side of the fork and the support stanchions are all critical. That said, if you have a notion to change wood sizes, it's best to sort out potential problems by making a cardboard-and-pins prototype.

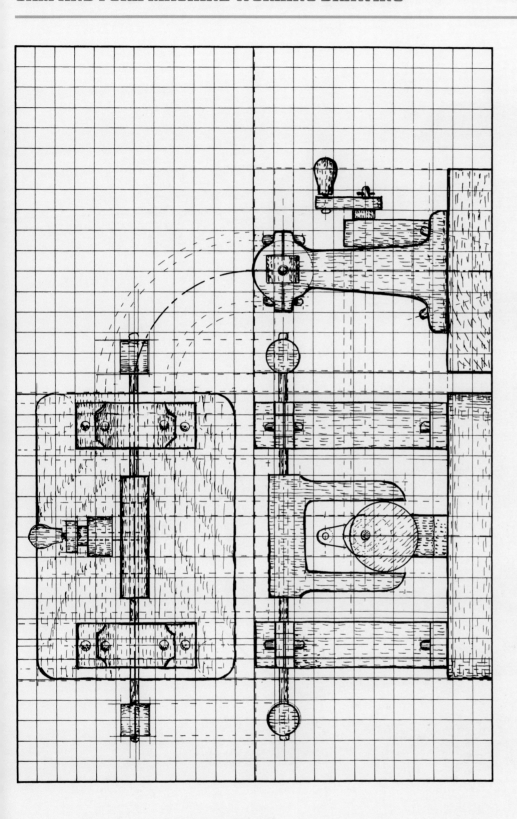

**FIGURE 3-1A**
At a grid scale of two squares
to 1", the machine stands
about 6" high and a little over
10" wide across the span of
the end-of-rod pill stops.

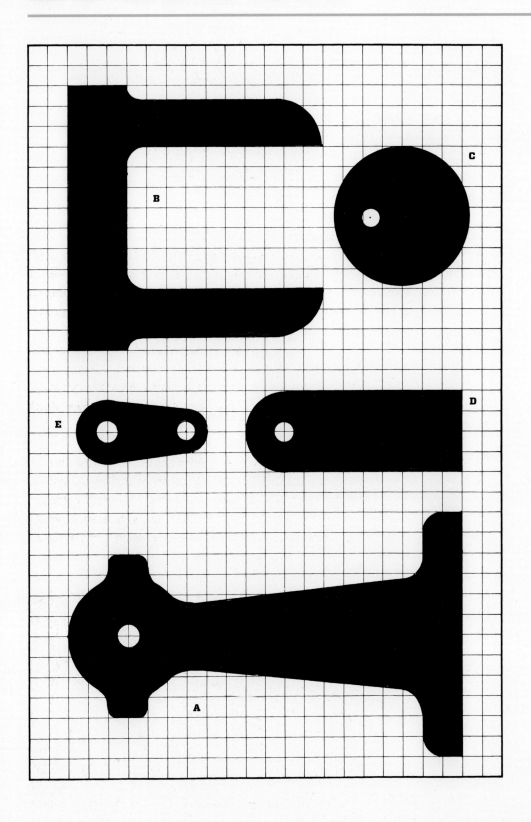

**FIGURE 3-1B**

**The scale is four grid squares to 1".**

**A** Stanchions or pillars.

**B** Fork.

**C** Disk cam.

**D** Cam post.

**E** Crank.

## CUTTING LIST

| A | Stanchions or pillars | 1 × 3 × 5 tulip |
|---|---|---|
| B | Fork | $^3/_4$ × $3^1/_4$ × 4 mahogany |
| C | Disk cam | $^5/_8$ × 2 × 2 mahogany |
| D | Cam post | $^3/_4$ × 1 × 3 pitch pine |
| E | Crank | $^1/_4$ × 1 × $1^3/_4$ mahogany |
| | Base | 1 × $5^1/_2$ × $7^1/_2$ tulip |
| | Crank handle and end-of-rod pills | 1 × 1 × 6 mahogany |
| | Rods | 24"—$^3/_8$" dowel |

## CHOOSING YOUR WOOD

This is one of those projects where you might—if you are pressed—reduce wood thickness to suit your stock or your wallet. For example, the base and the stanchions could be a bit thinner—say $^3/_4$" instead of 1"—while the fittings could be worked from offcuts.

We chose to use mahogany for the cam, fork, crank, crank handle and rod-end pills, and North American tulip for the base, stanchions, and one or two bits and pieces.

## MAKING THE BASE

**1** Take the piece of 1"-thick tulip wood—the piece for the base—and with the grain running along the length, use the pencil, ruler and square to mark it at 7" × 5".

**2** Set the compasses/dividers to $^1/_2$" radius, and scribe out the 1"-diameter circles that make up the design of the corner curves (Fig 3-1A). Use the tools of your choice to cut the wood to shape and size.

**3** When you have cut the base to size, use the graded sandpapers to rub down all faces and edges to a smooth finish. Pay particular attention to the top face and edges, and then pencil mark the underside.

## MAKING THE STANCHION PILLARS

**1** Draw the shape of the stanchions to size on the work-out paper, and then—being mindful that the grain must run from top to toe—use the pencil, ruler and compasses to mark the image on your chosen wood. Repeat the procedure so you have two identical images.

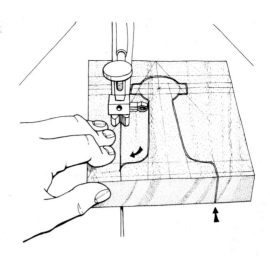

**FIGURE 3-2**

When using the scroll saw, control the rate of feed so the blade is always presented with the line of next cut. If the cut is ragged, the blade is too slack or the wood is too moist. If the wood is scorched, the blade needs changing or you are working at the wrong pace.

**2** Having double-checked from pillar to pillar that the circle center-points, meaning the points that mark the center of the rod hole, are the same distance up from the baseline, use the scroll saw to cut out the two identical forms (Fig 3-2).

**3** With the cutout securely clamped flat on the work surface, take the $^1/_4$" U-section carving gouge and lower the top-of-stanchion "lugs," or ear-like protrusions, by about $^1/_4$". Do this with both lugs on both faces, so when seen in edge-on view the wood curves down from the face to a thickness of about $^1/_2$" (Figs 3-3 and 3-1A).

**FIGURE 3-3**

With the workpiece secured flat on the work surface—with a clamp or up against a bench stop—use the U-section gouge to carve the scooped shape of the side lugs.

**FIGURE 3-4**

**With the workpiece supported on a waster to prevent exit damage, bore out the $^1/_4$" bearing hole and the $^3/_4$" blind hole. Note: we have removed the clamp for the photograph.**

**4** When you have carved the lugs to shape so the circle at the top of the stanchion looks to be standing slightly forward, use the pillar drill and the Forstner bits to bore out a $^1/_4$"-diameter rod-bearing hole and the decorative $^3/_4$"-diameter blind hole. Aim for a blind hole at about $^1/_4$" deep (Fig 3-4).

**5** Take your fine-grade sandpaper and bring all the edges to good order. Aim for edges that are slightly rounded.

**6** When the time comes to sink the decorative cut that runs around the top of the stanchion, firmly brace the workpiece against the bench hook, and use the fine-toothed saw to sink the cuts to a depth of about $^1/_8$" (Fig 3-5).

**FIGURE 3-5**

**Firmly butt the workpiece against the bench hook, adjust the angle of cut so the saw runs against the side of the hook, and then sink the cut to a depth of about $^1/_8$".**

**FIGURE 3-6**

**Clamp the workpiece between a couple of steel blocks so it is square with the surface and the drill bit, and run the lugs through with the $^1/_4$"-diameter bit. Note: if you like woodwork, you can't do better than set yourself up with a good selection of clamps. We have pincer action clamps for small work, toggle clamps for machine hold-downs, and so on.**

**7** Having drilled the two face holes, then comes the tricky task of drilling the lug and foot holes. I say tricky because, with both the lug and the foot, the holes need to be run into a curved face. When you come to drill the lug hole—and bearing in mind that the drill bit will try to push the curved surface to one side—first set the workpiece square between a couple of heavy blocks, and then hold it in place with a good clamp. This done, run the $^1/_4$"-diameter hole through the thickness of the lug (Fig 3-6).

**8** To drill the $^1/_4$"-diameter foot hole, set the workpiece on a stack of scrap so the hole is angled in toward center. Use a long, shanked bit so as to avoid contact between the chuck and the top of the pillar (Fig 3-7).

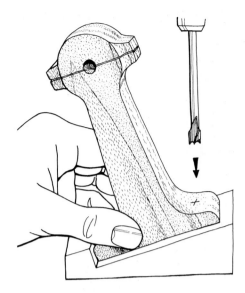

## MAKING THE CAM POST

**1** Have a look at the working drawing (Fig 3-1A) and templates (Fig 3-1B), and see that the controls, meaning the parts you turn, are made up of a fixed post, crank, crank handle, crank handle pin, or pivot, washer to distance the crank from the post, disk cam and pivot rod.

**2** Mark the size and shape of the post on your chosen wood—we use tulip wood—double-check the dimensions, and then cut out the curved-top front view on the scroll saw.

**3** Mark the position of the pivot rod hole, and run it through with the $1/4$"-diameter drill bit. It's important that the hole and the bottom of the hole are both square and true with the base, so aim to get it right the first time around.

**4** Draw in the "feet"—as seen in side view—and then cut them out on the scroll saw (Fig 3-8).

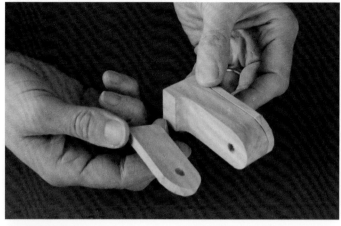

## TURNING THE HANDLE, PIVOT PIN AND ROD PILLS

**1** Take the length of square section mahogany, establish the end center points by drawing crossed diagonals, and set it securely on the lathe.

**2** Having made sure you and the lathe are in good, safe order, swiftly turn down the piece of mahogany to the largest possible diameter.

**3** Use the dividers to mark all the step-offs that make up the design. Working from left to right along the turning, allow a small amount for headstock waste—either for the chuck or for parting off—about $1/4$" for the handle pivot head, $3/4$" for the pivot, 2" for the handle, 1" for one pill, $1/4$" for waste, 1" for the other pill, and a small amount for tailstock waste (Fig 3-9A).

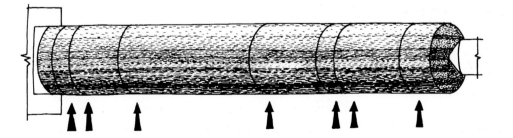

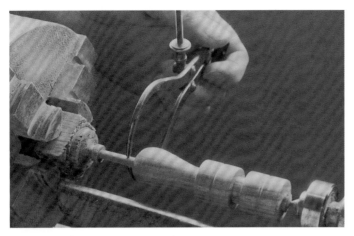

**FIGURE 3-9B**

**Use the calipers to check the diameters against the working drawings. Note: if you are working with a limited number of drill bit sizes, be sure to adjust the width of the pivot shank to suit your chosen bit diameter.**

**4** Having first removed the bulk of the waste, use the round-nosed gouge and the skew chisel to turn down the wood to shape and size. Make repeated checks with the calipers (Fig 3-9B).

**5** Turn and sand the string of turnings to a good finish, and carefully part off from the lathe.

## MAKING THE CRANK, HANDLE AND CAM

**1** Take a ¼"-thick piece of mahogany offcut and use a pencil, ruler and pair of compasses to draw the shape of the crank and the little washer spacer. Plan on the crank being about 1" between centers (Fig 3-1B).

**2** With all the lines of the design clearly established, first run ¼"-diameter holes through the crank and the spacer, and then use the scroll saw to cut out the shapes. While the drill is convenient, run a hole into the turned handle to a depth and size to suit your turned mushroom-headed peg.

**3** When you make the disk cam, you can either cut it out with a scroll saw or turn it on the lathe, as long as it is 1¾" in diameter, about ¾" thick, and as near as possible to a perfect circle.

**4** When you have what you consider is a good disk— nicely sanded to a smooth finish—run it through with a ¼"-diameter shaft hole, and then have a trial fitting (Fig 3-10).

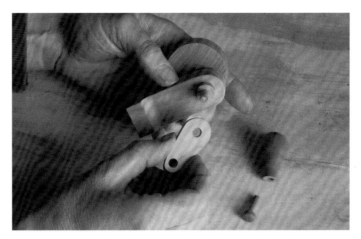

**FIGURE 3-10**

**Have a trial fitting to make sure all the control column parts come together for a smooth-working fit.**

**5** If you have followed our directions to the letter, you will need to adjust selected holes or parts of the dowel shaft to achieve a suitable fit. For example, the handle peg needs to be a tight fit in the handle and a loose fit through the crank. Then again, the dowel shaft needs to be a tight fit in the crank and disk cam, while being a loose easy fit through the little stanchion (Fig 3-11). Play around with the fit until you get it right.

**FIGURE 3-11**

**If need be, sand the holes or dowels to achieve an appropriate fit. The little pivot needs to be a loose fit through the shank and a tight push fit in the handle.**

## MAKING THE FORKED FOLLOWER

**1** If you have a look at the working drawing (Fig 3-1A) and templates (Fig 3-1B), you will see that the forked follower, or frame, is cut from ¾"-thick wood, with the grain running from top to bottom and the inside fork width being the same as the diameter of the disk cam.

**2** Having drawn the frame on your piece of prepared wood, give it a good checking over just to make sure you haven't made any mess-ups, and then carefully fret out the frame on the scroll saw.

**3** If you take it at an easy pace, all the while being ready to pull back if the blade snatches, the cut face will be so smooth it will only require the minimum of sanding.

**4** Take the cutout and carefully draw diagonals to establish the position of the through-top rod, or shaft, hole.

**FIGURE 3-12**
**Drilling the rod hole through the top of the forked frame is slightly tricky inasmuch as while the hole needs to run square and true, most drill bits are too short. A good method is to establish the center points for the holes, clamp the workpiece to a square iron block, and then run the holes through from both sides.**

**5** Hold the workpiece secure with blocks and a clamp so the hole is going to be well placed and true, and run it through with a long, shanked $1/4$" bit (Fig 3-12). If your bit isn't long enough, turn the whole works around, and drill it through from the other side.

## ASSEMBLY AND FINISHING

**1** When you have completed all the component parts that make up the design, then comes the exciting but finger-twisting task of putting everything together. You should have ten primary parts in all: the base, two stanchions, disk cam post, disk cam, washer, crank, handle, handle pin, two end-of-rod pills, or stops, and a whole heap of dowels cut to size (Fig 3-13).

**2** Before you do much else, take the finest-grade sandpaper and rub down all faces, edges and corners to a smooth finish. Give all the surfaces—barring the mating faces that are to be glued—a swift rubdown with a small amount of teak oil.

**3** Having cut all the rods and dowels to length, spend time rubbing them down with a scrap of sandpaper so they are an appropriate fit and all the on-view ends are nicely rounded. Have all the ends standing slightly forward by about $1/4$"–$3/8$".

**4** When you have generally brought everything to good order, start the fitting by pegging and adjusting the three posts.

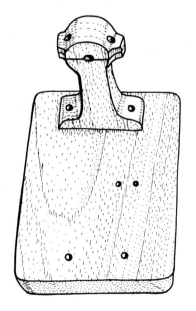

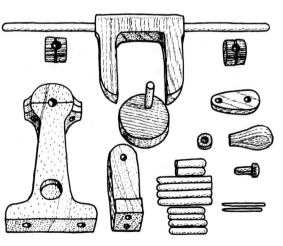

**FIGURE 3-13**
**When you have completed all the component parts that make up the project, check all the measurements against the working drawing and template design, and then sand all the surfaces down to a good, smooth finish.**

**FIGURE 3-14**

**Align the three posts so they are true, and fix with the pegs.**

**5** Glue, peg and fit the disk cam, crank and handle, and carefully adjust one with another so they are square and perfectly aligned (Fig 3-14).

**6** Slide the forked follower on its rod, and peg or glue. Slip the ends of the rods through the bearings so the fork straddles the disk cam (Fig 3-15).

**FIGURE 3-15**

**Slide the forked frame over the cam, and fit the other post. Note how the top of the frame has been rounded.**

**FIGURE 3-16**

**When you've finally put the whole machine together, spend time making sure all components are square and true to each other.**

**7** With all the parts variously glued or pegged in place, test for squareness, make sure the machine works, and then put it to one side until the glue is set (Fig 3-16). Finally, give the whole works another rubdown with the teak oil, and then the fun can begin!

### PROBLEM SOLVING

• If you like the idea of this project but want to change the design, no problem, as long as you make sure the cam and fork are compatible.

• Having made the project, Gill thinks the base and the stanchions would look even better if they were cut from slightly thinner wood. That said, I like the thickness of the wood, but I am not so keen about its color and texture.

• If you want to make the project but can't get use of a lathe, settle for making the crank handle from a shop-bought dowel.

• As the distance between the side ends of the forked follower and the inside faces of the stands is critical—the machine won't work unless it's right—make sure everything is smooth running before you glue up.

# In-the-Round Combustion Engine

## PROJECT BACKGROUND

Although the in-the-round combustion machine is in essence much like the reciprocating machine, as shown in project 6, it is in many ways all the more exciting in that it can—like a piece of sculpture—be seen and enjoyed from all angles. The turn-handle movement attractively illustrates how the up-and-down operation of a piston is converted, by way of a crank, into rotary motion (right).

## PROJECT OVERVIEW

Have a look at the working drawing (Fig 4-1) and the templates (Fig 4-2), and see that at a grid scale of two squares to 1", the machine stands almost 12" high and over 6" wide across the span of the drive shaft. Consider that the greater part of the machine is made up of three beautifully complex turnings: the base, which is drilled and hollow turned; the quatrefoil top, which is both drilled and fretted halfway through the turning stage; and the cylinder, which is turned, drilled and then sawn.

Though the project is challenging, a lot of the tricky procedures relate not so much to your skill level, but to your equipment. Modify the stages to fit your tool kit. OK, so it might take a lot longer, but then the pleasure is in the doing!

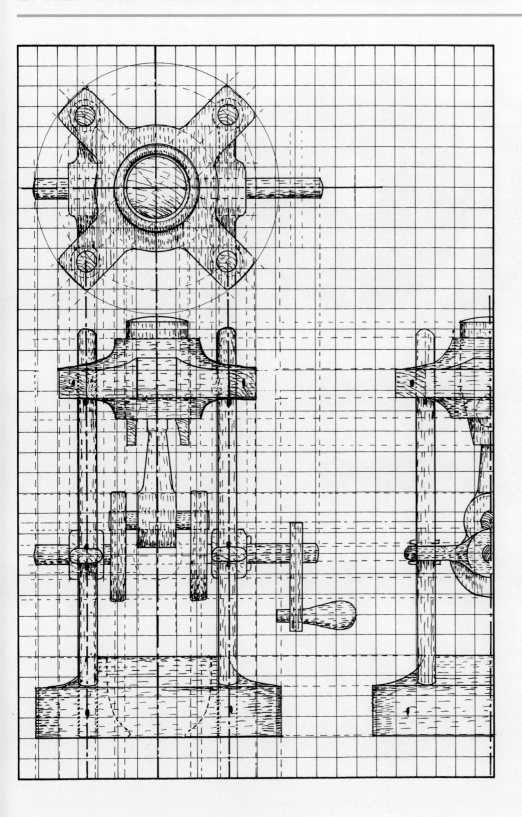

**FIGURE 4-1**

At a grid scale of two squares to 1", the machine stands almost 12" high and about 6" wide across the diameter of the base.

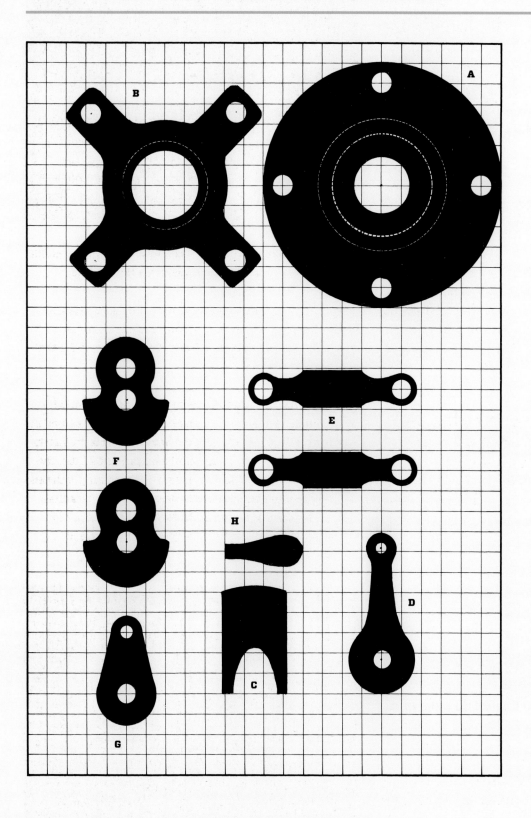

## FIGURE 4-2

**The scale is two grid squares to 1". Note that we have only shown what we consider are the most difficult-to-visualize views.**

**A** Base.

**B** Top.

**C** Piston.

**D** Piston/connecting rod.

**E** Crankshaft bearings (2).

**F** Crank plates.

**G** Handle crank.

**H** Knob.

## CUTTING LIST

| | | |
|---|---|---|
| A | Base | 2 × 7 × 7 easy-to-turn beech |
| B | Top | 2 × 7 × 7 easy-to-turn tulip |
| C | Piston | $2\frac{1}{2}$ × $2\frac{1}{2}$ × 6 beech |
| D | Piston rod | $1\frac{1}{4}$ × $1\frac{1}{2}$ × 5 beech |
| E | Crankshaft bearings (2) | 1 × $3\frac{1}{2}$ × 6 mahogany |
| F | Crank plates | $\frac{3}{8}$ × 3 × 7 cherry |
| G | Handle crank | $\frac{3}{8}$ × $1\frac{1}{2}$ × $2\frac{3}{4}$ |
| H | Knob | 2"—$\frac{3}{4}$" dowel |
| | Stand rods and shaft | 60"—$\frac{1}{2}$" dowel |

## CHOOSING YOUR WOOD

This is one of those projects where the choice of wood is all important; it's got to be just right. We have chosen European beech for the piston and base, because it's easy to turn and yet strong across the short grain, and tulip for the top, because it's both easy to turn and easy to work on the scroll saw.

## MAKING THE ENGINE CASE AND BASE

**1** Have a good, long look at the working drawing (Fig 4-1) and templates (Fig 4-2), and see that the quatrefoil component at the top of the engine—we call it the engine or piston case—is both turned on the lathe and worked with the saw and drill. Note also the shape of the base.

**2** Take the 2"-thick slabs of tulip and fix the center point by drawing crossed diagonals.

**3** Mark the slab with a $6\frac{1}{2}$"-diameter circle. Cut away the waste on the scroll saw or band saw. Screw the resultant disk on the 6" faceplate using short, fat screws.

**4** With the tool rest set over the bed of the lathe, turn down the wood to a smooth 6"-diameter disk and true up the face.

**5** Use the dividers to mark the disk with a $2\frac{1}{2}$"-diameter circle, and then turn down the waste so the $2\frac{1}{2}$" circle stands up as a $\frac{1}{2}$"-high plateau (Fig 4-3).

**6** Mount the drill chuck on the tailstock, fit the $1\frac{5}{8}$" Forstner bit, and run a hole through the center of the plateau (Fig 4-4A).

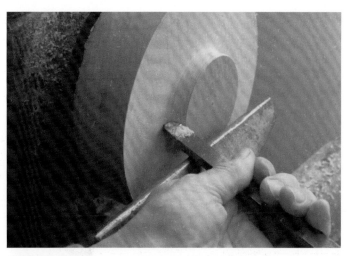

**FIGURE 4-3**

Mount the blank on the lathe, and turn down the edge and profile. See how I use a round-nosed scraper for the inside curve.

**7** Mark the lowered area with a couple of guideline circles, one at about $\frac{1}{2}$" from the edge, for the postholes, and one about $\frac{3}{8}$" outside the plateau, for the profile line.

**8** Having first rubbed down the turning to a smooth finish, take it off the lathe—off the faceplate—and set to work on the turned face of the wood, drawing in all the lines that make up the quatrefoil design. Pencil label the turned face "bottom," fix the position of the four postholes on the guideline circle—at 90° intervals—and establish the shape of the cross-arms. Make the arms about $1\frac{1}{4}$" wide and all the corners and angles nicely rounded (Figs 4-1 and 4-2 top).

**FIGURE 4-4A**

Bore out the piston hole with a Forstner bit. Advance and retreat with the tailstock so as not to burn or clog the bit.

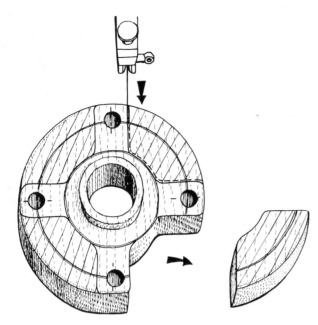

**FIGURE 4-4B**

**Having drawn the quatrefoil profile, use the scroll saw to clear the waste. Have the workpiece flat on the cutting table so the cut faces are at right angles to the working face.**

**9** Run the ,holes through with the $^1/_2$"-diameter drill bit, and cut the quatrefoil profile out on the scroll saw (Fig 4-4B).

**10** When you have completed the cross—all drilled and cut—mount it on the expanding jaws option of the chuck, and set to work turning down what will be the "top" face (Fig 4-5). I used the small, round-nosed gouge and the round-nosed scraper.

**11** Rub down the whole works with the fine-grade sandpaper. Do one face of the turning, then turn it over on the chuck and do the other face. If you rub down one face as it points toward the bed of the lathe plus the difficult-to-reach face between the whole piece and the chuck, you will find that the change of direction ensures that all the edges are well rounded.

**12** Having achieved a well-turned and finished component, redo the same procedures and turn the beech wood base. That is to say, turn down the wood to a $6^1/_2$" disk and run a $1^5/_8$" borehole through the disk.

**13** Turn down the top-of-base profile so the underside rim of the cross is a neat fit in the hole (Fig 4-6).

**FIGURE 4-5**

**With the workpiece held securely on the expanding jaws of the chuck, use a round-nosed tool to turn down what will be the underside of the casing. Go at it nice and easy, all the while being mindful that this is a stage that needs to be worked with extreme care and caution.**

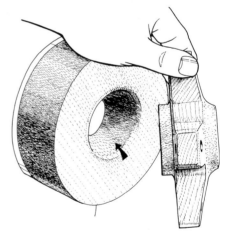

**FIGURE 4-6**

**Turn out the base hole until the neck of the top casing is a nice slide fit.**

**14** Take the whole works off the lathe—the turning on the faceplate—set the cross component in place so the cross plateau is in the hole, and then use the four holes on the cross to drill four matching holes through the base (Fig 4-7).

**15** Finally, remount the base on the lathe and drill, and turn the profile in much the same way as already described. Check your turning against the working drawing (Fig 4-1 bottom).

**FIGURE 4-7**

**With the base still screwed to the faceplate, and using the quatrefoil casing as a pilot guide, bore out the four postholes.**

## MAKING THE CRANKSHAFT BEARINGS

**1** When you have studied the working drawing (Fig 4-1) so you know what you are doing, take the 1"-thick piece of mahogany and use the pencil, ruler, square and compasses to mark the design as seen in side view.

**2** With all the lines in place, and having first established the exact position of the various holes— both the bearing holes and the postholes—bore the holes out with the $1/2$"-diameter bit. Be careful when you run the postholes down through the 1" thickness of the wood; be sure they are well aligned and true.

**3** Take the wood, all marked and drilled, and fret out the two side-view profiles (Fig 4-8).

**4** Mark the plan-view imagery on the newly revealed cut faces, and then begin shaping and sculpting with the scroll saw, knife and tube rasp (Fig 4-9).

**5** Continue whittling, rasping and sanding until you have two well-matched forms (Fig 4-10).

## MAKING THE CRANK AND CONNECTING ROD

**1** Have a look at the working drawing (Fig 4-1), templates (Fig 4-2) and the various photographs, and see that the crank is achieved by having two identical plates and offset dowels.

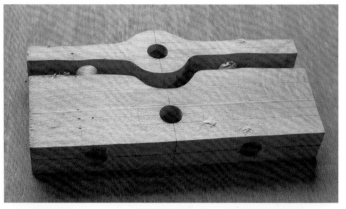

**FIGURE 4-8**

**See how the postholes run through the thickness of the wood.**

**FIGURE 4-9**

**Use the knife, rasp and sandpaper to whittle the crankshaft bearings to shape. Be careful not to force the blade at the relatively fragile short-grained areas.**

**FIGURE 4-10**

**Have repeated fittings until the components come together for a good fit.**

**2** Cut the $3/8$"-thick cherry into two crank-sized pieces, draw the imagery out on one of the pieces, and then fix them together with a single pin at one corner. Keep the pin out of the design area.

**FIGURE 4-11**

**Fitting the single pin and two dowels at the presaw stage ensures that the two crank plates are identical mirror-image cutouts.**

**3** Bore and dowel plug the two $1/2$"-diameter shaft holes right through both pieces of wood, first one hole and then the other. Use lengths of scrap dowel.

**4** With the holes in place, begin fretting out the crank shape on the scroll saw. Work at a steady, even pace, all the while feeding the wood into the blade so the line of cut is a little to the waste side of the drawn line (Fig 4-11).

**5** Having first drawn the shape of the connecting rod on the 1"-thick beech and variously fixed the position of the rod holes, fret out the connecting rod profile as drawn (Fig 4-12).

**6** Draw the side-view imagery of the rod on the sawn face, mark in the waste, and then slice it off on the saw (Fig 4-13).

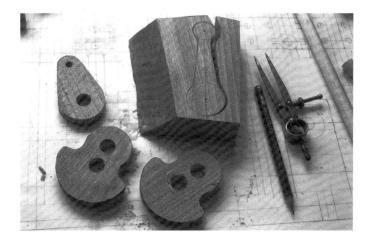

**FIGURE 4-12**

**While you are busy at the scroll saw, you might as well fret out the connecting rod and crank handle.**

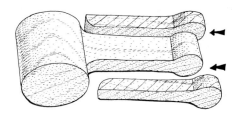

**FIGURE 4-13**

**Slice away the connecting rod waste—as seen in top view.**

**7** Use the knife and rasp to shape the connecting rod. Take your small, sharp knife and whittle the straight part of the rod to a roundish section. The best technique is to set the circle lines of the ends in with a stop-cut on both sides of the wood and at both ends and then to carefully slice the blade into the stop-cut so the waste falls away.

**8** When you have shaped and lowered the round section so the flat faces of the end circles stand somewhat in relief, take a scrap of sandpaper and generally rub down the whole workpiece to a smooth, slightly round-edged finish.

**9** When you have finished fretting and shaping the connecting rod, and drilled out the two holes, go back to the crank plates and wedge the $1/2$" shaft dowels in place (Fig 4-14). The dowels have to run true, so spend time making sure everything is aligned.

## MAKING THE PISTON

**1** Set your chosen square section length of wood on the lathe, and use the large gouge to swiftly turn down the wood to a diameter of $1^3/4$". If all is correct, $1^3/4$" will be slightly larger than the hole that runs through the cross-shaped unit at the top of the engine.

**FIGURE 4-14**

**Slot and wedge the drive shaft stubs into the crank plate. Don't glue at this stage.**

**FIGURE 4-15**

**When you think the piston turning is to size, wind back the tails tack and have a trial fitting.**

**FIGURE 4-16**

**Aim for a nice, smooth-sliding fit.**

**2** This done—and having first set the calipers to the exact diameter of the crosspiece hole—take the skew chisel and turn down the piston so it is an easy-slide fit in the case hole. The best procedure is to carefully draw the tailstock out of the way and then to try the cross casing on for size (Figs 4-15 and 4-16).

**3** Fit the tailstock drill chuck on the lathe, and use the $1^1/_8$"-diameter bit to run a hole down into the cylinder (Fig 4-17).

**4** Push the piston through the scroll saw—or you might prefer to use a handsaw—and take an angled slice from each side (Figs 4-18 and 4-2).

**5** Run a pencil guideline up, down and around the piston, and drill out the $1/_4$"-diameter pinhole—through one side and out the other. It might be a good idea to plug the center of the piston with a length of waste to minimize exit damage.

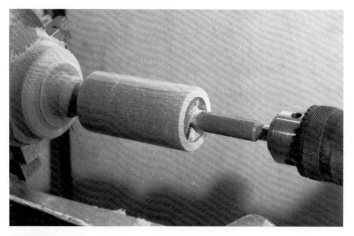

**FIGURE 4-17**

**Use the tailstock drill chuck to bore out the piston waste. Advance cautiously so as not to knock the workpiece off-center.**

**FIGURE 4-18**

**Slice the sides away from the bottom of the piston pot, and sand them to a smooth finish.**

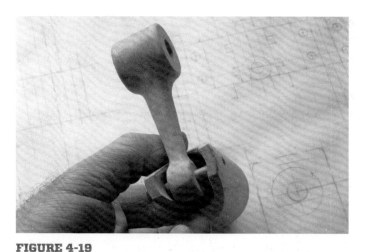

**FIGURE 4-19**

**Have a trial fitting of the connecting rod small end in the piston. The pin needs to be a tight fit in the piston and a loose fit through the small end.**

**6** Have a trial fitting of the small end of the connecting rod in the piston (Fig 4-19).

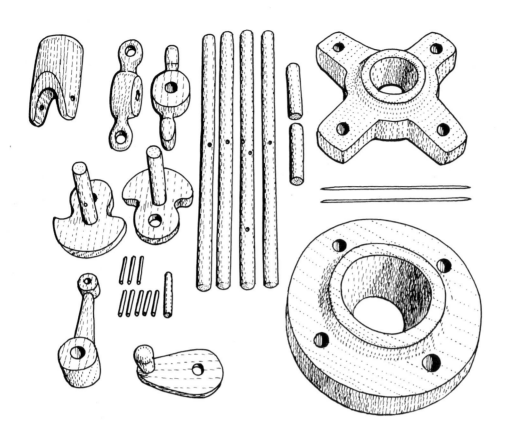

## ASSEMBLY AND FINISHING

**1** When you have before you all the component parts that make up the project (Fig 4-20), then comes the difficult task of putting the machine together.

**2** Start by fitting the small end of the connecting rod in the piston. Aim for a tight fit of the pin through the sides of the piston and a loose fit of the pin through the small end. If need be, rub out selected holes or parts of the pin until everything fits just right (Figs 4-21 and 4-22) .

**3** When you are happy with the fit of the small end in the piston, take the two crank plates—complete with their lengths of drive shaft dowel—and link them with a short length of dowel that runs through the big end bearing at the end of the connecting rod. Make the rod about 2" long (Fig 4-23). Don't glue at this stage.

**4** One piece at a time, fit the piston in the cross-shaped casing, set the crankshaft bearings in place on the dowel ends (Fig 4-24), and set the pair of bearings on the four support dowels (Fig 4-25). Fit little pegs to hold the various components at the correct height.

**5** Continue fitting and sanding and generally easing until the whole machine comes together.

**FIGURE 4-21**

**Pass the short length of crank dowel through the big end, and check for an easy, well-aligned fit.**

**6** Finally, wipe all nonglued surfaces with the teak oil, glue, clamp, burnish the machine to a dull sheen finish, and... hurrah—everything is finished and ready for showing!

**FIGURE 4-22**

**Fit the crank plates so there is a small space between the plate and the flat face of the big end.**

**FIGURE 4-23**

**The crank plates need to have perfect mirror-image alignment.**

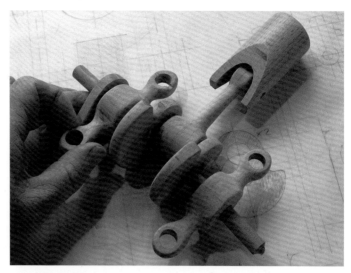

**FIGURE 4-24**

**Fit, check and ease the crankshaft bearings.**

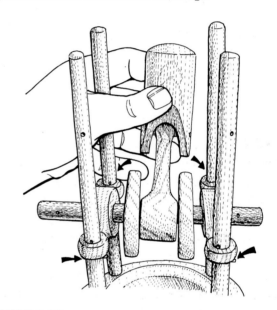

**FIGURE 4-25**

**Set the component parts in place on the posts, and hold them in position with small pegs.**

## PROBLEM SOLVING

• If you like the idea of this project but want to change the design, be mindful that it's not so easy to redesign a single element in isolation. This being so, we would always advise that you make a prototype.

• Any time you are ordering wood, it's always a good idea to ask for wood that is well seasoned and dry, but it's all the more important when you are ordering wood for turning.

• Warning: fitting the crank plates to the drive shaft stubs is difficult—the sort of task that requires a lot of time, a lot of patience, and not too much glue!

# Ward Lock and Key

## PROJECT BACKGROUND

When I was a kid—I must have been about seven years old—I was absolutely fascinated by locks and keys. As I remember, I spent a good deal of my time collecting keys, mending locks, and generally showing friends and family just how easy it was to escape from a locked room.

Most of us are literally surrounded by locks; we can hardly move without first finding our keys. Yet, few of us know how locks work. The good news is our simple ward-and-tumbler locking machine illustrates all the essentials of the archetypal locking mechanism. There is a key, a ward to block the passage of the wrong key, a sliding latch plate, and a tumbler that holds the latch in place. In action, the shaped key is pivoted past the blocking ward knob, with the effect that, in its turning, it lifts the tumbler out of the way and pushes the latch forward (right). So there you go. If you want to know a little more about one of our most common mechanisms, now's your chance.

## MAKING WOODEN MECHANICAL MODELS PROJECT OVERVIEW

Have a look at the working drawing (Fig 5-1) and the templates (Fig 5-2), and see that the locking machine stands about 6" high with a base slab at 8" long and 4½" wide. Note that we have reduced the workings, meaning the number of moving parts, to a minimum in an attempt, as it were, to show the "bones." Of course, most ward locks have a number of springs that bear down on a series of tumblers, but in the context of our machine we feel that a single heavy tumbler falling down under its own weight is enough to demonstrate the basic principle.

Consider how the cavity has been constructed by setting a fretted front plate against a solid back plate. As for the overall design, we have consciously gone for a solid, easy-to-make, good-to-hold structure. All in all, we have kept the fixings to a minimum so everything is in view.

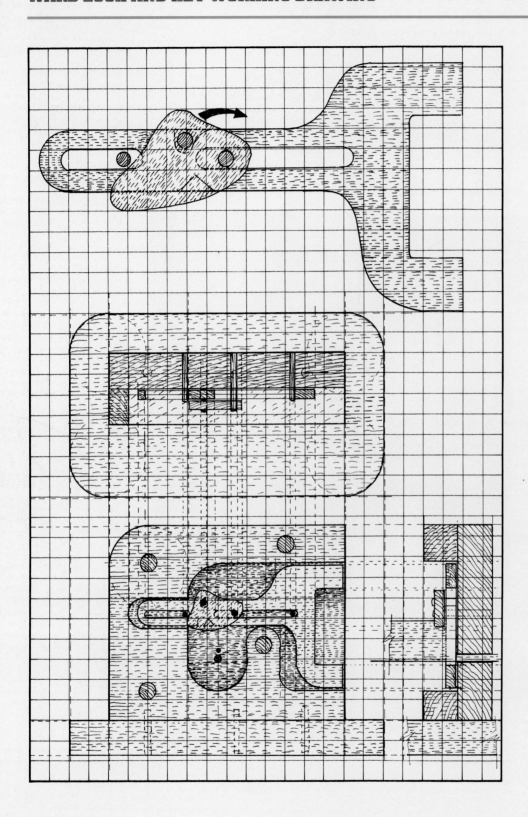

**FIGURE 5-1**
The finished machine stands
about 6" high and about
8" long.
(top) Latch plate and tumbler
at a scale of four grid squares
to 1".
(bottom) Views and section at
a scale of two squares to 1".

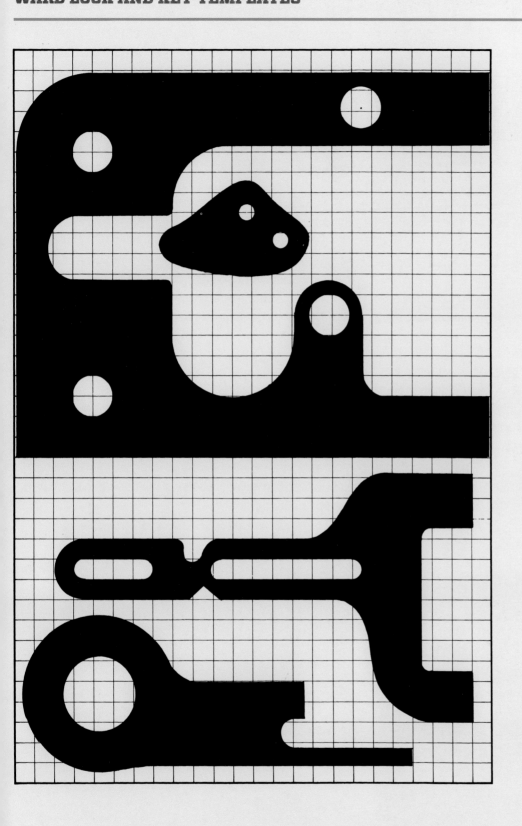

**FIGURE 5-2**

The scale is four grid squares to 1". With a project of this character—where success might hinge on the width of a saw cut or the placing of a dowel hole—you must take it that these profiles are only broad guides.

## CUTTING LIST

| A | Box front | $^7/_8 \times 5 \times 6$ oak |
|---|---|---|
|   | Box back | $^7/_8 \times 5 \times 6$ oak |
| B | Tumbler | $^1/_4 \times 1^1/_4 \times 2$ maple |
| C | Latch plate | $^1/_4 \times 3^1/_4 \times 5^1/_4$ maple |
| D | Key | $^1/_4 \times 2^1/_4 \times 5^1/_4$ cherry |
|   | Base | $^7/_8 \times 4^1/_2 \times 8$ oak |
|   | Pivots | $^1/_4$" dowel |
|   | Decorative pins | 12"—$^1/_2$" dark wood dowel |
|   | Fixing pins | round toothpicks |

## CHOOSING YOUR WOOD

As this is a project that is best made from a hard, straight-grained wood, we have gone for oak for the box and base and maple for the moving parts: the sliding latch and tumbler.

## MAKING THE BOX AND BASE

**1** Have a good, long look at the working drawing (Fig 5-1) and templates (Fig 5-2), and see that the main structure is made up of three pieces of wood: a single slab for the base and two glued and pinned slabs for the box.

**2** With your workshop in good order, and when you are clear in your own mind as to the procedures, take the three slabs of wood—for the base and the box—and use a pencil, ruler and pair of compasses to mark the design. Mark the base with the corner radius curves and the front box slab with the single corner curve and interior shape that needs to be cut away.

**3** Having first pinned the two box slabs together so you have them as if they were a single slab nearly 2" thick, move to the scroll saw and carefully cut out the single radius curve. While you are working on the machine, cut the four curves that make up the base.

**4** Take the two-layer box slab, ease the layers apart, partially withdraw the pins so the points are out of harm's way, and then cut away the central area of waste so you are left with the profile that makes up the front of the box (Fig 5-3).

**5** Align and repin the two box slabs, and run the various holes through with drill bits of a size to fit your dowel (Fig 5-4).

**6** Finally, take the two slabs that make up the box, set them on the base slab, and mark in the position of the three fixing dowels, meaning the three dowels that fix the box to the base.

**FIGURE 5-3**

Having cut the two slabs of wood to the same shape, fret out the front slab to make the latch box cavity.

**FIGURE 5-4**

Drill out all the primary holes, and have a trial fitting of the box to the base slab.

## MAKING AND FITTING THE LATCH PLATE

**1** Take the front-of-box cutout, set it on the ¼"-thick maple—like a template—and use a pencil to transfer the imagery.

**2** Having drawn the shape of the sliding latch plate to size and made a good tracing, use the tracing to press transfer the drawn image through to the box shape you've marked on the maple (Fig 5-5).

**3** If you have a close-up look at the photograph—in this and many other projects—you will perhaps wonder at there being a great number of differences between our initial prototype drawings, as seen on the tracing paper, and the actual workpiece. The project changes a bit as we work on it. If you have a notion that such and such a shape or way of working is the best way, then that is the best way for you.

**4** With the shape of the latch plate clearly marked within the shape of the box, and having made adjustments to allow for easy movement, fix the position of the various holes and pilot piercing within the plate, and run them through with the ¼" drill bit (Fig 5-5).

**5** When you feel all is correct, fret out the latch plate on the scroll saw. Don't bother at this stage to cut the fine details; just go for the main profile.

**6** With the plate partially cut out, wipe the edges with a fine-grade sandpaper to remove any rough edges that might get in the way, and have a trial fitting in the lock box (Fig 5-6). The latch plate should slide neatly backward and forward without sticking or racking.

## MAKING THE KEY AND TUMBLER MECHANISM

**1** When you have completed the basic sliding latch profile and have succeeded in getting it to slide smoothly in the box, then comes the not-so-easy business of fitting the key and tumbler. Start by looking at the working drawing (Fig 5-1) and templates (Fig 5-2), and seeing that the key needs to be cut and worked so the end-of-key profile, or ward, is able to pass over a ward stud that is set in the body of the box.

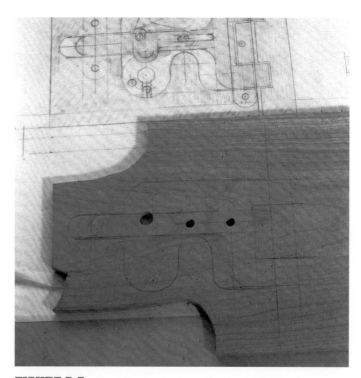

**FIGURE 5-5**

**Having transferred the shape of the box cavity through to the ¼"-thick wood, set to work transferring and modifying the latch profile to ensure a smooth-sliding fit.**

**FIGURE 5-6**

**Fret out the latch plate, and try it out for size. If it's too tight, it won't move, and if it's too loose, it twists and gets stuck—so go at it slowly.**

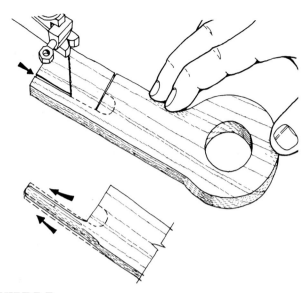

**FIGURE 5-7**

**Cut out the key shape on the drill and scroll saw, and whittle the stalk so it's an easy-to-turn fit in the ¹⁄₄"-diameter box hole.**

**2** Having first cut out the basic shape of the key blank (Fig 5-7), whittle the stem to a round section so it fits in the keyhole, and shape the leading edge of the key (Fig 5-8) so, when it is turned, it catches the notched underside of the latch plate, with the effect that the latch slides forward.

**3** The trick to fitting the key is to trim back little by little, stop and have a fitting, trim back some more and so on (Fig 5-9) until the movement is just right.

**4** When you have cut the key to a good fit, then comes the frustrating task of fitting the tumbler. If you look at the mechanism (Fig 5-10), you will see that the little, shaped profile of the tumbler has two dowels: the one on the far right, which is the pivot, and the one at top center, which is a peg or knob. In action, the turning key catches and lifts the curved underside of the tumbler, with the effect that it swings up on its pivot. And, of course, as the tumbler rises, the peg is lifted out of the notch on the top edge of the latch, and the turning key goes on to move the latch.

**5** Once again, you might well have to cut two or three tumbler plates and play around with the position of the pivot hole and the shape of the underside curve before you get it just right.

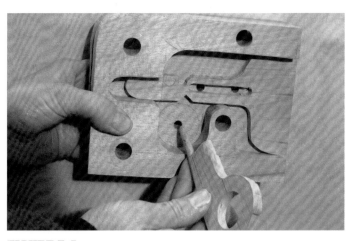

**FIGURE 5-8**

**Whittle away the leading edge of the key so it fits in the notch on the underside of the latch.**

**FIGURE 5-9**

**Continue whittling the leading edge of the key to shape so when it turns, it catches and moves the sliding latch plate.**

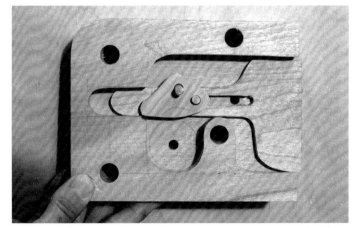

**FIGURE 5-10**

**Shape and fit the tumbler. Eventually, the pivot peg needs to be glued into the tumbler plate and held in place with a round toothpick with the heel end of the pivot running back through the box. The other dowel is no more than a stub that sticks out at the back of the tumbler plate—to rest in the latch notch.**

## ASSEMBLY AND FINISHING

**1** When you have achieved a smooth movement of the key, tumbler and latch, take the latch plate back to the drill and the scroll saw and finish cutting the other location slot and the two-pronged bolt profile on the leading edge of the latch (Fig 5-11).

**2** Having fretted out all the component parts that make up the project, spread them out (Fig 5-12) and check them over for potential problems.

**3** When the whole movement is smooth running, fit the ward knob in the back of the box, and whittle a little bridge ward on the bottom edge of the key so it just clears the knob. The idea is, of course, that only your key will fit into the lock (Fig 5-13).

**FIGURE 5-13**

**With the latch being held in place with a couple of temporary dowel pegs, fit the ward stub in the back plate, and whittle the key ward to shape—like a little bridge.**

**4** Finally, when you are happy with all the moving parts, fit and glue the dowels and pins that hold the sliding latch in place, glue and peg the two layers that make up the box, glue and peg the box to the base, and so forth (Fig 5-14). When the glue is completely dry, rub down all surfaces to a smooth finish, wipe the whole works with the teak oil, and the project is finished.

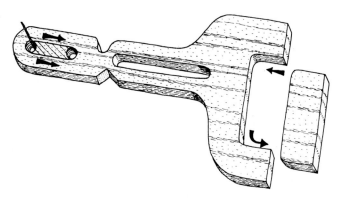

**FIGURE 5-11**

**Having established the position of the slot at the back end of the latch, go back to the scroll saw and finish cutting the profile.**

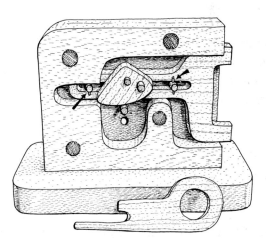

**FIGURE 5-14**

**Finally, glue and dowel the whole works together. Note how the latch is held in place by dowels that are end pinned.**

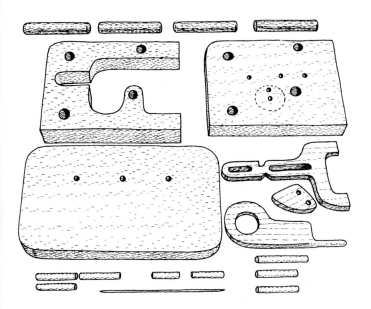

**FIGURE 5-12**

**The component parts—all ready for the final fitting.**

### PROBLEM SOLVING

• If you like the idea of this project you can adapt it to fit other kinds of locks.

• When we designed this project, we had in mind that we would cut and fit a wooden leaf spring to firmly hold the tumbler on the latch. It's still a good idea; you could use a piece of springy wood, like bamboo.

• This is one of those projects where you need to hold back with the sanding until the mechanism is up and working. I say this because you might well need to make several keys or several tumblers before you get everything just right.

# Reciprocating Engine

## PROJECT BACKGROUND

The reciprocating machine beautifully illustrates all the movements that make up the archetypal combustion engine. At the turn of a handle, it's plain to see how the up-and-down movement of a piston is converted, by way of a crank, into rotary motion (right).

If you are looking to make a relatively easy project, this is the one for you.

## PROJECT OVERVIEW

Having said the project is easy to make—and it really is—this is not to say you can do it with your eyes closed. Yes, the various cuts are straightforward, and no, you don't need a fancy tool kit, but the cutting and shaping procedures do need to be completed with care. For example, although the fretted side runners can be cut on the fret saw—and this is swift and easy—the various layers that make up the sections of the runners need to be carefully drawn out.

The working action is pretty to watch. As the handle is turned—either clockwise or counterclockwise, it makes no difference—the crank turns on its pivot, with the effect that the piston slides up and down in its runners. But don't forget, when you are giving that science fair lecture, to mention that the real-life in-car movement is reversed, with the combustion pushing down on the piston and the rotary crank driving the road wheels.

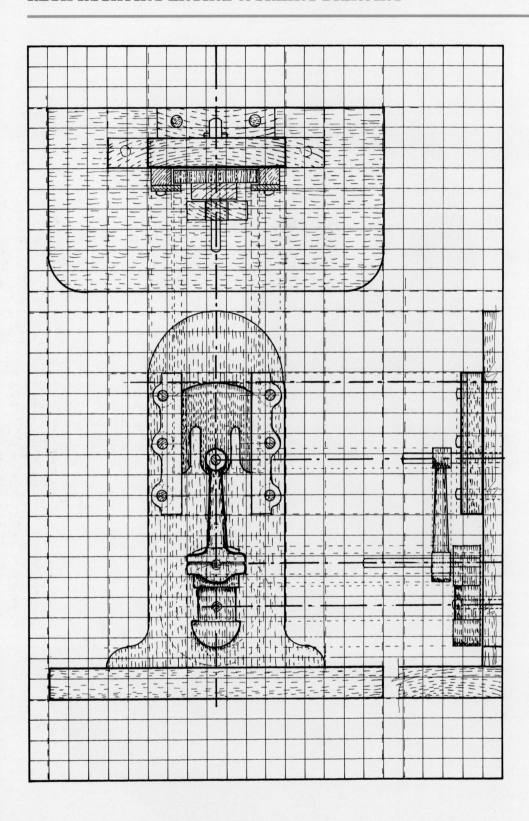

**FIGURE 6-1**

At a grid scale of two squares to 1", the machine stands about 9" high, 8$\frac{1}{2}$" wide across the span of the base and 4$\frac{1}{2}$" in depth.

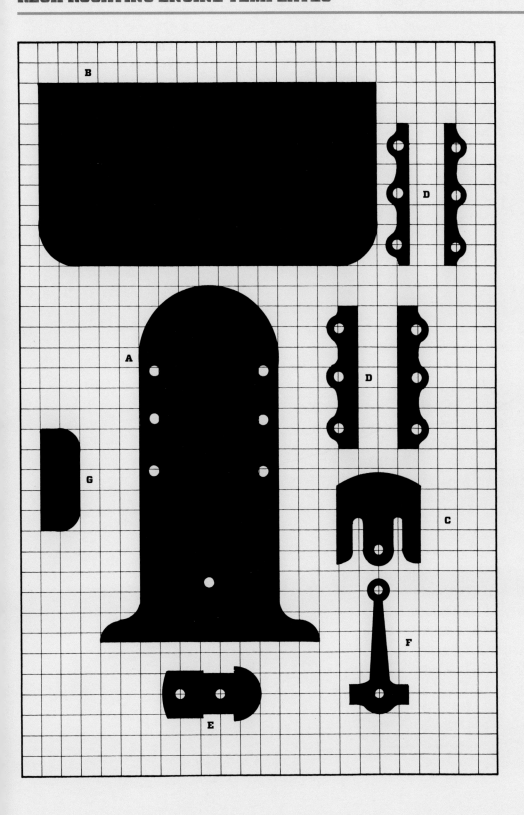

**FIGURE 6-2**

The scale is two grid squares to 1". Note that, as with all the templates in the book, the profiles are more a diagrammatic guide than actual templates. This being so, it's always a good idea to check out the sizes and the placings of the various fixing and pivot holes before cutting your wood.

**A** Backboard.

**B** Base.

**C** Piston.

**D** Slide rails.

$^3/_{16}$" thick.

$^1/_8$" thick.

**E** Crank.

**F** Connecting rod.

**G** Buttress.

## CUTTING LIST

| | | |
|---|---|---|
| A | Backboard | $3/4 \times 5^1/_2 \times 9$ straight-grained, knot-free tulip |
| B | Base | $3/4 \times 4^1/_2 \times 8^1/_2$ tulip |
| C | Piston | $3/8 \times 2^1/_4 \times 3^1/_4$ mahogany |
| D | Slide rails | $5/8 \times 1 \times 8$ cherry |
| | $3/_{16}$" thick | |
| | $3/8$" thick | |
| E | Crank | $3/4 \times 3/8 \times 2^1/_2$ pitch pine |
| F | Connecting rod | $1/2 \times 2 \times 3^3/_4$ pitch pine |
| G | Buttress | $3/4 \times 1 \times 2^1/_2$ |
| | Pegs and pivots | $1/4$" dowel |

## CHOOSING YOUR WOOD

If you are anything at all like us—like most woodworkers, in fact—the never-ending question is what to do with the ever-growing pile of offcuts. Yes, it does seem a pity to throw out small pieces of exotic wood left over from large projects, but what to do with them? Well now, no such problems here. This is a great project for using up odds and ends! After searching through our stockpile, we decided to go for straight-grained tulip for the base and backboard (it needs to be strong); cherry for the runners, pitch pine for the crank and connecting rod; mahogany for the piston; and dowels for the various pins and pivots. Note: if you look through the various photographs, you will see that the top, back edge of the backboard is shaped. Don't worry about it. It's not important. It's just a bit left over from another project.

## MAKING THE BASE AND BACKBOARD

**1** Having carefully studied the working drawing (Fig 6-1) and templates (Fig 6-2), take the two pieces of tulip and use the pencil, ruler, square and compasses to mark all the lines that make up the design.

**2** Spend time carefully marking in the position of the center lines, the crank pivot hole, and any other guidelines you think are necessary. If you are at all unsure as to what goes where and how, shade in the areas that need to be cut away.

**3** When you feel all is correct, move to the scroll saw, and set to work cutting out the profiles. Having made sure the blade is well tensioned, run the workpiece into the saw so the blade is always presented with the angle of best cut and the line of cut is fractionally to the waste side of the drawn line.

**4** Drill and peg the backboard to the base with the pegs run in at a slight angle, check with a square, and generally see to it that everything is square and stable.

## MAKING AND FITTING THE SLIDE RAILS

**1** Before you do anything else, have another good, long look at the working drawing (Fig 6-1) and the sequence of photographs, and see that the pair of slide rails are achieved by being first sliced into four layers—two for each rail—and then marked out, drilled, fretted to shape and reassembled. Note how the order of work—first drilling and pegging and then fretting—ensures that profiles and holes match up.

**2** When you have sliced the slide rail wood into four 4"-long, 1"-wide layers—two at $3/_{16}$" thick and two at a little over $3/8$" thick—draw the imagery on one or other of the layers.

**3** With the four pieces of wood sanded down and clamped securely together, drill the three dowel holes through all four thicknesses of wood.

**4** Push lengths of $1/4$" dowel through the holes to hold the four pieces of wood together, and fret out the total three-curve shape on the scroll saw (Fig 6-3).

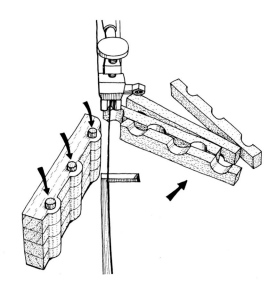

**FIGURE 6-3**

**With the dowels to hold the layers in place, carefully fret out the shape of the runners, or rails. If the blade starts to wander off course, it's a sure sign either the blade is worn or the tension is too slack.**

**FIGURE 6-4A**

Having carefully pencil labeled the layers so they are nicely matched up and you know what goes where and how, slice away the strip of waste from the back layer. It's easy to make a mess-up, so be sure to get it right the first time around.

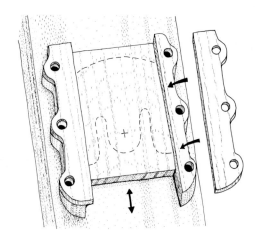

**FIGURE 6-4B**

The piston needs to be a good fit—not so sloppy it tilts to the side nor so tight there is any friction, just an easy, comfortable fit.

**5** Slice a ¼"-wide strip from the straight edge of both thick layers (Fig 6-4A), and have a trial fitting. Label the layers so you know precisely what goes where (Fig 6-4B).

**6** Having completed two identical, two-layer rails, carefully set the rails in place on the backboard, and mark in the position of the six peg-fixing holes. While you are at it—if you haven't already done it—mark in the position of the crank pivot hole, run the holes through with the ¼" bit and have another fitting (Fig 6-5).

## CUTTING THE PISTON

**1** Take your chosen piece of wood and check its thickness by sliding it in the rails. It needs to be an easy, smooth-running fit between the rail and the backboard. If need be, reduce the thickness to fit.

**FIGURE 6-5**

Drill the seven holes, and have a trial fitting of the rails. Aim to have the rail pegs standing slightly proud. Note that the crank peg as shown is no more than a tryout.

**2** Draw the design on the working face of your chosen piece of wood, mark the center line, and fix the position of the pivot. Shade in the area that needs to be cut out.

**3** When you have double-checked that everything is well placed—the profile lines and the position of the pivot point—go back to the scroll saw and fret out the shape (Fig 6-6). As always, work at a nice, easy pace, all the while being ready to ease back if the blade starts to bend or if the line of cut looks to be running away from the drawn line.

**4** Finally, take a scrap of fine-grade sandpaper and rub down the edges of the piston cutout to a slightly rounded finish to create a good, sliding fit between the rail tracks and the backboard.

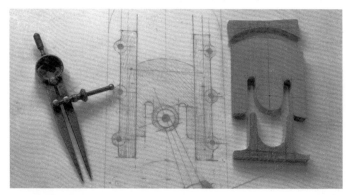

**FIGURE 6-6**

It's important you go for a straight-grained wood, and equally important you mark the profile so the grain is aligned with the center line. This way of working ensures that there is a minimum of weak, short-grained areas.

## CUTTING AND WHITTLING THE CRANK AND CONNECTING ROD

**1** Have a look at the working drawing (Fig 6-1) and templates (Fig 6-2), and consider that the two components—the crank and the connecting rod—are first cut out on the scroll saw and then whittled.

**2** One piece at a time, draw the lines of the design, fix the position of the various pivot holes, and fret out the profiles on the scroll saw (Fig 6-7).

**3** With all the lines and center points in place, and having carefully checked for accuracy, run the four $1/4$"-diameter holes through on the drill press.

**4** Starting with the connecting rod, take your knife and set to work whittling the cutout to shape. And just in case you are a beginner to whittling, if your knife is sharp, and if you are working with an easy-to-cut piece of wood, you won't have any problems.

**5** Having once again studied the working drawing (Fig 6-1), templates (Fig 6-2) and photographs, take your small, sharp knife and start whittling the straight part of the rod to a roundish section. The best technique is to set in the circle lines of the ends with stopcuts—on both sides of the wood and at both ends—and then to carefully slice the blade into the stop-cut so the waste falls away. If you work with a careful thumb-braced paring cut, you won't have any problems with the knife slipping (Fig 6-8).

**6** When you have shaped and lowered the round section so the flat faces of the end circles stand somewhat proud, take a scrap of sandpaper and generally rub down the whole workpiece to a smooth, slightly round-edged finish.

**7** Run a V-cut around the big end to achieve the illusion that—just like a metal casting—the form is made up of two parts.

**8** When you are pleased with the overall shape and feel of the connecting rod, follow through with more or less the same whittling procedures for the crank. That is to say, set the ends in with stop-cuts, and then pare away the central portion so it is half-round in section. Make sure the square, flat end stands slightly higher than the rest of the piece.

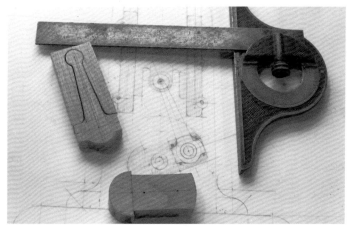

**FIGURE 6-7**

**Run the center line in the direction of the grain, and then have the profile set square and symmetrical with the line. Be sure to double-check the position of the dowel holes.**

**FIGURE 6-8**

**Work with a careful thumb-braced paring stroke, all the while being ready to brake if the blade slips. Tip: a razor-sharp blade is much safer to use than a blunt blade that needs to be bullied into action.**

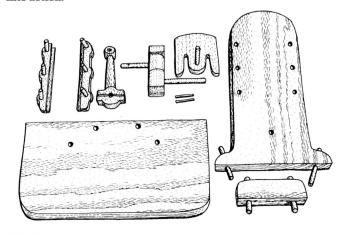

**FIGURE 6-9**

**When you have completed all the component parts that make up the project, spread them out on the work surface, and check them over just to make sure everything is correct.**

## ASSEMBLY AND FINISHING

**1** When you have completed all the component parts that make up the project (Fig 6-9), then comes the pleasure of putting the machine together.

**2** Having rubbed down all faces and edges with a sheet of fine-grade sandpaper, wiped away the dust, and had another trial fitting—just to make sure everything comes together for a good fit—give all nonglued surfaces a swift wipe with the teak oil, and put the whole works to one side to dry.

**3** Glue and peg the backboard to the base so it's at right angles, and glue and peg the buttress in place. It's important everything is true, so spend time checking with the ruler and square (Fig 6-10).

**4** Glue and peg the rails in place, check that the piston still fits, wipe away any excess glue and clamp up.

**5** Glue the three pivot rods in place: the small end rod that stands out from the piston, the rod that runs out from the back of the crank, and the handle or big-end rod that stands out from the front of the crank. Wipe away excess glue, check alignment, and put the rods to one side until the glue is set (Fig 6-11).

**6** Finally, slide the crank rod through the backboard, fit the fixing pin, slide the piston down in place between the rails, set the connecting rod on both the crank rod and the piston rod, and . . . the project is finished.

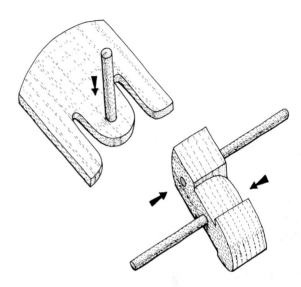

**FIGURE 6-11**

**The movement hinges on the dowel rods being carefully placed so they are square with the working face. Make several checks. (left) Piston. (right) Crank.**

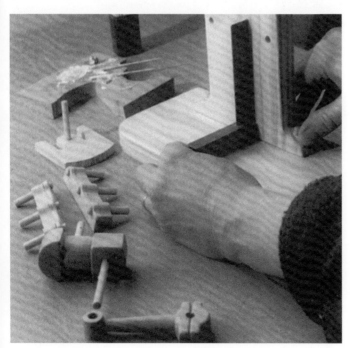

**FIGURE 6-10**

**Having glued, check for squareness before clamping.**

### PROBLEM SOLVING

• If you like the idea of this project but want to change the design, no problem, as long as there is clearance between the bottom of the piston and the rounded end of the crank and between the square end of the crank and the base slab. If in doubt, it's always a good idea to make a working model.

• When you are ordering your wood, always ask for wood that is well seasoned and dry. I say this because partly seasoned wood is likely to split, warp or shrink, and damp wood is difficult to work.

• Having said the straight-grained tulip is suitable for the backboard and the base, this is not to say it is suitable for the small parts that are to be whittled. If you have any doubts as to the suitability of such and such a wood for whittling, it's a good idea to try a sample with your knife.

• Shop-bought dowel rod is a problem inasmuch as the sizing is variable and unreliable. For example, my so called $1/4$"-diameter dowel is a very loose fit in a $1/4$" hole, whereas my $1/2$" dowel is too big for a $1/2$" hole and a sloppy, loose fit for a $3/8$" hole. This being so, it's always a good idea to check out your dowel supply at the start of a project, and then modify the project accordingly.

# Oil Pumping Rig

## PROJECT BACKGROUND

We have tried in this project to capture the essential imagery—the tower, or derrick, seesaw beam, crank and nodding donkeylike head. The movement is beautifully direct: when the handle is turned, the crank revolves, with the effect that the beam oscillates and the loose-pivoted donkey head at the end of the beam slowly nods up and down.

## PROJECT OVERVIEW

Have a look at the project picture (right), the working drawing (Fig 7-1) and the templates (Fig 7-2), and note that the machine is made up of six primary elements: a base slab, tower, balance beam at the top of the tower, pivot plate that holds the beam, crank, and connecting rod. And, of course, there are secondary elements like the donkey head and the various pins and pivots.

This project is ideally suited for the beginner, inasmuch as it can be cut and worked with nothing more complicated than a scroll saw and pillar drill. What else to say, except that this machine is great fun to make and great fun to watch in action.

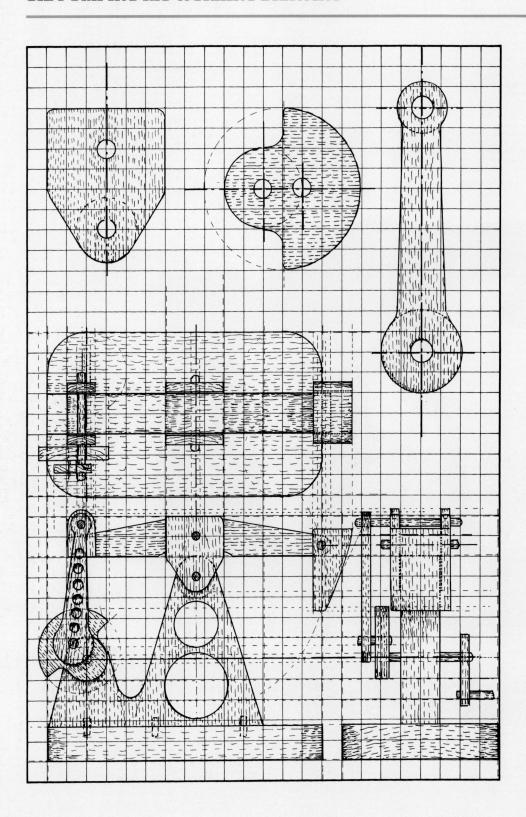

**FIGURE 7-1**

The machine stands about 6" high and 7" long.

(top) The grid scale is four squares to 1".

(bottom) The grid scale is two squares to 1".

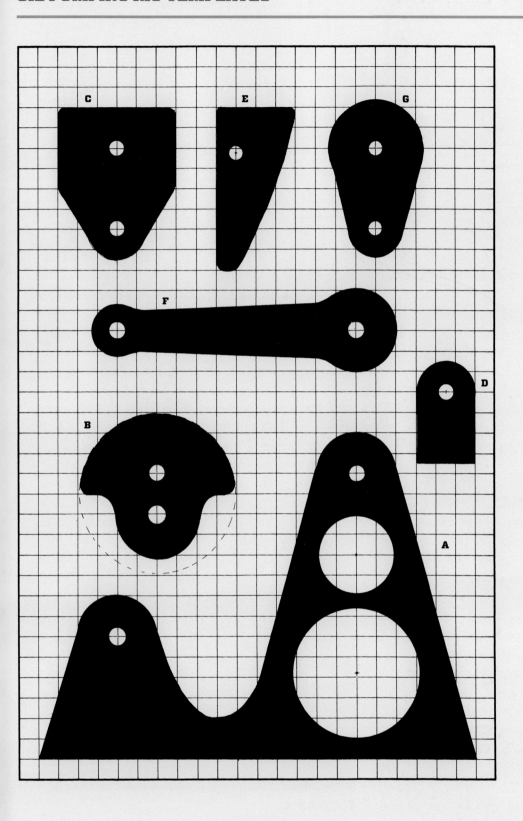

**FIGURE 7-2**

**The scale is four grid squares to 1".**

**A** Derrick tower.

**B** Crank plate.

**E** Center pivot plates.

**F** End pivot plates.

**E** Donkey head.

sides.

center.

**F** Connecting rod.

**G** Handle.

## CUTTING LIST

| A | Derrick tower | $7/8 \times 6 \times 7$ tulip |
|---|---|---|
| B | Crank plate | $1 \times 3/8 \times 2 \times 2$ pitch pine |
| C | Center pivot plates | $2\text{—}1/4 \times 1^{1}/_{2} \times 2$ mahogany |
| D | End pivot plates | $2\text{—}1/4 \times 3/4 \times 1^{1}/_{4}$ mahogany |
| E | Donkey head: sides | $2\text{—}1/4 \times 1 \times 2$ mahogany |
| | center | $7/8 \times 1 \times 2$ cedar |
| F | Connecting rod | $1/4 \times 1^{1}/_{4} \times 4$ mahogany |
| G | Handle | $1/4 \times 1^{1}/_{4} \times 2$ mahogany |
| | Base | $7/8 \times 4 \times 7$ tulip |
| | Beam | $7/8 \times 1 \times 8$ cedar |
| | Pivot rods | $1/4$" dowel |
| | Fixing pins | round toothpicks |

## CHOOSING YOUR WOOD

In the context of this easy-to-make project—no wood turning or fancy carving—all that is required of the wood is that it be easy to cut and work. That said, what better woods to use than tulip and mahogany? We chose tulip for the base and derrick; scraps of mahogany for the pivot plates, donkey head cheeks, connecting rod and handle; cedar for various bits and pieces, and shop-bought dowel for the pins and pivots.

## MAKING THE BASE, DERRICK AND BEAM

**1** Having spent time studying the working drawing (Fig 7-1) and the templates (Fig 7-2), bringing your tools to good order, and generally making sure your chosen wood is in tip-top condition, draw the design to size and make a clear tracing.

**2** Take your chosen $7/8$"-thick wood, note how the grain needs to run in relation to the profiles, meaning the shape of the base, beam and derrick, and then carefully transfer the imagery accordingly. The best procedure is to first establish the position of the baseline and the center lines, then fix the position of the centerpoints for the holes and curves, and then finalize the profiles with the compass and ruler.

**3** Having marked the base slab, beam and derrick, and being satisfied with the way the imagery relates to your chosen pieces of wood, move to the scroll saw and set to work cutting out the profiles (Fig 7-3).

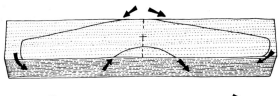
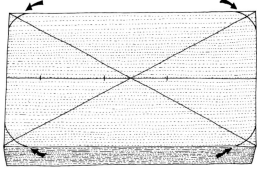

**FIGURE 7-3**

**Although both the base and the beam are simple structures, this is all the more reason they need to be carefully marked. If you decide to redesign such and such a detail, bear in mind that smooth, easy curves are much easier to cut and work than small, tight angles.**

**4** Having fretted out the three primary profiles, move to the bench drill and set to work sinking the various holes that make up the design. Don't worry too much about the two large pierced holes in the derrick (Fig 7-4)—they can be larger or smaller or even placed in a different position; it makes no difference—but do make sure the pivot and fixing holes in the derrick and beam are precisely placed.

**FIGURE 7-4**

**When you come to sink large-diameter holes, the working procedure is to run the bit in for about $1/8$", then bring it up and out and clear the waste, run the drill in another $1/8$", clear the waste and so on until the hole has been cut. If you try to force the pace and run the hole through in one great thrust, you risk splitting the wood or doing damage to the drill bit.**

**FIGURE 7-5**

**It's always a good idea to stop along the way and try out the component parts for size. This method of working gives you time to assess your progress.**

**5** Finally, having cut out the three primary components and drilled the holes, have a trial fitting and set them in place one on top of another (Fig 7-5). It's important the derrick stands true to the base and the beam sits square. To this end, spend time sanding and adjusting to a good fit.

## MAKING THE PIVOT PLATES AND DONKEY HEAD

**1** Before you put tool to wood, cast your eyes over the working drawing (Fig 7-1) and templates (Fig 7-2), and see how various plates and parts come together. Note how the pivot plates at the tail and center of the beam are cut and worked in pairs and pinned and glued at either side of the beam, while the donkey head is made up of three layers and loose pivoted on the end of the beam.

**2** When you have a clear understanding of just how the parts need to be worked, meaning the order of work and the procedures, take the two ¼"-thick pieces of wood that make up the tail and center plates and pin them together with a couple of tacks so you have a two-layer sandwich.

**3** Now, having drawn the imagery, fixed the center points, and drilled out the ¼"-diameter center plate pivot hole, tap a length of dowel in the hole to ensure that the holes are identically placed, and run the wood through the scroll saw (Fig 7-6). Repeat the procedure with the tail plates.

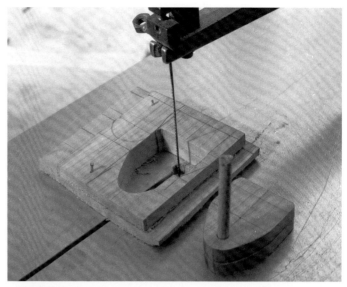

**FIGURE 7-6**

**If you need to cut out a number of multiple parts, meaning identically matched parts, it's a good idea to layer up the wood, drill out any holes, and cut out all the parts at once.**

**4** When you have completed the two sets of plates—all cleanly fretted and drilled—set them in place on the beam, and have a trial fitting. Pencil label the plates with alignment marks so you know what goes where and how, and decide which of the surfaces are to be glued.

**5** To make the donkey head, rerun the layering and cutting procedures as already described, only this time, cut through three layers of wood rather than two.

**FIGURE 7-7**

**Having achieved the three identical profiles that make up the donkey head, cut away the waste from the middle layer.**

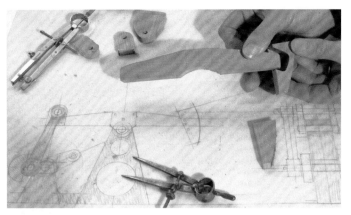

**FIGURE 7-8**

The head needs to be a loose-rocking fit on the end of the beam. Spend time variously rounding over the end of the beam or cutting the hole bigger.

**6** Having achieved the three identical scroll-sawn profiles that make up the donkey head, carefully saw away the waste from the middle layer (Fig 7-7). If you have done it correctly, when you reassemble the three layers—the thin layers on the outside and the thicker, partially cutaway layer at the center—you should finish up with a little hatlike structure that sits neatly on the end of the beam (Fig 7-8). Check the head for size.

## MAKING THE CONNECTING ROD, CRANK PLATE AND HANDLE

**1** Have a look at the working drawing (Fig 7-1) and templates (Fig 7-2), and see how the connecting rod needs to be cut and worked. Note that the row of blind holes is no more than a decorative feature.

**2** Draw the profiles to size, and transfer them through to your chosen pieces of wood.

**3** The crank and handle plates (Fig 7-9) are straight-forward: establish the position of the pivot holes, drill them, and then fret out the profiles on the scroll saw .

**4** When you have fretted out the handle plate, check it out for size, and decide how it is going to be placed in relation to the whole structure. For example, if you look at the photograph (Fig 7-10), you will see that in the first instance, we considered having the handle on what came to be the front of the machine.

**5** The connecting rod is simple enough to make: All you do is fret out the total shape, run the pivot holes through with the $^{1}/_{4}$"-diameter bit, and then sink the blind holes at regular step-offs along the center line (Fig 7-11).

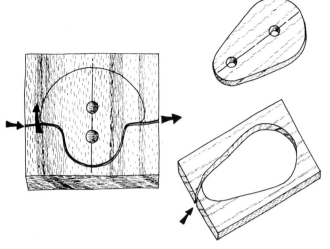

**FIGURE 7-9**

The precise shapes of the crank plate and the crank aren't too important, as long as the profiles are well placed with the run of the grain and the position of the holes is positively established. To this end, you must double-check the position of the hole center points and see to it that the initial marking relates to the grain.

**FIGURE 7-10**

Try the handle plate for size, and make sure there is enough clearance between the swing and the base.

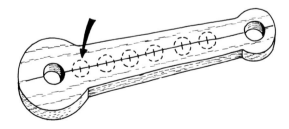

**FIGURE 7-11**

To mark the connecting rod, draw in the center line, establish the distance between the two pivot points, and decide on the best size of drill bit for the blind holes.

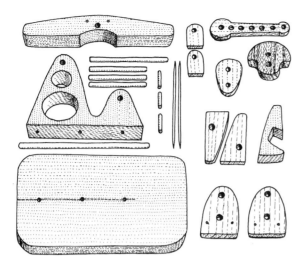

**FIGURE 7-12**

Set out all the component parts—all drilled and with most of the raw edges sanded back—and check them for potential problems.

## ASSEMBLY AND FINISHING

**1** When you have completed all the component parts that make up the design, spread them out on the work surface, and check them for potential problems (Fig 7-12).

**2** When you are pleased with all the component parts, take the finest-grade sandpaper and swiftly rub down all the faces, edges and corners. Pay particular attention to bearing faces, meaning surfaces that are going to rub together.

**3** Having drilled, pegged, glued and clamped the derrick to the base—and put it to one side so it is out of harm's way—then comes the tricky task of gluing and fitting the donkey head.

**4** Being mindful that the head needs to be a loose-pivoted fit on the end of the beam and the beam and middle layer are both cut from the same $^7/_8$" inch wood, it follows that the head end of the beam will need to be reduced in thickness. The best procedure is to glue and clamp the head, try it on the end of the beam for size (Fig 7-13), and then reduce the beam thickness accordingly.

**5** Have a trial placement of the various beam plates, and make sure you are clear in your own mind as to how the parts need to come together.

**6** Fit, drill, glue and peg the two pivot plates in place, set the two connecting-rod bearing plates at the tail end of the beam, and glue and clamp them in place.

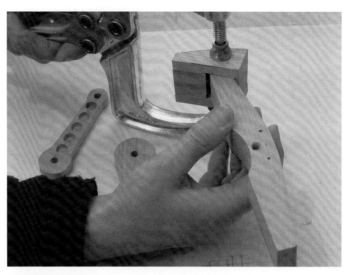

**FIGURE 7-13**

Having glued and clamped the donkey head, try it on for size, and reduce the width of the beam end for a loose fit.

**7** When you are happy with the placement of the various plates, set the donkey head on the beam, and fit with a pivot rod. Make sure the head is a loose-nodding fit (Fig 7-14).

**8** Finally, glue the two rods in place in the crank plate, set all the pins in place, and have a trial run to test out the movement.

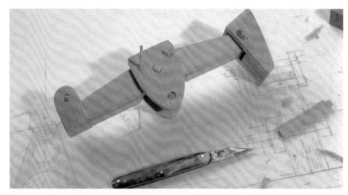

**FIGURE 7-14**

Drill and pivot the donkey head so it is a loose-nodding fit. If you have got it right, the peg should be a tight fit through the beam and a loose fit through the sides of the head.

### PROBLEM SOLVING

• As always, much will depend on your tool kit. If you can't get use of large drill bit sizes or you have to make your own dowels or whatever, you will of course have to modify the techniques accordingly.

# Centrifugal Impeller Pump

## PROJECT BACKGROUND

The poor, old, impeller pump is one of those clever little bits of unsung machinery that's been around for such a long time that we either take it for granted or simply don't know it's there! Centrifugal impeller pumps are used primarily to move liquid along pipes. And they aren't too particular about the liquid: water, oil, petroleum, beer—it's all the same to them.

The classic centrifugal impeller pump consists of a wheel enclosed within a hollow chamber or reservoir, with the wheel having sliding gates and the chamber having slots or holes. In action, when the wheel spins around, the gates fly outward, with the effect that the liquid within the box is suddenly caught up in an enclosed space that is getting smaller. And, of course, when the body of fastmoving liquid passes one of the slots or holes, it is forced out under pressure.

With our pump, when the crank handle is turned, the centrifugal force causes the little gates to slide out of their slots and follow the casing profile (right).

## PROJECT OVERVIEW

Have a look at the working drawing (Fig 8-1) and the templates (Fig 8-2), and see that, in essence, the machine is made up of four primary elements: a fretted base slab, cradle and collar, turned tube, or chamber, that sits in the cradle, and turned shaft with integral vanes, or gates, that pivot within the chamber.

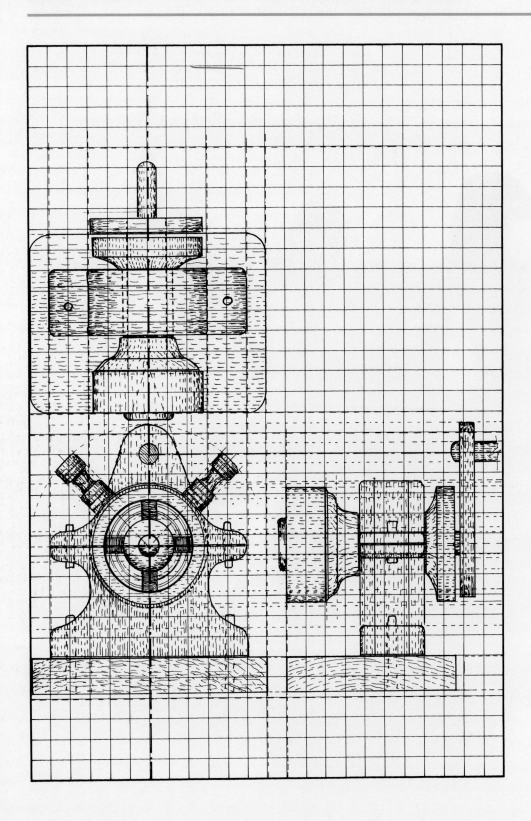

**FIGURE 8-1**

At a grid scale of two squares to 1", the machine stands about 7" high with a slab at 6" long.

# CENTRIFUGAL IMPELLER PUMP TEMPLATES

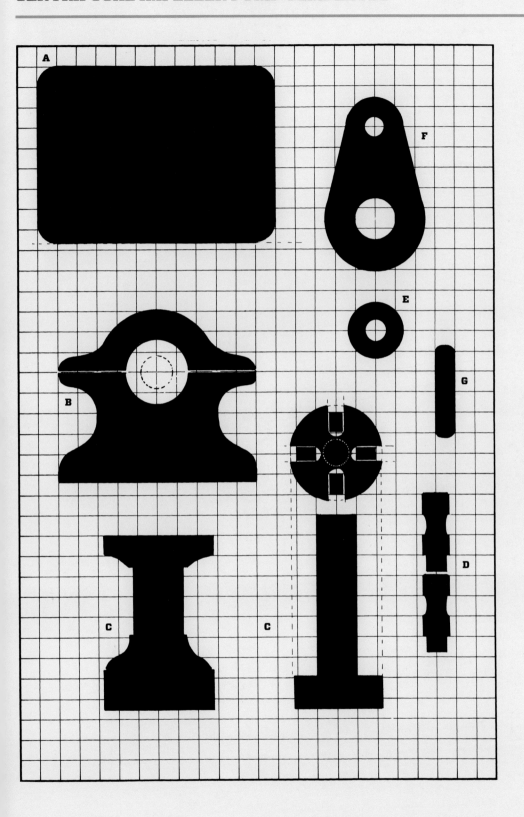

**FIGURE 8-2**

**The scale is two grid squares to 1".**

**A** Base slab.

**B** Cradle.

    sides.

    center.

**C** Main turnings.

    chamber.

    shaft.

**D** Pipes.

**E** Boss ring.

**F** Crank plate.

**G** Crank handle.

## CUTTING LIST

| A | Base slab | $^7/_8 \times 4^1/_2 \times 7$ cedar |
|---|---|---|
| B | Cradle: | |
| | sides | $2{-}^1/_2 \times 6 \times 6$ plum |
| | center | $^7/_8 \times 6 \times 6$ beech |
| C | Main turnings | $4 \times 4 \times 20$ tulip |
| | chamber | |
| | shaft | |
| D | Pipes | $1 \times 1$ beech |
| E | Boss ring | $^1/_2 \times 1^3/_4 \times 1^3/_4$ plum |
| F | Crank plate | $^3/_8 \times 2^1/_2 \times 4^1/_4$ plum |
| G | Crank handle | $2^1/_4" {-}^1/_2"$ white dowel |

## MAKING THE BASE, CRADLE AND CRANK HANDLE

**1** When you have studied the working drawing (Fig 8-1), templates (Fig 8-2) and the various hands-on illustrations, and when you have gathered your wood and brought your tools to order, draw the design to size, and make a tracing.

**2** Take your chosen pieces of wood—the piece for the slab and the piece for the crank plate—and use the square, ruler and compasses to mark the profiles.

**3** Having marked the slab and crank handle, take the three layers that make up the cradle, and sandwich them together so that you have a total slab thickness of about $1^3/_4"$.

**4** Take the pencil, ruler and compasses and mark the shape of the cradle on the topmost layer of the sandwich. Make sure you arrange the profile so the grain runs through the cradle from the top down to baseline.

**5** With the design carefully drawn out, tap three or four thin pins through the sandwich—down through the area of waste that is to be cut away—to ensure the three layers stay put.

**6** When you are happy with the layout, use the scroll saw to cut out the profile.

**7** Continue feeding the wood into the saw, slowly maneuvering around the curves, cutting out the circle of waste and so on until the profile is cut out (Fig 8-3).

**FIGURE 8-3**

**Secure the sandwich with pins and fret out the form on the scroll saw. Be careful at the end of the cut—when the layers are no longer pinned—that the layers don't slide out of kilter.**

**8** Take the crank plate, drill the holes through on the drill press, and then fret out the shape on the scroll saw (Fig 8-4).

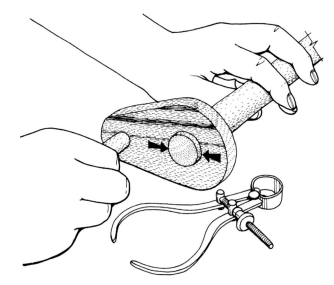

**FIGURE 8-4**

**Check the crank handle for shape and size—I use a length of dowel—and take an accurate caliper reading of the shaft hole.**

**9** Finally, sand the parts to a good, smooth, round-edged finish.

## TURNING THE CHAMBER AND SHAFT

**1** Before you put tool to wood, have a look at the working drawing (Fig 8-1), the templates (Fig 8-2) and various hands-on photographs, and see that the main body of the pump is made up of two components: a hollow chamber and shaft. Note the way the outside of the shaft is spigoted and the inside of the chamber is stepped so the two come together for a smooth-turning, sliding fit. Having noted that we've turned the two component parts from a single length of wood, this is not to say you can't go for two separate turnings.

**2** When you are clear on the order of work and the procedures, take your 4" × 4" square section of easy-to-turn wood—we use tulip—and establish the end center points by drawing crossed diagonals.

**3** Turn down the wood to a round section of about 3", then take the ruler and dividers and mark along the cylinder all the step-offs that make up the design. Working from right to left, that is, from the tailstock end, allow a small amount for tailstock waste, $^1/_2$" for the back end of the chamber, $^3/_8$" for the first cove, about $1^7/_8$" for the neck, $^3/_8$" for the next cove, $^3/_8$" for the bead, 1" for what will be the front band of the chamber, about $^3/_8$" for waste, $^7/_8$" for what will be the spigoted end of the drive shaft, meaning the bit with the sliding gates, 4" for the length of the shaft, and the remainder for headstock waste (Fig 8-5).

**4** With all the primary step-off guidelines in place, use the parting tool and round-nosed gouge to sink the main blocks of waste (Fig 8-6). Aim to finish up with a chamber neck at about $1^1/_2$" in diameter so it's a nice, comfortable fit in the cradle collar. Sink the between-component waste so you are left with a central core at about 1".

**5** With the chamber profile crisply roughed out, take the tool of your choice—we use a round-nosed scraper—and carefully turn the decorative coves and beading to shape (Fig 8-7). As to the precise shape of the coves and beads, look to the templates (Fig 8-2) and see that they are really open to your own interpretation.

**6** When you have achieved what you consider is a good chamber profile, follow through the sizing and roughing out procedures as already described, and turn down the shaft and spigot to shape. The spigot needs to fit the hole made by a $2^1/_8$"-diameter bit, while the shaft needs to be a sliding fit in a 1"-diameter hole.

**FIGURE 8-5**

Mark all the step-offs that make up the design, and shade in the bands of part-off waste so as to avoid mess-ups. If you think it helps, pencil label the other areas.

**FIGURE 8-6**

Use the parting tool to swiftly sink the large areas of waste. Be wary when you are sinking the narrow trench of waste that the tool doesn't get stuck and bind. To this end, best cut the trench slightly wider than your tool.

**FIGURE 8-7**

Use a round-nosed gouge or scraper to turn the rounded cove curves to shape. Be watchful that the tool doesn't snag and jump.

**FIGURE 8-8**

**Having brought the turning to a good finish, fit the 1"-diameter bit in the tailstock drill chuck and run the shaft hole into a depth of a couple of inches. Be careful when you enter and exit that you don't knock the workpiece off-center.**

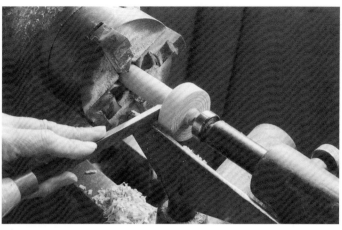

**FIGURE 8-9**

**When you have turned off the boss and the rings at the front of the spigot, spend time generally tidying up. Make a point of cleaning out the step so the back face of the spigot is at right angles to the shaft.**

**7** When you have completed both turnings—the chamber and shaft—sink the 1"-diameter hole in the end of the chamber to a depth of about 2", and part them off from the lathe (Fig 8-8).

**8** Take the shaft and mount it on the lathe so the stem of the shaft is held secure in the jaws of the chuck and the spigot end is centered and pivoted on the live center at the tailstock. This done, use the parting tool and the skew chisel to turn the boss and decorative rings and to generally clean up (Fig 8-9).

**9** When you are pleased with the shaft, remove it from the lathe, and mount the chamber with the back end of the chamber held in the chuck—the end with the blind hole—and the front end pivoted on the live tailstock center.

**FIGURE 8-10**

**If you sink the hole in stages by repeatedly running the bit in and out, you will avoid burning the wood or the bit. Be careful when you exit that you don't throw the workpiece off-center.**

**10** Face up the front end of the chamber, fit the drill chuck in the tailstock, and set to work boring out the two holes—the large one at $2\frac{1}{8}$" diameter and the other end of the 1" shaft hole. First sink the large-diameter hole to a depth of 1", then follow up with the 1"-diameter hole, and then finally tidy up with the large-sized bit (Fig 8-10).

**11** Now have a trial fitting. The shaft needs to be a smooth-sliding fit through the chamber, the face of the spigot needs to be set back a little from the front rim of the chamber, and the whole works has to be a snug fit in the cradle (Fig 8-11).

**FIGURE 8-11**

**Have a trial fitting. The chamber needs to be a tight-gripped fit in the cradle, while the shaft needs to be able to turn freely within the chamber.**

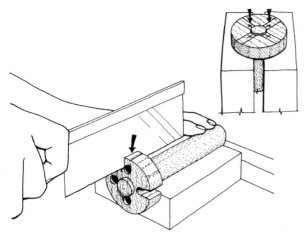

**FIGURE 8-12**

**(top) With the spigot shaft well gripped and supported between a couple of wooden V-blocks, run the 3/8"-diameter drill holes all the way down through the thickness of the spigot end. (bottom) Support the shaft in or on the V-block, and clear the waste with a small, fine-toothed gents or brass-backed handsaw.**

**12** Having marked on the front face of the spigot the size and position of the four gate slots, the tricky task of cutting them out comes. The best method is to first clear the ends of the slots with the 3/8"-diameter drill—this establishes the width and depth of the slot—and then use the back saw to run parallel cuts from the rim of the spigot through to the drilled holes (Fig 8-12).

**13** Finally, run two 1/2"-diameter holes through the rim of the chamber for the pipes, and cut a slice out of the handle end of the shank in readiness for fitting the crank with a tenon wedge.

## TURNING THE PIPES AND BOSS RING

**1** With the greater part of the project made, now is the time to look to the working drawing (Fig 8-1) and then perhaps to modify the unmade components, because if your way of working is anything like mine, then chances are some part will need to be reshaped or resized.

**2** When you have a clear understanding of precisely how the remainder of the project needs to go, take the length of 1" × 1" square section wood, meaning the piece you have chosen for the pipes, and mount it in the lathe as already described.

**3** Swiftly turn down the wood to a diameter of about 3/4", then take the ruler and dividers and mark all the step-offs that make up the design. It's beautifully easy; all you do is allow about 1/8" for tailstock waste, and then mark eight 1/2" step-offs.

**4** With the step-off guidelines in place, take the skew chisel and round-nosed gouge and set to work systematically turning off all the little curves and grooves.

**5** After turning the string of repeat cuts that make up the two little pipes, burn in the decorative V-cuts with the wire, and clean up with the skew chisel (Fig 8-13).

**6** Finally, fit the 1/4" Forstner bit in the tailstock drill chuck, run a hole through the whole length of the turning and then part off.

**7** With the two pipes made and off the lathe, use the scroll saw to swiftly cut a little disk blank of plum to size—it needs to be about 1/2" thick and 1 1/2" in diameter—and mount it in the jaws of the chuck.

**8** Now turn down one face of the blank to an accurate disk, reverse the disk in the chuck and turn the other face round over the edge of the disk so you have a little domed shape. Drill the turning through with the 5/8"-diameter drill bit (Fig 8-14).

**FIGURE 8-13**

**Use the toe of the skew chisel to set in the various steps and grooves.**

**FIGURE 8-14**

**Use the 5/8" bit to run the hole all the way through the boss. If you are working in the way described, you should be able to run the bit through without touching the inside face of the chuck jaws.**

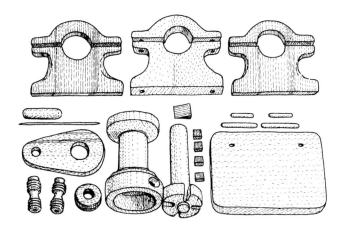

**FIGURE 8-15**

**The component parts—all cut and ready for putting together.**

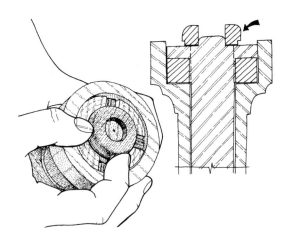

**FIGURE 8-16**

**Set the ring on the boss so the gates are nicely contained; they need to be a loose, sliding fit.**

**9** Lastly, having first checked that the boss does in fact fit into the ring, rub it down with the graded sandpapers and take it off the lathe.

## ASSEMBLY AND FINISHING

**1** Check the component parts for potential problems and make sure they fit together (Fig 8-15).

**2** Cut the little sliding gate blocks to size, note how they fit in place, and generally rub down all the mating faces so the gates are a well-contained sliding fit.

**3** Set the gates in the slots, and hold in place with the boss ring (Fig 8-16); set the pipes in their holes; and set the crank handle on the end of the shaft (Fig 8-17).

**4** Set the chamber in the cradle, and draw a couple of registration marks so you know what goes where

and how (Fig 8-18). Generally pencil mark the position of the cradle on the base and the crank on the shaft so you will be able to complete the gluing stage without giving much thought to the positioning.

**5** Finally, when you are pleased with the look and fit of the whole project, glue it together (Fig 8-19). Drill and fit the decorative dowel pegs (Fig 8-1), wipe the whole workpiece with the teak oil, and burnish it to a sheen finish.

## PROBLEM SOLVING

• If you are new to wood turning I strongly recommend you get a four-jaw chuck, a tailstock drill chuck, and a really good set of Forstner drill bits.

**FIGURE 8-17**

**Set the pipes in the holes so that they are aligned with the axis or center of the turning.**

**FIGURE 8-18**

**The chamber needs to be a tight-gripped fit between the cradle and the collar.**

**FIGURE 8-19**

**Glue fit the chamber in place in the cradle, and then glue mate surfaces and set the collar in position.**

# Sector Wheel Bearing Machine

## PROJECT BACKGROUND

Sector wheel bearings are, in many ways, at the very heart of engineering systems.

Sector wheels are the "wheels within wheels" that keep everything moving. Their primary function is to smooth out the operation by reducing friction, in much the same way as roller bearings and ball bearings. In fact, sector bearings were invented before all the rest; they were the prototype for bearings that were to follow.

The working movement of this machine is wonderfully simple and direct: as the crank handle is turned on the fixed pivot, the captured wheels within the sector frame will follow the fixed path defined by the edge of the pan (right).

## PROJECT OVERVIEW

Have a good, long look at the working drawing (Fig 9-1) and the templates (Fig 9-2), and consider that, at a grid scale of two squares to 1", the machine stands about 5" in total height and 7" across the diameter of the wheel pan.

The machine is made up almost entirely of turned components—the pan, bearing wheels, handle and knobs.

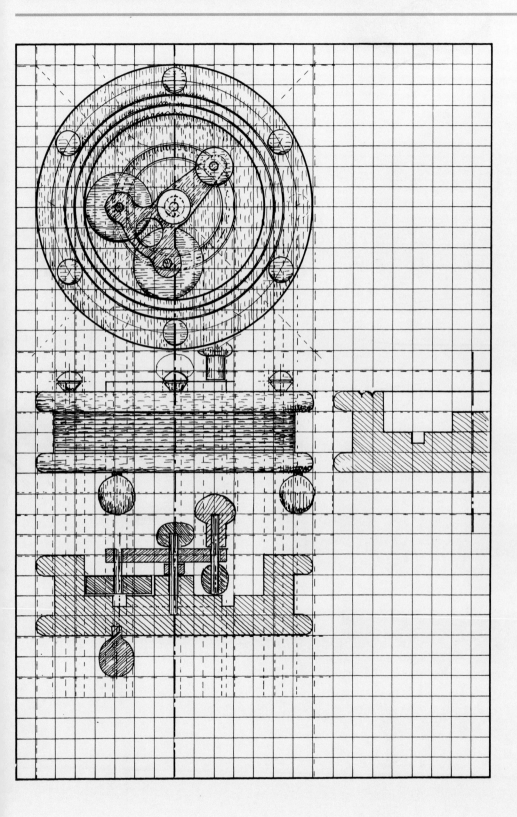

## FIGURE 9-1

At a grid scale of two squares to 1", the machine stands about 5" high from the underside of the bun feet through to the top of the handle and about 7" wide across the diameter of the pan.

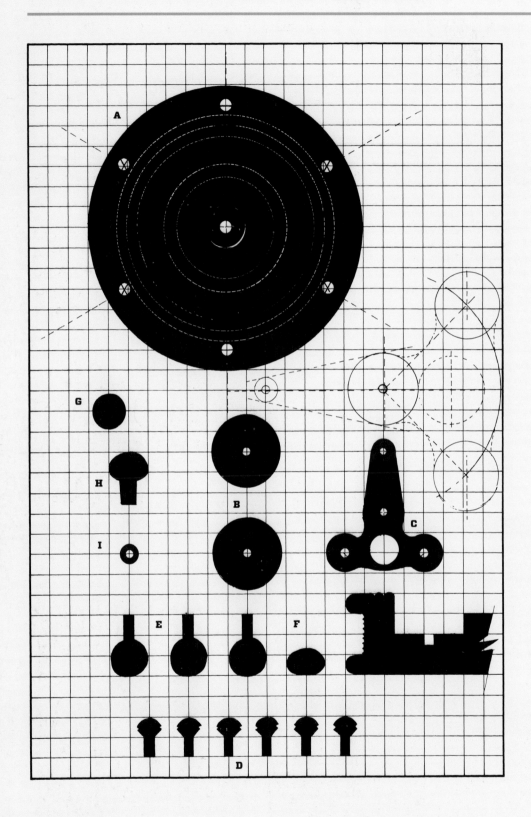

**FIGURE 9·2**

**The scale is two grid squares to 1" for the black silhouettes and four squares to the inch for the line drawing.**

**A** Large pan.

**B** Bearing wheels.

**C** Sector frame.

**D** Decorative knobs (6).

**E** Buns (3).

**F** Bun knobs.

**G** Handle base.

**H** Handle.

**I** Washer.

## CUTTING LIST

| A | Large pan | 2 × 8 × 8 maple or beech |
|---|---|---|
| B | Bearing wheels | 2 × 2 beech |
| C | Sector frame | $3/8$ × 4 × 4 cherry |
| D | Decorative knobs (6) | $3/4$ × $3/4$ × 9 walnut |
| E | Buns (3) | $1^1/4$ × $1^1/4$ × 10 beech |
| F | Bun knob | |
| G | Handle base | 1 × 1 × 6 cherry |
| H | Handle | 1 × 1 × 6 cherry |
| I | Washer | 1 × 1 × 6 cherry |
| | Pivots and pegs | $1/8$" dowel (or round toothpicks) |

## CHOOSING YOUR WOOD

As with all the wood-turning projects, the wood must be easy to turn. The wood must be well seasoned, straight grained, and generally described as being easy to turn. We settled for beech for the large pan and the bearing wheels, American walnut for the decorative knobs, and beech for the feet.

## MAKING THE PAN

**1** Having studied the working drawing (Fig 9-1) and the templates (Fig 9-2), carefully selected your wood, and painstakingly planned the sequence of work so you know how to proceed, take the 2"-thick slab of beech—the piece for the base—and mark it with a 7"-diameter circle.

**2** Cut out the blank on the band saw, and mount it on a 6"-diameter faceplate. Use short, fat screws at about $3/4$" long for fixing, with about $3/8$" of the screw going into the wood.

**3** Mount the whole works on the lathe, set out all your tools so they are readily available, and check that you and the lathe are in good, reliable working order.

**4** Position the tool rest over the bed of the lathe, and use a large gouge to swiftly turn down the blank to a smooth diameter of 7".

**5** Mark the center point with the toe of the skew chisel, and then fix the dividers—first to a radius of $3/8$" and then $1^3/4$"—and mark the face of the wood with the various lines that make up the design (Fig 9-3). Move the tool rest out to the side of the lathe, and mark the band that runs around the edge of the wheel.

**6** Use the parting tool and skew chisel to sink the $1^3/4$"-wide wheel track to a depth of 1". Bring the whole area to a good, smooth, sharp-sided finish. The best working procedure is to first establish the depth at the sides and then to clean up the rest (Fig 9-4).

**7** Continue turning the decorative beads that run around the rim, continue turning the edge, and so on (Fig 9-5).

**FIGURE 9-3**

Use the ruler and dividers to mark the central pivot point, the width of the track, and the decorative band that runs around the turning.

**FIGURE 9-4**

Use the parting tool to lower the waste to the desired depth. Hold the tool so the inside face is at right angles to the bottom of the pan.

**FIGURE 9-5**

Use the tool of your choice to turn the decorative beads that run around the face of the pan. Note that I'm using an old file I've ground to a beaklike point.

**8** When happy with the profiles and finish, take a length of wire and friction burn the grooves that decorate the channel that runs around the edge of the pan (Fig 9-6). Warning: on no account should you wrap the wire around your fingers or have loop handles; use sticks so the wire can be swiftly released if there are snarls.

**9** Finally, having first rubbed down all surfaces to a smooth finish, leave the turning on the faceplate, and take it off the lathe.

## TURNING THE WHEELS

**1** Take the length of 2" × 2" square wood you've selected for the wheels, establish the end center points by drawing crossed diagonals, and mount it securely on the lathe.

**2** Having turned down the wood to the largest possible round section, use the dividers and parting tool to cut the two wheel thicknesses. Aim for two $1/2$"-thick wheels at $1^3/_4$" diameter. It is best to clear the bulk of the rough with the gouge and then to use the skew chisel to shave the turning to a good fit and finish (Fig 9-7).

**3** When you think the wheels are to size, carefully draw the tailstock out of the way, and have a trial fitting of the wheels in the pan (Fig 9-8). Be cautious that you don't knock the workpiece off-center.

**4** With the wheel diameter marginally smaller than the width of the pan track, rub down the wheels to a smooth finish, and part them off one piece at a time (Fig 9-9). Note: if you have a tailstock drill chuck, you could bore out the pivot holes prior to parting off.

**FIGURE 9-7**

**Use the left hand both to support the workpiece and to control the cutting pressure.**

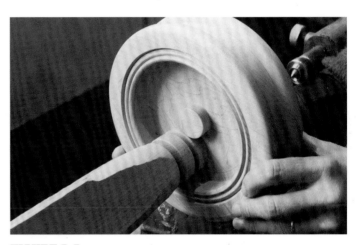

**FIGURE 9-8**

**When you think the wheels are to size, stop the lathe, back the tails tack out of the way, and have a trial fitting. Aim for a small space between the side of the heel and the center of the pan.**

**FIGURE 9-6**

**Firmly hold the copper wire on top of the spinning workpiece to friction burn a series of decorative rings. Warning: on no account should you wrap the wire around your fingers or have loop handles; you must be able to swiftly drop the wire if it snarls.**

**FIGURE 9-9**

**Having cleaned up the face of the first wheel, back the tails tack out of the way and carefully part off.**

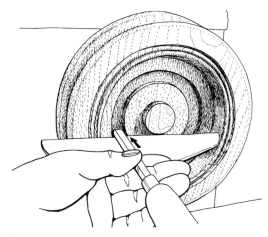

**FIGURE 9-10**
**Use the parting tool to sink the channel at the bottom of the pan.**

**FIGURE 9-11**
**Turn down the cylinder so you have a beadlike string of little drum shapes. Note how the wood is securely held in the chuck and pivoted on a live tailstock center.**

**5** Lastly, having first run $1/8$"-diameter holes through the wheel centers, mark the position of the wheel centers on the bed of the pan track. This done, remount the pan on the lathe, and cut the center-of-wheelline with a $1/2$"-wide, $1/4$"-deep channel (Fig 9-10).

## TURNING THE DECORATIVE KNOBS AND BUNS

**1** First of all, have a look at the working drawing (Fig 9-1) and the project photographs, and see that there are six decorative knobs set at 60° intervals around the top rim of the pan and three knobs, or buns, set at 120° intervals around the underside of the base.

**2** Feel free to change the shape and size of the turnings to suit your needs, select the length of wood for the decorative knobs, and mount it on the lathe.

**3** With the wood securely mounted between the four-jaw chuck and the tailstock, turn it down to a diameter of about $1/2$".

**4** Use the dividers to mark the string of beadlike repeats that make up the six knobs. I used a $1/4$" module—$1/4$" for the top of the knob, $1/4$" for the bottom, and $1/4$" for the stalk or spigot (Fig 9-11). Sink the waste, meaning the width of the spigot, to match one of your drill bit sizes. Aim for a diameter between $1/8$" and $3/8$".

**5** With the little blanks all cut to size, take the skew chisel and set to work systematically turnmg them to the desired shape. Work along the turning in one direction and then rerun in the other direction. Turn off the bottom shoulder on all six forms, then cut in the decorative lines on all six forms (Fig 9-12).

**FIGURE 9-12**
**Use the heel of the skew chisel to turn off the sharp shoulders. The best procedure is to work along the turning in one direction and then rerun in the other direction. If you have doubts about your turning skills, turn off more shapes than you need and select the choice set.**

**6** When you have achieved what you figure are six well-turned knobs, take the wire and mark each midline with a decorative, friction-scorched stripe.

**7** Having first of all parted the knobs off the lathe with the toe of the skew chisel, set them one piece at a time in the jaws of the chuck, and sand the cutoff points to a smooth, rounded finish.

**8** Have a look at the working drawing (Fig 9-1) and the various photographs, and see that we turned off four buns—three to be used as feet and one to be used as a support under the handle end of the little wheel frame.

**9** Working in much the same way as already described, mount the wood on the lathe, turn it down to a cylinder, use the dividers to set out the step-offs that make up the design, reduce the waste at the spigot and so on until you have four identical little drum-shaped blanks (Fig 9-13).

**10** To turn the buns to the roundish nutlike shape you should:
• Set the skew chisel flat down on the workpiece so the heel is on the midline and looking in the direction of cut.
• Gently rotate the tool until the blade begins to bite.
• Lift and rotate so as to cut away the sharp shoulder. If you are doing it properly, the lifting-rolling action will cut off a ribbon of waste, while at the end of the pass the tool should be in the valley with the toe uppermost.

**11** Continue to repeatedly set the heel of the skew on the midline, lifting and rotating—first to the left to remove all the shoulders on one side and then to the right to remove the shoulders on the other side—until you finish up with four well-turned forms (Fig 9-14).

**12** Sand each bun to a smooth finish, then part off the turnings from the lathe, remount them one at a time in the jaws of the chuck, and sand the part-off area to a smooth finish (Fig 9-15).

## MAKING THE WHEEL SECTOR BEARING FRAME

**1** First of all, have a good look at the working drawing (Fig 9-1) and the line drawing (Fig 9-2), and see how the form is drawn with a compass and ruler. Note how the main pivot point is set at the center of a large circle, while the bearing wheel centers are set on the circumference of the circle.

**2** When you have a clear understanding of how to achieve the image, draw it on your chosen piece of ³⁄₈"-thick wood so the center line runs in the direction of the grain.

**3** Fix the position of the four holes, and run them through with the ¹⁄₈"-diameter drill bit. Then move to the scroll saw and fret out the profile. Being mindful that the speed of cut will change as you cut alternately with and across the grain, run the line of cut a little to the waste side of the drawn line.

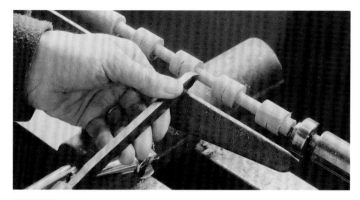

**FIGURE 9-13**

**Use the parting tool to swiftly sink the areas of waste.**

**FIGURE 9-14**

**When you have achieved what you consider to be a well-matched set of buns, tidy up the spigots with the parting tool, and use the toe of the skew chisel to very nearly part off the turnings one from another.**

**FIGURE 9-15**

**Hold the bun by its spigot, and use the sandpaper to rub down the part-off point to a smooth finish.**

**4** Using a large-sized drill bit—or you could cut a hole on the scroll saw—reduce the weight and lighten up the appearance of the form by piercing the center area (Fig 9-16). Be careful not to weaken the structure by having the pierced window too near the edge of the profile.

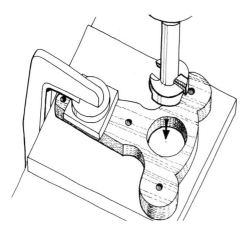

**FIGURE 9-16**

**Being careful not to get too near the edge of the profile, use a large-sized drill bit to bore out the pierced window.**

## ASSEMBLY AND FINISHING

**1** When you have made all the component parts that make up the machine—the disk shape pan, two wheels, sector frame, and various decorative bits and knobs—check them over just to make sure they are free from damage, give them a light rubdown with the teak oil, and then clear the work surface to prepare for putting the pieces together (Fig 9-17).

**2** Before you do anything else, especially if there is a likelihood that one of the component parts is made from suspect wood—it might be damp or have a knot or whatever—set the wheels in the frame and the frame on the main pivot, and try out the movement. If all is correct, the contact between the wheels and the inside face of the pan should be such that there is just enough friction to set the wheels in motion but not so much that they stick (Fig 9-18). If need be, take a fold of the finest-grade sandpaper and rub down the wheel rims to fit.

**3** Glue the three bun feet and the six knobs in place, glue the main pivot in the center of the pan, glue the ends of the wheel pivots in the sector frame, fit and glue the handle in place, fit the wheels in the frame and the frame on the center pivot and so on until the task is done. And, of course, if and when you find that such and such a component part sticks or is deformed or whatever—which sooner or later you most certainly will—then be ready to ease and modify the offending part accordingly.

**4** Finally, wipe away the dust, burnish the oiled surface to a sheen finish, and the machine is ready for action.

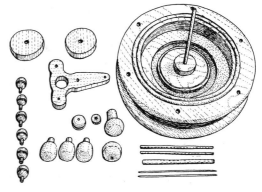

**FIGURE 9-17**

**Set out all the component parts, and check them over for potential problems.**

**FIGURE 9-18**

**When you are ready for glue, dip the points of round toothpicks, wedge the points in loose-fit holes, make adjustments for a good fit, and trim back when the glue is dry.**

## PROBLEM SOLVING

• I think it fair to say that the innate character of this project is such that it needs to be made on the lathe. But what to do if you haven't a lathe? Well, if you are really keen, you could possibly seek out a lathe at the local school or join a group or build your own lathe.

• Being mindful that as wood dries it shrinks across the width of the grain, this is all the more reason you must use well-seasoned wood for making disks and wheels. If you find that the wheels jam when you bring the machine into the house—even though they started out as a perfect fit—this is a good indication that the wood is still drying, shrinking and moving. Avoid using woods that are so inherently unstable that they never stop moving.

• If at any point along the way you find that a component part splits or doesn't seem to want to come out right or looks wrong or whatever, always be ready to give it another try.

# Flywheel Propeller Machine

## PROJECT BACKGROUND

This machine is made up of two key engineering devices, namely, a flywheel and a propeller. Flywheels must surely be one of the most commonly used engineering mechanisms of all time; they are everywhere … in clocks, in automobiles, in motors, and in just about everything from toys and tools to tram cars and traction engines.

The dictionary says of a flywheel: "a flywheel is a heavy wheel that stores kinetic energy and smooths the operation of a reciprocating engine by maintaining a constant speed of rotation over the whole cycle" (right).

## PROJECT OVERVIEW

Have a good long look at the working drawing (Fig 10-1A) and the templates (Fig 10-1B). Note that the propeller boss, flywheel, bell-shaped distance hubs at either side of the flywheel, pull cord ring, and ball stop at the end of the shaft are all turned.

If you don't have a lathe, you can modify the forms and make them from flatwood cutouts. The efficiency of the movement hinges primarily on the flywheel's precision and any nonturned modifications must be made with extra special care.

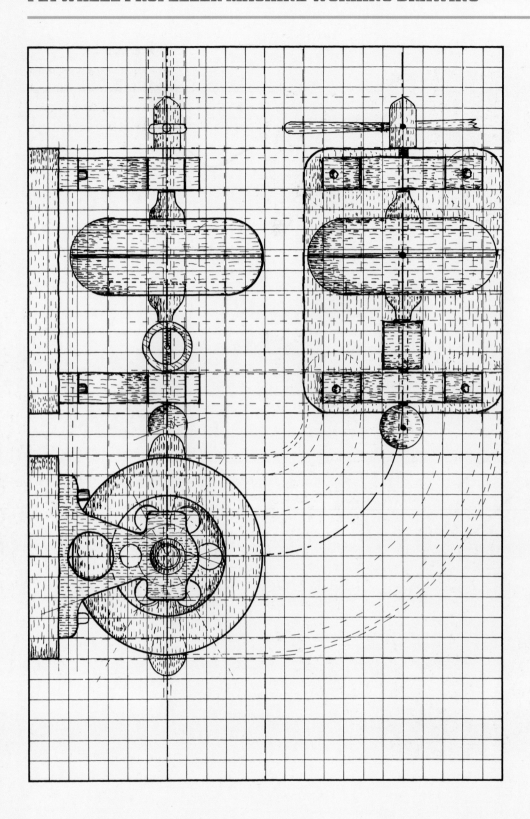

**FIGURE 10-1A**
At a grid scale of two squares to 1", the machine stands 6" high from the underside of the base through to the top of the flywheel, about 9" long, and about 6" wide across the span of the propeller.

# FLYWHEEL PROPELLER MACHINE TEMPLATES

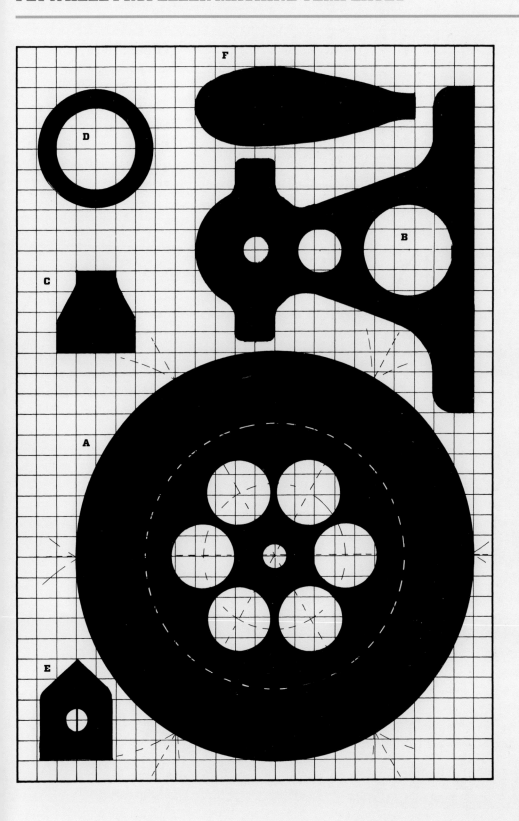

FIGURE 10-1B

**FIGURE 10-1B**

**The scale is four grid squares to 1". Note that the position of the six holes on the flywheel is fixed with a compass.**

**A** Flywheel.

**B** Stanchions (2).

**C** Spacers (2).

**D** Pull ring.

**E** Boss.

**F** Propellers.

## CUTTING LIST

| A | Flywheel | 2 × 6 × 6 maple |
|---|---|---|
| B | Stanchions (2) | $^3/_4$ × 8 × 9 cherry |
| C | Spacers (2) | $1^1/_4$ × $1^1/_4$ cherry |
| D | Pull ring | $1^3/_4$ × $1^3/_4$ cherry |
| E | Boss | 1 × 1 beech |
| F | Propellers | 2—$^1/_4$ × 1 × 3 beech |
|   | Base | $^3/_4$ × 5 × $6^1/_2$ beech |
|   | Ball stop | 1 × 1 |
|   | Main shaft | 9"—$^3/_8$" dowel |
|   | Pegs | 6"—1/4" dowel |
|   | Fixing pins | round toothpicks |

## CHOOSING YOUR WOOD

Two considerations influenced our choice of wood: the need for the flywheel to be as heavy as possible and the fact that the wheel was going to be made on the lathe. We settled for European beech for the base slab, North American cherry for the stanchions and the small turnings, and North American maple for the flywheel.

## MAKING THE BASE

**1** Having studied the working drawing (Fig 10-1A) and templates (Fig 10-1B), take the $^3/_4$"-thick slab of beech—the piece for the base—and mark it with all the measurements that make up the design.

**2** Cut the base to size with your chosen tools and sand it down to a smooth finish.

**3** Have another look at the working drawing (Fig 10-1A) so you know what goes where and how, and then use a soft pencil, ruler and square to mark the base with all the guide and placement lines. For example, label the propeller end, draw in an end-to-end center line, establish the position of the two stanchions, and so on.

## MAKING THE STANCHIONS

**1** Take your chosen piece of wood and transfer the lines of the design from the working drawings through to the wood. Tip: I usually draw the design up to full size on the work-out paper, make a tracing, and then use the tracing to establish the primary reference points. Some woodworkers paste a paper pattern on the wood and then cut through the paper, wood and all.

**2** Use the scroll saw to cut out the profiles.

**3** Mark the position of the three holes: the $^3/_8$"-diameter shaft hole and the other two holes at $^1/_2$" and $1^1/_8$" diameters.

**4** When both cutouts have been identically marked, run the holes through on the drill press. It's important from workpiece to workpiece that the shaft holes are the same distance up from the baseline, so spend time getting it right.

**5** Pencil label the stanchions for the propeller end and which direction the faces are looking.

## TURNING THE FLYWHEEL

**1** Take your 2"-thick slab of wood, fix the center point by drawing crossed diagonals, and then use the compasses/dividers to mark it with a circle at a little over 5" in diameter (Fig 10-2a).

**2** Cut out the blank on the band saw, and mount it on a 3"-diameter screw chuck.

**3** Mount the whole works on the lathe, and check that you and the lathe are in good, safe working order.

**4** Position the tool rest over the side of the lathe, and use a large gouge to swiftly turn down the blank to a smooth diameter of a little over 5".

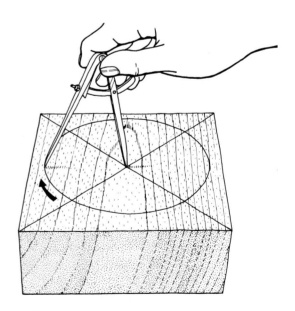

**FIGURE 10-2A**

**Fix the center of the slab by drawing crossed diagonals, draw out the circle, and then clear the waste with the band saw.**

**5** Move the rest over the bed of the lathe so you can work the wood face on, and use your chosen tools to turn off the face of the disk.

**6** Mark the center point with the toe of the skew chisel; then fix the dividers to a radius of about $1^5/_8$", and mark the face of the wood with a $3^1/_4$"-diameter circle. Note: the circle must be slightly bigger than the diameter of your screw chuck.

**7** Use the parting tool and skew chisel to sink and waste the center of the disk to a depth of at least $^1/_4$". Bring the whole central area to a good, smooth finish.

**8** Use the gouge and skew chisel to round over the edge so you have a radius curve of about $^7/_8$" (Fig 10-2b).

**9** Having turned down one radius curve, flip the tool over, and start the curve on the other side of the wheel (Fig 10-3).

**10** Spend time cleaning up one side of the turning (Fig 10-4) so the profile is crisp and sharp, and then record the diameter of the sunken area with the dividers (Fig 10-5). Turn the wood over on the screw chuck, and rerun the whole procedure on the other side.

**11** When you have what you consider is a nicely turned flywheel, rub it down to a smooth finish, and take it off the lathe.

**FIGURE 10-3**
When you have completed the curve at one side, turn the skew chisel so it is nose down, and tidy up the V-section midline.

**FIGURE 10-4**
Use the parting tool to clean up the edge of the sunken area.

**FIGURE 10-2B**
Use the skew chisel to cut the quarter-circle curve that runs from the center line and around to the rim of the sunken area. I use the side of the skew chisel like a scraper; it's not very good for the cutting edge, but it gets the job done without the need for changing tools.

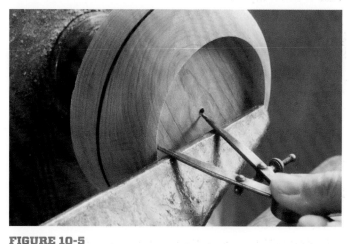

**FIGURE 10-5**
Before you turn the workpiece over on the screw chuck and work the other side, use the dividers to take a radius reading.

**FIGURE 10-6**

**Having used a compass to fix the position of the six holes, set the flywheel on a disk of waste wood, and run the holes through with a ³/₄" bit. Everything needs to be well clamped and secure.**

**12** Use the compasses to position the six holes, and drill them with a ³/₄"-diameter Forstner bit. Lastly, drill out the central ³/₈"-diameter shaft hole (Fig 10-6).

## TURNING THE BELL-SHAPED SPACERS

**1** Have a look at the working drawing (Fig 10-1A) and templates (Fig 10-1B). Apart from the flywheel, there are five secondary turnings: two bell-shaped distance spacers—one either side of the fly-wheel—a ring that holds the pull string, a boss for the propeller blades, and a ball stop at the back end of the shaft.

**2** Take your piece of wood for the two bell-shaped spacers and turn it down to a diameter of 1".

**3** Use the dividers to mark the cylinder with all the step-offs. Allow a small amount at each end for chuck waste, 1" for each of the spacers, and about ¹/₄" at center for part-off waste (Fig 10-7).

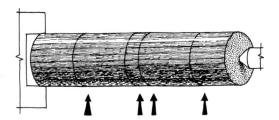

**FIGURE 10-7**

**When you have achieved the 1"-diameter cylinder, use the dividers to mark the step-offs. Allow a small amount on each end for chuck waste, 1" for each of the turnings, and about ¹/₄" at the center for part-off waste.**

**4** Study the shape of the bell (Fig 10-1B), then use the small, round-nosed gouge and the skew chisel to turn down the two little forms to shape (Fig 10-8).

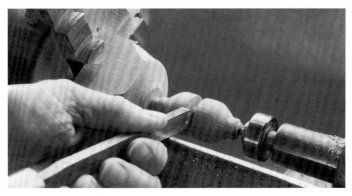

**FIGURE 10-8**

**If your workpiece is supported in a chuck, you will be able to cut the turnings one piece at a time from the lathe. Note the way that we achieve symmetry by turning the two items as mirror-image profiles. The idea is that we move swiftly backward and forward from side to side, all the while making sure each stage is well matched.**

**5** Rub down the turnings to a smooth finish, part them off from the lathe, and run them through with a ³/₈"-diameter hole—a hole to match the diameter of your shaft.

## TURNING THE PULL STRING RING

**1** Mount your chosen length of wood on the lathe—use a four-jaw chuck—and swiftly turn it down to a diameter of about 1¹/₂" (Figs 10-1A and B).

**2** Use the dividers to scribe the 1" length. Mark a center line with the toe of the skew chisel, and part off from the tailstock.

**3** With the workpiece still secure in the jaws of the four-jaw chuck, mount a 1"-diameter Forstner bit in a drill chuck at the tailstock end of the lathe, and run a 1"-diameter hole through your turning (Fig 10-9).

**FIGURE 10-9**

**Drilling out the ring using a tailstock chuck and Forstner bit, advance the tailstock at a steady rate, every now and again pulling back to clear away the waste shavings.**

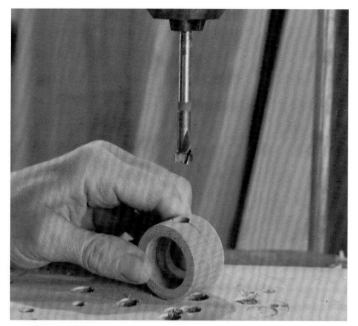

**FIGURE 10-10**

Although, as the photograph shows, we ran the hole straight through the ring, it's really best to support the ring by sliding it on a length of waste dowel.

**4** Now rub down the turning to a smooth finish, and part off from the lathe.

**5** Lastly, using the center line as a guide, and being sure to drill across the grain, run a $3/8$"-diameter hole through the ring—down through one side and on down through the other (Fig 10-10).

## TURNING THE PROPELLER BOSS AND MAKING THE BLADES

**1** Mount your carefully selected length of 1" × 1" square wood securely on the lathe.

**2** Before you go any further, have a look at the various drawings and photographs, and see that the boss is only partially turned—at the nose and the corners—with the sides left flat. The idea is that the propeller blades can be more easily fitted if they are located on flats.

**3** When you have a clear understanding of just how the wood is to be worked, swiftly turn off the corners of the 1" × 1" square section.

**4** Having used the dividers to mark a single $1\frac{1}{2}$"-long step-off, take the skew chisel and turn down one end of the workpiece to a smooth, round-nosed, or dome, finish. Make the nose about $1/2$" long and the flats about 1" long (Fig 10-11).

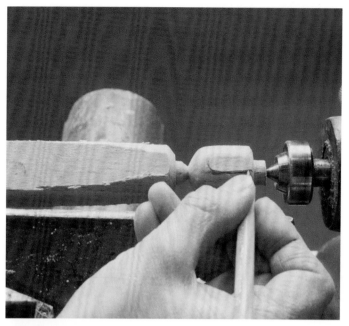

**FIGURE 10-11**

Turn down the square section so there are unturned $1/2$"-wide flats on all four sides.

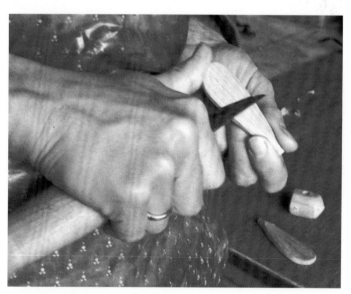

**FIGURE 10-12**

Use a sharp knife and a safe thumb-braced cutting action to whittle the blades to shape and size.

**5** Bring the turning to a good, smooth finish, and part off from the lathe. Sink a $3/8$"-diameter hole into the flat end of the boss to a depth of about $1/2$" and run a $1/4$"-diameter hole through one flat side and out of the other.

**6** Finally, when you have considered the shape of the propeller blades (Fig 10-1B), take a knife and a couple of lengths of wood at about $1/4$" thick by 1" wide by 3" long and whittle the blades to shape and size. Aim for a couple of well-matched paddle-blade shapes (Fig 10-12).

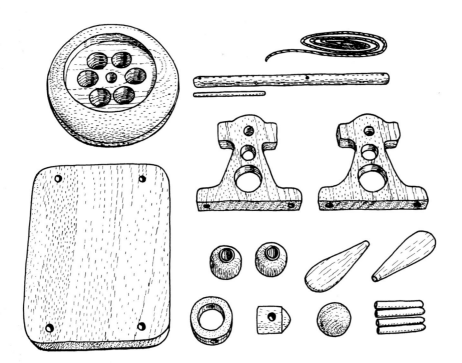

**FIGURE 10-13**

**When you have completed all the component parts that make up the project, give them a good rubdown with the finest-grade sandpaper and a swift wipe with the teak oil. Be careful not to get the oil on surfaces that are to be glued.**

## ASSEMBLY AND FINISHING

**1** When you have made all the component parts—the base slab, two stanchions, flywheel, two spacers, pull cord ring, boss, propeller blades, and all the little dowel pegs and pins—then comes the fun task of putting everything together (Fig 10-13).

**2** Start by dry fitting and pegging the two stanchions in place on the base. Set the propeller end stanchion in place, and then slide the shaft through the bearing, and make sure it runs free and easy.

**3** Make sure the shaft is a smooth, accurate fit, then slide the other component parts on the shaft, drilling and pegging as you go. From the boss end, the order goes: front stanchion, spacer, flywheel, spacer, pull string ring and back stanchion (Figs 10-14, 10-15, 10-16 and 10-17).

**4** Check the spacing and the movement and, if need be, rub down the shaft or the holes until everything is a smooth fit. You might also have to reduce the length of one or both of the bell-shaped spacers.

**5** With all the components in place on the shaft, spend time adjusting for best fit. Make sure the pin-fixing holes run through the center of both the component and the shaft.

**6** Fit the boss. Angle the propeller blades in the boss so they look like fan blades (Figs 10-18 and 10-19).

**FIGURE 10-14**

**Peg the first stanchion in place, and slide the shaft and the first spacer in position.**

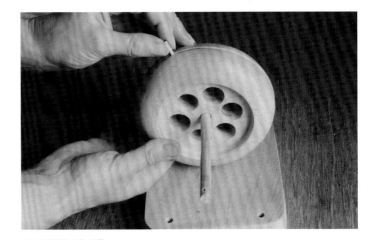

**FIGURE 10-15**

**Do your best to see that the fixing pin runs between rather than across the holes.**

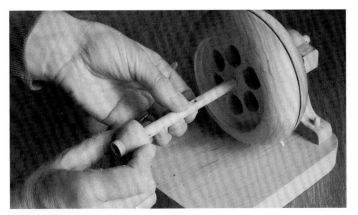

**FIGURE 10-16**

Cut off the flywheel pin so the wheel is able to turn, and slide the other spacer in position.

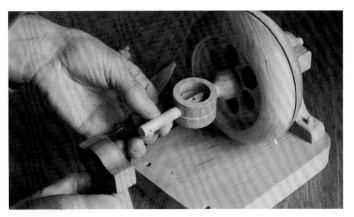

**FIGURE 10-17**

Slide the pull ring in place, and then follow up with the second stanchion.

**7** When everything is a good fit, pass the end of the cord through the pull hole and have a tryout. All you do is wind the string good and tight around the shaft, firmly hold the base on the work surface—with your knuckles well clear of the flywheel—and then give a good, smooth pull on the cord. If all is well, the flywheel will spin into action and then carry on spinning.

**8** Lastly, when you are pleased with the running action, glue and peg everything into place, and give the whole works a swift wipe with the teak oil. Now the machine is finished and ready for action.

## PROBLEM SOLVING

- If you like the idea of this project but can't get use of a lathe, you could use shop-bought items for the turned parts: a large, wooden wheel for the flywheel; a length from the end of a broomstick for the boss; large, wooden beads for the spacers and end stop; and so on.
- If you decide to use a different wood for the flywheel, make sure it is a good weight and strong across the grain. In the context of this project, avoid loose, lightweight wood like jelutong and ragged, knotty wood like pine.
- Be careful not to get the glue on areas that are to be oiled or oil on areas that are to be glued.
- If by chance your flywheel fixing hole runs across one of the six large holes, making the round toothpick visible, then glue the round toothpick in place, and cut away the bit when the glue is set.
- If you have a tailstock drill chuck, you could maybe modify the order of work and drill out the bell-shaped spacers while they are still on the lathe.

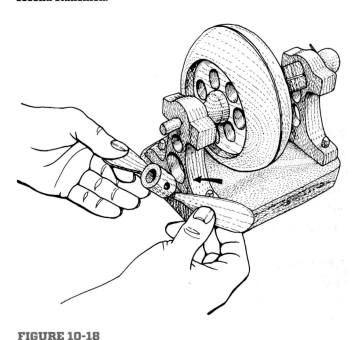

**FIGURE 10-18**

Trim the propeller blade ends to a tight push fit, and glue them in place in the boss holes.

**FIGURE 10-19**

Finally, glue fix the boss and the tail ball with round toothpicks, and trim back when the glue is dry.

# Pyramid Roller-Ball Machine

## PROJECT BACKGROUND

The sphere, or ball, is perhaps one of the most perfect and dynamic of all forms. Wheels, disks, spheres, balls and all circle-related forms are complete, self-contained and full of energy.

This machine is made up of fourteen balls: three groups of three small balls, pivoted and captured in the base frame, all topped off by five loose, larger balls. In use, the handle is turned, with the overall effect that the three balls on the drive shaft revolve and in so doing set all the other balls in motion (right).

## MAKING WOODEN MECHANICAL MODELS PROJECT OVERVIEW

Have a good, long look at the working drawing (Fig 11-1) and the templates (Fig 11-2), and consider how this machine beautifully illustrates a number of key engineering principles that have to do with bearings, friction drive and movement. And, of course, it is also a machine that poses a number of pretty gritty engineering questions. For example, can you guess what direction the top balls will roll if you turn the handle counterclockwise? Or what will happen if you top off the whole stack of balls with yet another ball?

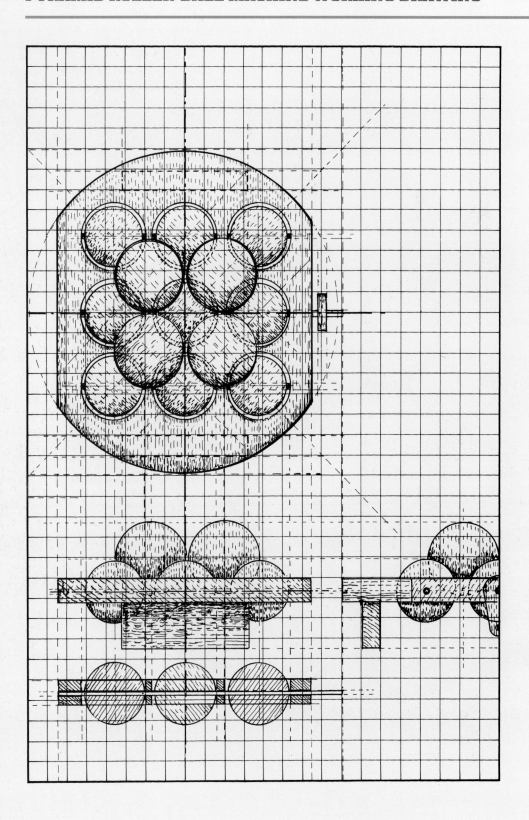

**FIGURE 11-1**

At a grid scale of two squares to 1", the machine stands about 4" high and 6³/₈" across the flats of the frame.

# PYRAMID ROLLER-BALL MACHINE TEMPLATES

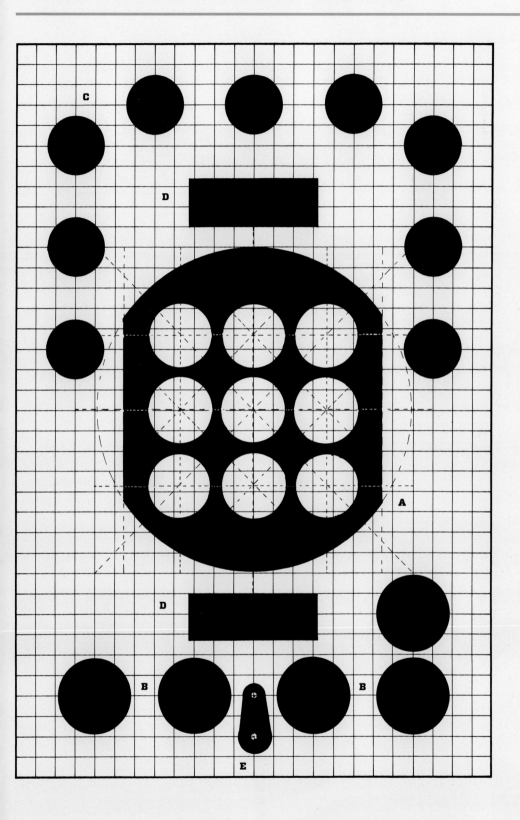

**FIGURE 11-2**

**The scale is two grid squares to 1".**

**A** Base frame.

**B** Large balls (5).

**C** Small balls (9).

**D** Foot bars (2).

**E** Handle crank.

## CUTTING LIST

| | | |
|---|---|---|
| A | Base frame | $^5/_8 \times 9 \times 9$ tulip |
| B | Large balls (5) | $2 \times 2 \times 16$ beech |
| C | Small balls (9) | $2 \times 2 \times 36$ beech |
| D | Foot bars (2) | $1^1/_4 \times 1^1/_4 \times 7$ |
| E | Handle crank | $1 \times 2$ mahogany |
| | Pivot rods | $24"—^1/_4"$ dowel |

## CHOOSING YOUR WOOD

This project calls primarily for three wood types: a strong, heavy, tight-grained wood for the base frame; a heavy-weight, easy-to-turn wood for the nine small balls; and a heavy, easy-to-turn wood for the large balls. We settled for using tulip for the frame, beech for all the balls, and mahogany for the crank handle.

## MAKING THE BASE FRAME

**1** After looking at the working drawing (Fig 11-1) and templates (Fig 11-2), selecting your wood, and just as carefully planning out the order of work, take the $^5/_8$"-thick slab of tulip—the piece for the base—and fix the center by drawing crossed diagonals. This done, use the compass to mark the slab with an 8"-diameter circle.

**2** Cut out the circle with your chosen tool. Now mount it securely on the faceplate. Use short, fat screws to minimize damage (Fig 11-3).

**3** Mount the whole works on the lathe, set out all your tools so they are readily available, and check that you and the lathe are in good, safe working order.

**4** Position the tool rest at an angle to the bed of the lathe, and use a large gouge to swiftly turn down the blank to a smooth diameter of 8".

**5** Move the rest over the bed of the lathe so you can work the wood face on, and use your chosen tools to turn off the face and edge of the disk. Aim for an edge that is nicely rounded over at the working face (Fig 11-4).

**6** When you are happy with the disk, rub it down to a smooth finish, mark the center point with the toe of the skew chisel, and take the disk off the lathe.

**7** Use the compasses, square and ruler to draw all the lines that make up the design (Fig 11-2) and to fix the precise position of the nine holes. Be sure to have the straight sides aligned with the run of the grain.

**8** Having made sure that all is correct, run the holes through with a $1^3/_4$"-diameter Forstner bit (Fig 11-5). It's important the holes are well placed and cleanly cut.

**9** With all nine holes well placed and cleanly cut, run the disk through the band saw, and slice away the two areas of part-circle waste.

**FIGURE 11-3**

**Align the faceplate with the center point, and screw it securely in place. Try to place the screws so they occur in areas of waste, which are to be cut away.**

**FIGURE 11-4**

**Turn down the disk to a smooth, round-edged finish.**

**FIGURE 11-5**

**Run the holes through with the $1^3/_4$" Forstner bit.**

**FIGURE 11-6**

**Having made sure the workpiece is standing square and true—so the drill bit is perfectly aligned with the face of the wood—carefully run the pivot rod holes down through the thickness.**

**10** Now for the most difficult part of the project! Look at the working drawing (Fig 11-1) and templates (Fig 11-2). The notion of giving the base frame two flat edges that are perfectly square and parallel to each other has to do with the actual procedure of drilling the pivot holes through the thickness of the wood. Without the edges, how else could you make sure the holes are aligned?

**11** When you have made sure the edges are parallel and marked as many guidelines as you think necessary, fit the $1/4$" bit in the drill, set the workpiece on edge—with blocks and clamps—and run the pivot holes down through the wood so they are well placed in the thickness of the wood and run across the centers of the holes (Fig 11-6).

**12** Still working on the drill press, sink a $3/4$"-wide, $1/4$"-deep stopped hole at the intersections between the holes.

**13** Take the hooked knife—or you might use a scoop or spoon gouge—and carve away the edges of the $3/4$"-diameter hole. Aim for a sculptured surface that runs in a smooth sweep from the top face of the frame down into the dip and up again (Figs 11-7 and 11-8).

**14** When you have a good frame, rub it down to a super-smooth finish, and cut the two little foot bars to fit.

## TURNING THE NINE SMALL BALLS

**1** Taking your length of 2" × 2" square section beech—the length for the small balls—establish the end centers by drawing crossed diagonals, and mount it securely on the lathe.

**FIGURE 11-7**

**Use a hooked knife to carve the smooth-curved dips at the intersections. Do not cut through into the pivot rod holes.**

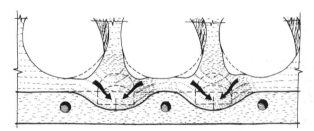

**FIGURE 11-8**

**Cross section showing the depth of the carved dips.**

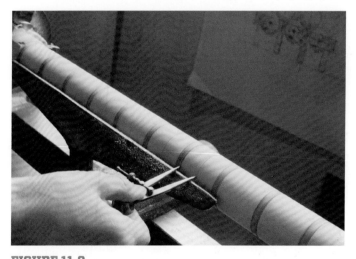

**FIGURE 11-9**

**Mark the cylinder with all the divider step-offs that make up the design.**

**2** With the wood at a smooth $1^1/2$"-diameter cylinder, set the dividers to $1^1/2$" and step off all the guidelines that make up the design. Starting at the chuck, allow $1/4$" for chuck waste, $1^1/2$" for the first ball, $1^1/2$" for waste, $1^1/2$" for the second ball, $1/4$" for waste and so on along the length of the wood. Now reset the dividers to $3/4$" and mark each step-off with a midline (Fig 11-9).

**FIGURE 11-10**
Use the parting tool to sink the waste to a depth of about ¹/₂".

**FIGURE 11-11**
Do your best to make sure the string of balls are well matched.

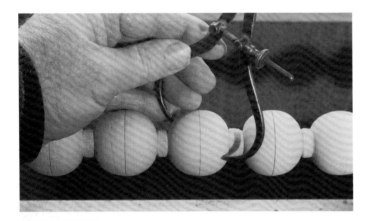

**FIGURE 11-12**
Use the calipers to check the turnings. Note that at this stage the balls look to be slightly egg shaped.

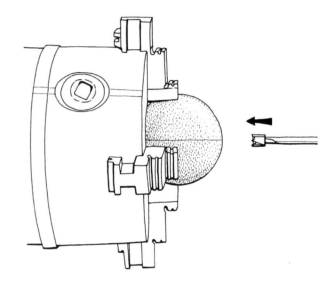

**FIGURE 11-13**
Drill out the ¹/₄"-diameter pivot hole; use the turned midline as an alignment guide.

**3** Take the parting tool and sink the bands of between-ball waste to a depth of ¹/₂" so you are left with a central core at about ¹/₂" (Fig 11-10).

**4** When you are happy with the markings, take the skew chisel and turn down the ball shapes. The sequence of work along the length of the wood is:
• Hold the skew chisel flat on the workpiece—on the mid-line—on the first ball nearest the headstock such that the heel is looking toward the headstock.
• Lift the handle until the blade begins to bite, and then advance in a smooth rolling action.
• Repeat the cut—from midline and down into the valley—until the ball begins to take shape.
• Having turned down one half of the ball, move on to the next ball in line, and rerun the action.
• When you have turned down the left-hand side of every ball, go back to the first ball in line, flip the chisel over so the heel is looking toward the tailstock, and then rerun the sequence of cuts for the other side of the balls.

**5** When you have turned the whole string of balls more or less to shape (Fig 11-11), go back to the first ball in line, and use the calipers (Fig 11-12) and skew chisel—and maybe also a cardboard template—and fine-turn each ball to the best possible shape and finish.

**6** Take the whole string off the lathe and use a fine-bladed saw to cut the balls apart.

**7** Take the balls one at a time, set them in the jaws of the chuck, and rub down the part-off points.

**8** Finally, one piece at a time, hold the balls in the chuck—this time with the midline in the horizontal plane—and use the tailstock drill chuck and the ¹/₄"-diameter bit to sink the pivot holes (Fig 11-13).

## TURNING THE LARGE BALLS

**1** The main difference between the small and large balls is not so much in the shape—although the small balls can be slightly flat faced at the holes—but more in the turning technique. For example, the small balls are turned off as a string, while the large balls are turned off one at a time.

**2** Having mounted the wood on the lathe, cut a cardboard template, and marked off the sequence of step-offs (Fig 11-14)—all as already described in the previous section—lower the waste at either side of the ball at the tailstock end.

**3** With the diameter of the midline defined by the width of the cylinder and the diameter across the poles defined by the bands of waste, all you have to do now is turn off the shoulders with the skew chisel, as already described.

**4** Having more or less turned off the ball nearest the tailstock—first one half and then the other—and checked it with the cardboard template (Fig 11-15), wind back the tailstock so you can approach the ball end on, and carefully bring the ball to the best possible finish (Fig 11-16).

**5** Finally, part off the ball with the toe of the skew chisel, wind back the tailstock so the workpiece is once again supported at both ends, and rerun the sequence for the other four balls.

## ASSEMBLY AND FINISHING

**1** When you've completed all the component parts that make up the project—the base frame, two foot bars, nine small balls, five large balls, little crank bar and pivot rods—spread them out on the surface, and check them over for potential problems (Fig 11-17). Pay particular attention to the movement of the small balls on the pivot rods. The three central balls need to be a tight fit on the drive rod with the rod being a loose fit through the frame holes, while the outside balls need to be an easy-to-turn, loose fit on the rods with the rods being a tight fit in the frame holes.

**2** Start by gluing and pegging the foot bars in place on the underside of the frame.

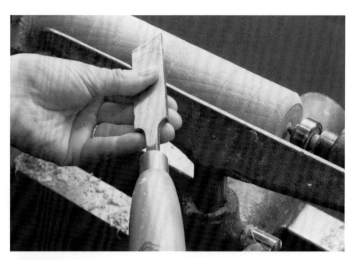

**FIGURE 11-14**
Use the skew chisel to shave the wood to a good, smooth finish.

**FIGURE 11-15**
Use a cardboard template to check the profile.

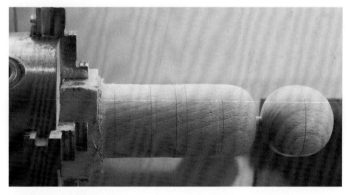

**FIGURE 11-16**
With the workpiece still held firmly and securely in the jaws of the chuck, back the tailstock out of the way and turn down the end face of the ball to a good profile and finish.

**3** When the glue is dry, take the finest-grade sandpaper and spend time rubbing down the whole frame to a smooth finish (Fig 11-18). Pay particular attention to the carved dips on the top and the inside edges of the nine holes. Make sure the pivot holes are clean and free from jags.

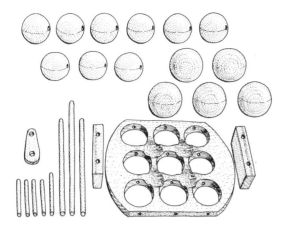

**FIGURE 11-17**

**Set out all the component parts, and check them over for shape and size and possible faults.**

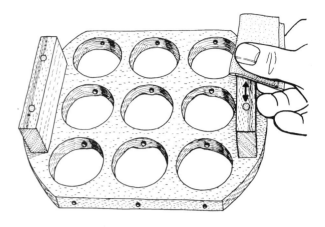

**FIGURE 11-18**

**Having pegged and glued the foot bars in position and waited for the glue to dry, clean up the surface with a fold of sandpaper.**

**4** Having sanded the pivot rods so the balls are an easy-to-turn fit, fit the nine balls in place. The best procedure is to slide the rods through both the frame and the balls, fitting and easing as you go. Continue fitting and modifying until everything comes together. For example, you might fit one ball, then decide that another is a better fit, then spend time sanding a ball so it turns freely (Fig 11-19), and so on.

**5** When you have fitted all nine balls and their pivot rods in place and glued the little crank handle on the central rod, give the whole works a rubdown with teak oil, and burnish to a dull, sheen finish.

**6** Set the five large balls in place, turn the handle, and watch the movement of the balls as they revolve.

**PROBLEM SOLVING**

• If you like the idea of this project but can't get use of a lathe, you could use shop-bought balls and settle for making only the frame.

• If you decide to use a different wood for the balls, make sure it is a good weight, strong across the grain and suitable for turning.

• Be careful not to get the glue on areas that need to revolve freely. A good tip is to generously oil everything except the faces that are to be glued before you start putting the parts together.

• If you can't use a crooked knife, you could use a scoop gouge.

**FIGURE 11-19**

**Experiment with the placement of the balls on the pivot rods until you achieve the best fit. If need be, use a fold of sandpaper to ease the fit.**

# Rack and Pinion Machine

## PROJECT BACKGROUND

This is one of our favorite projects. Rack and pinion is a device for converting rotary movement into linear motion and vice versa in which a gear wheel—the pinion—engages with a flat-toothed bar—the rack. When the crank handle is slowly turned—clockwise or counterclockwise—the cog wheel teeth engage, with the effect that the rack slides along its frame.

## PROJECT OVERVIEW

Before you put tool to wood, have a good, long look at the project picture (right), photographs, working drawing (Fig 12-1A) and templates (Fig 12-1B), and note that the machine is made up of three primary parts: a small gear wheel, large gear wheel, and long, toothed bar. Consider how the two wheels are pivoted on dowel shafts, with the smaller wheel being operated by a crank and handle. See that while the rack needs to be a nice, smooth-sliding fit between the bed rails, it also has to be held captive by means of a dowel rod that runs through the front rail, through a slot in the rack, and on through into the back rail.

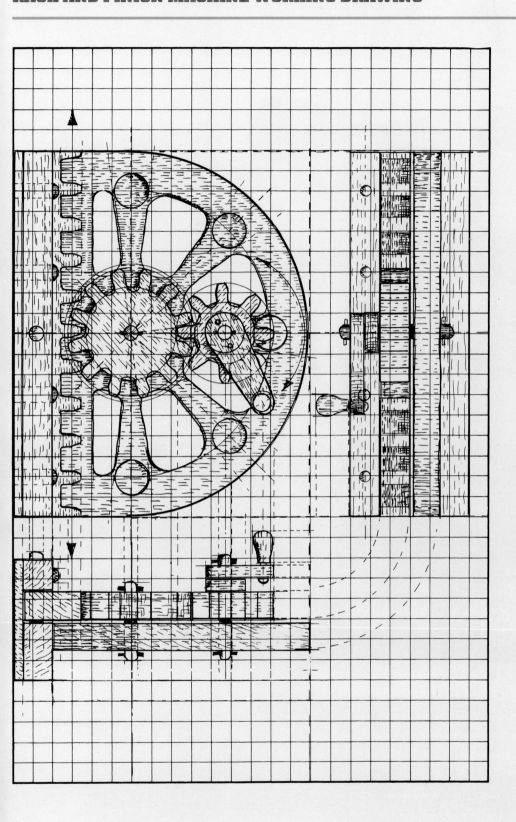

**FIGURE 12-1A**

At a grid scale of two squares to 1", the machine stands 7³/₄" high and 9" wide. Note that in side view the design primarily uses ³/₄"-wide stock.

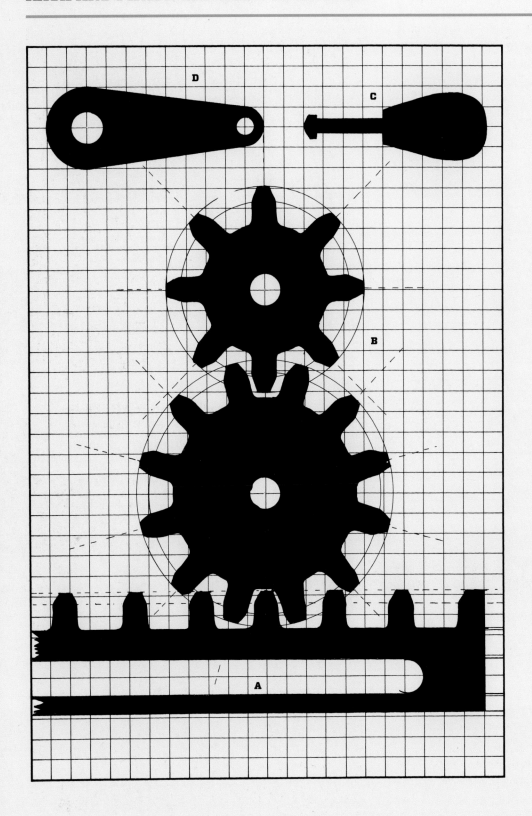

**FIGURE 12-1B**

**The scale is four grid squares to 1". Although it is important you do your best to copy the profile and spacing of the teeth, we have shaped the design so there is plenty of leeway.**

**A** Rack.

**B** Wheels (2).

**C** Crank handle.

**D** Crank.

## CUTTING LIST

| | | |
|---|---|---|
| A | Rack | ³/₄ × 1¹/₂ × 9 beech |
| B | Wheels (2) | ³/₄ × 4 × 6 cherry |
| C | Crank handle | 1 × 1 × 6 walnut |
| D | Crank | ³/₄ × 1 × 2³/₄ |
| | Back plate | ³/₄ × 9 × 7 beech |
| | Base | ¹/₄ × 3 × 9 beech |
| | Rails | ³/₄ × 2 × 9 beech |
| | Washer | ³/₄ × 1¹/₄ × 1¹/₄ |
| | Rods | 24"—³/₈" dowel |

## CHOOSING YOUR WOOD

In this project the character of the wood is important. The wood for the gear wheels needs to be strong across the short grain, and must be smooth grained, free from knots, attractive in color, and easy to work. We chose to use North American cherry for the wheels; European beech for the base, rails and back plate; North American walnut for the crank handle; and various offcuts for all the little bits and pieces.

## MAKING THE BACK PLATE

**1** Take the 7" length of ³/₄" beech at 9" wide. With the grain running from top to bottom, use the pencil, ruler, square and compasses to mark the lines that make up the design. We use an adjustable square and a washer for the radius curves. It's important the baseline is square and the pivot points are correctly placed, so double-check everything (Figs 12-1A and B and 12-2).

**2** Having shaded in all the areas that need to be cut away and pierced, use the drill and a suitably sized drill bit to drill pilot holes through all the enclosed "windows" of the design.

**3** Now cut out the profile, making sure the blade is running slightly to the waste side of the drawn line.

**4** When you cut out the enclosed "windows," the order of work is:
- Unhitch the scroll saw blade.
- Pass the blade through the pilot hole.
- Refit and retension the blade.

**5** Now sand all inside radius curves to a good, smooth finish (Fig 12-3).

**FIGURE 12-2**

When you prepare to use the adjustable square to mark the design on the wood, make sure you start off with a square baseline and a reasonably smooth surface.

**FIGURE 12-3**

We use a small rotary carver—a small drum sander—to finish the difficult-to-reach, inside-radius curves.

**FIGURE 12-4**

**Forstner drill bits are perfect for sinking smooth-sided, flat-bottomed blind holes.**

**6** Use the $^3/_4$" -diameter Forstner bit to drill the five decorative blind holes that make up the design. Drill holes that are about $^1/_4$" deep (Fig 12-4).

**7** Now smooth the back plate with sandpaper.

## MAKING THE PINION GEAR WHEELS AND RACK

**1** Trace the gear wheel and rack patterns on to your wood. It's important the teeth are accurately placed, so spend time getting it right.

**2** Cut out the profiles on the scroll saw.

**3** Check fit the wheels and movement (Fig 12-5). We used a couple of pencil stubs—and check out the movement by turning the wheels by hand. Make sure the three primary components, the two wheels and the rack, are a good, smooth-moving fit.

## MAKING THE CRANK

**1** Now draw out the washer spacer and crank. The washer needs to be 1" in diameter. The crank is 2" long from center to center, 1" in diameter at the big end, and $^1/_2$" in diameter at the small end (Figs 12-1A and B).

**2** With all the lines of the design clearly established, run $^3/_8$"-diameter holes through the spacer washer and through the big end of the crank and a $^1/_4$"-diameter hole through the small end of the crank.

**3** Use the scroll saw to cut out the two components.

**4** When you have completed the two cutouts, both at $^3/_4$" thick, run them through the band saw—or you might use the scroll saw—so you have two spacers and two cranks, all at about $^3/_8$" thick (Fig 12-6).

## TURNING THE CRANK HANDLE AND MUSHROOM PIVOT

**1** Take the 6" length of 1" × 1" square section walnut, establish the end center points by drawing crossed diagonals, and mount it securely on the lathe.

**2** Having checked through your safety checklist, turn down the wood to the largest possible diameter.

**3** When you have completed a cylinder at about $^7/_8$" diameter, take the dividers and mark the cylinder with all the step-offs that make up the design. Working from the tailstock end, allow about $^1/_2$" for tailstock waste, $1^1/_4$" for the handle, $1^1/_4$" for the pivot stalk, $^1/_4$" for the little mushroom head, and $^1/_4$" for part-off waste (Fig 12-7).

**4** Sink the step-offs to the required depth, and then turn the rounded shape of the handle, the $^1/_4$"-diameter stalk and the mushroom head.

**FIGURE 12-5**

**Spend time making sure the three primary components, the two wheels and the rack, are a good, smooth-moving fit.**

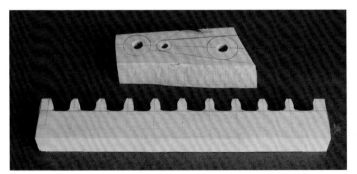

**FIGURE 12-6**

**The use of $^3/_8$"-thick wood allows for two $^3/_8$" spacers and two $^3/_8$" cranks—one pair for this machine and one for another project.**

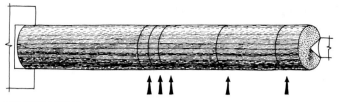

**FIGURE 12-7**

Working from the tailstock end, use the dividers to carefully mark the cylinder with all the step-offs that make up the design. Allow $^1/_2$" for tailstock waste, $1^1/_4$" for the handle, $1^1/_4$" for the pivot stalk, $^1/_4$" for the mushroom-shaped head, and $^1/_4$" for part-off waste.

**FIGURE 12-8**

When you have sanded to a good finish, use the toe of the skew chisel to part off the workpiece from the lathe.

**5** Sand the turning and then part off so you have two components: the handle and pivot (Fig 12-8).

## ASSEMBLY AND FINISHING

**1** Mount the backing plate on the base, position the two slide rails, and set the rack in place. When you are sure all is correct, drill and dowel (Fig 12-9).

**2** With the rack a nice, smooth-running fit, set the two pinion wheels in place with a couple of temporary dowels, and test out the movement. Turn the small wheel, and mark any teeth that look to be a problem.

**3** When you are happy with the movement, cut the dowel rods to size, drill peg holes, drill out the handle for the mushroom pivot, and sand all the parts (Fig 12-10). Use round toothpicks for fixing everything in place.

**4** With the back plate square to the base (Fig 12-11) and the rack free to move in its track, glue, fit, peg and clamp the project together and let it dry.

**5** Finally, give the whole works a swift wipe with the teak oil; fit and peg the wheels, dowels and handle; and the machine is finished.

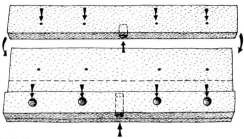
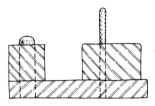

**FIGURE 12-9**

Place and align the base components so they are true to each other, and drill out the various fixing holes.
(top) Plan view showing position of holes.
(right) Cross section.

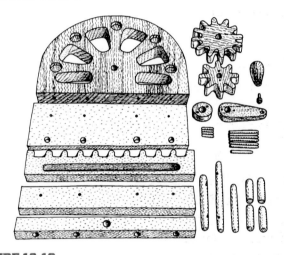

**FIGURE 12-10**

Check the component parts for potential problems.

**FIGURE 12-11**

Be sure to check that the back plate is square to the base.

## PROBLEM SOLVING

• If you want to make the project but can't get use of a lathe, settle for making the crank handle from a shop-bought dowel.

# Pendulum Recoil Escapement Machine

## PROJECT BACKGROUND

The tick, tick, ticking that measures time passing is controlled in the traditional clock by a mechanism known as the pendulum recoil escapement. This wonderfully simple device is made up of a toothed wheel on a pivot, a pivoted anchorlike form we term an anchor escapement, a swinging weight on an arm we call a pendulum, and a falling weight that acts in much the same way as a spring.

The working movement is beautifully simple: as the toothed wheel is set into motion by the falling weight, or "spring," and the pendulum is set swinging, the clawlike pallet fingers at the end of the anchor and the teeth of the wheel all complement each other in keeping the machine in motion. One side of the swinging anchor gives a little push or recoil on the wheel teeth that in turn gives a little push on the other side of the anchor that in turn gives another push on the next wheel tooth, and so on. In this manner, the movement is paced by the recoil energy as it bounces backward and forward between the two components. Of course, there is a great deal more to it than that, and if you are interested go to a book on horology and refer to "pendulum recoil escapement."

## PROJECT OVERVIEW

The size of the pendulum, the length of the pendulum arm, and the size of the "spring" weight in relation to the swing of the pendulum are all critical factors that relate to the success of the movement. Get one or other of the factors wrong—too much or too little weight, not enough swing or whatever—and everything grinds to a halt. That said, if you have doubts about your skills, proceed anyway and view this whole project as a prototype—an adventure that will lead on to other things.

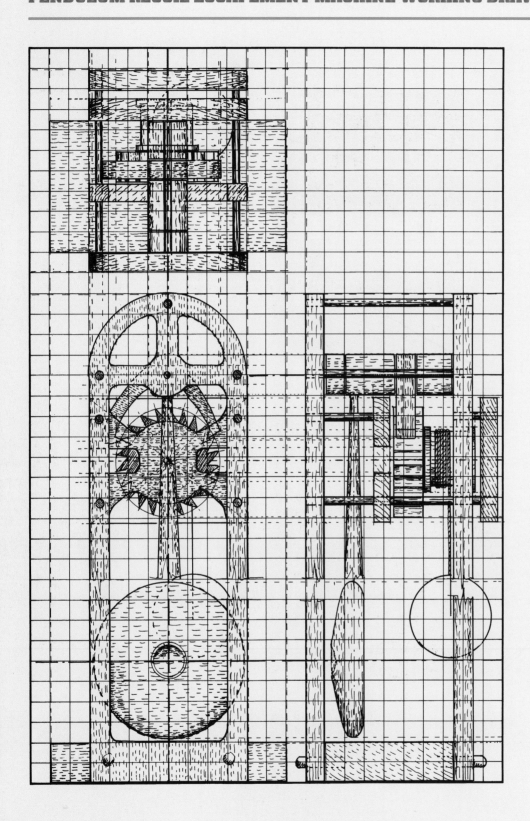

**FIGURE 13-1**

At a grid scale of two squares to 1", the machine stands about 15" high and 6" wide across the span of the base slab.

# PENDULUM RECOIL ESCAPEMENT MACHINE TEMPLATES

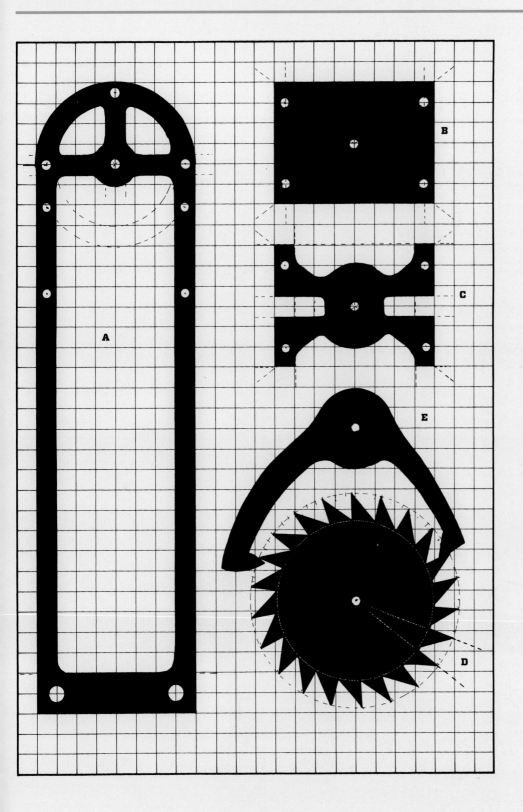

**FIGURE 13-2**

**The scale is two grid squares to 1" (A, B, C). The scale is four grid squares to 1" (D, E).**

**A** Tall, fretted frames (2). Frames in between fretted frames (2).

**B** Blank plate.

**C** Fancy plate.

**D** Toothed wheel.

**E** Anchor.

## CUTTING LIST

| | | |
|---|---|---|
| A | Tall, fretted frames (2) | $3/8 \times 4 \times 15\frac{1}{2}$ plum |
| | Frames in between fretted frames (2) | |
| B | Blank plate | $3/8 \times 4 \times 3$ plum |
| C | Fancy plate | $3/8 \times 4 \times 3$ plum |
| D | Toothed wheel | $3/4 \times 2^3/4 \times 2^3/4$ mahogany |
| E | Anchor | $1/2 \times 2^1/4 \times 3^1/4$ walnut |
| | Spacer drum (3) | $1 \times 1$ |
| | Base | $3/4 \times 3^1/4 \times 6$ cedar |
| | Pendulum arm | $1 \times 1 \times 12$ tulip |
| | Pendulum weight | $1 \times 4 \times 4$ tulip |

## CHOOSING YOUR WOOD

Being mindful that the woods variously need to be strong across the grain, close grained, free from knots, attractively colored, and relatively easy to work, we decided to go for European tulip for the pendulum; English plum for the frame; mahogany for the toothed wheel, walnut for the anchor; and pine for the dowels. That said, you could use just about any wood type that takes your fancy, as long as you consider it structurally and technically fitting. For example, if you are trying to cut costs, you could use soft pine for the pendulum weight, arm, frame, and just about everything except the toothed wheel and anchor that need to be made from a close-grained, dense wood.

Note that we used a metal weight (a brass film container) for the "spring" for the simple reason that we couldn't find a lump of wood that was heavy enough.

## MAKING THE FRETTED PLATES AND BASE

**1** Have a good, long look at the working drawing (Fig 13-1) and the templates (Fig 13-2), and study the two views. Note that we have cut through the views—through the height—so they fit on the page. Study all the illustrations—the photographs and pen drawings—until you are completely clear in your own mind as to how the various parts of the project come together.

**2** When you have an understanding of what goes where and how, draw the design imagery to size, make tracings, and transfer the traced lines through to your chosen wood. Note that in the context of the two identical frames—the two tall support frames—you need only draw the frame on one piece of wood.

**3** Take the two lengths of wood that make up the two primary frames and pin them together so the drawn imagery is on the top layer.

**4** On the drill press, use the $1/4$" bit to bore out the eight fixing-rod holes that occur at the top of the frame. Run the holes through both layers of wood. While the drill is in use, run $1/4$"-diameter pilot holes through all windows of waste and $3/8$"-diameter holes through the bottom of the frame—for fixing the base.

**5** Push dowels through at least two of the holes to ensure the holes and the cutouts are identically placed, and use the scroll saw to cut out the profiles.

**6** To cut out the enclosed windows, the order of work is (Fig 13-3):
- Unhitch the scroll saw blade.
- Pass the blade through the pilot hole.
- Refit and retension the blade.
- Cut out the window.
- Reverse the procedure and remove the wood.

**7** Having fretted through both layers of wood and removed the holding dowels, sand all the sawn edges—all the inside and outside radius curves and straight sides—to a smooth finish.

**8** To cut the cradle plates that support the escapement, rerun the same procedures.

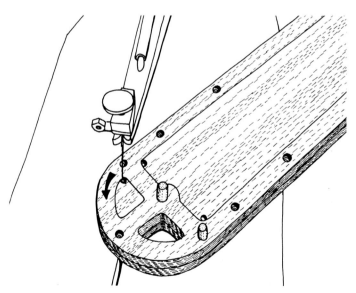

**FIGURE 13-3**

**To pierce a window, unhitch the blade, pass it through a pilot hole, rehitch and retension and start the cut. Reverse the procedure when the window has been fretted out.**

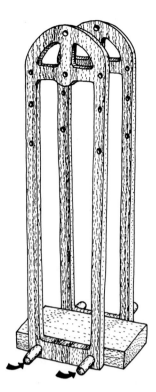

**FIGURE 13-4**

**Have a trial fitting of the two main frames to the base slab.**

**9** Cut the base slab to size, and have a trial fitting of the two main plates (Fig 13-4). Pencil label the underside of the base slab and the inside faces of the frames so you can fit everything back in the same position.

## MAKING THE ESCAPEMENT

**1** Start by looking at the working drawing (Fig 13-1) and templates (Fig 13-2) and noting that the escapement mechanism is made up of three primary components—the toothed wheel, the anchor with the finger pallets and the cord drum—all supported on pivots and rods.

**2** Now take your chosen piece of prepared ³/₄"-thick wood and use the pencil, ruler and compasses to mark the lines that make up the design (Fig 13-2). Draw the two circles—the large outer circle and the inner circle—run 22 equal step-offs around the outer circumference, and then draw radius lines and diagonal lines across the resultant intersections, all as illustrated. Although it's easy enough to work out with a calculator that each of the 22 step-offs springs from a part-circle angle of 16.3636°, meaning 360 divided by 22 equals 16.3636, it's not so easy to divide up the circle as drawn on the wood. We found that the best procedure is to set the dividers to a guesstimate size and then to fix the size of the step-offs by trial and error.

**3** With all the lines carefully drawn, move to the band saw and set to work cutting the teeth. Work at a slow pace, all the while making sure the tooth points occur on the outer circumference (Fig 13-5). Be mindful that perhaps more than anything else, the success of the movement depends on the length and spacing of the teeth.

**4** To make the drum and spacers, swiftly turn the wood down to a 1¹/₂"-diameter cylinder, and then use the dividers to step off the guidelines that make up the drum. From right to left along the length of the wood, allow a small amount for tailstock waste, about ¹/₄" for the first rim, about 1" for the central area, and another ¹/₄" for the other rim (Fig 13-6). In fact, the spacing isn't too important, as long as the total length of the drum is as near as possible to 1¹/₂". Sand the drum to a good finish, and then part off from the lathe.

**FIGURE 13-5**

**Cut out the toothed wheel with a series of straight cuts. Make sure the points all occur on the circumference line.**

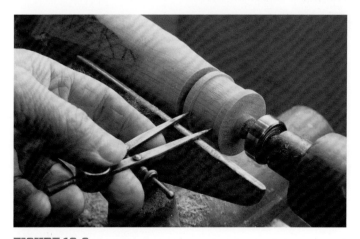

**FIGURE 13-6**

**Use the dividers to check the various step-offs that make up the design.**

**5** Follow basically the same turning procedures to cut the three spacer drums that hold and distance the anchor on its pivot. Turn down the wood to a circumference of about ³/₄", and run it through with the ¹/₄" bit (Fig 13-7). Cut the two primary spacers to length, and then cut an extra length so you can use additional slices as fine shim adjustments.

**6** When you prepare to make the anchor, first have a look at the working drawing (Fig 13-1) and the templates (Fig 13-2), and see that the characteristic asymmetrical profile needs to be cut with a fair degree of precision.

**7** Draw the imagery to shape and size, make a tracing, and press transfer the traced lines through to your chosen piece of wood. Have the profile arranged so there is a minimum of fragile short grain at the pallet points. Fix the position of the pivot point, and run it through with the ¹/₄"-diameter drill bit.

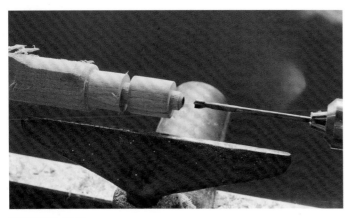

**FIGURE 13-7**

**Fit the bit in the tailstock drill chuck, and run the pivot hole through the length of the turning.**

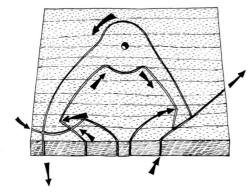

**FIGURE 13-8**

**When you prepare to fret out the anchor escapement on the scroll saw, make sure the line of cut is true to the drawn line, meaning the line of cut is fractional to the waste side of the drawn line.**

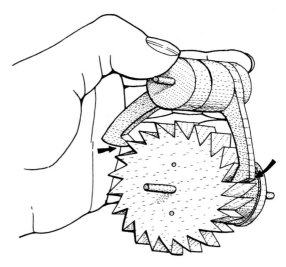

**FIGURE 13-9**

**At every step along the way, stop and make sure the parts come together for a good fit.**

**8** When you are happy with the image, use the scroll saw to carefully cut out the profile (Fig 13-8).

**9** When you have completed all the component parts that make up the escapement—the drum, toothed wheel, anchor and spacers—slide the anchor and spacers in place on their pivot rod, fix the wheel to the drum with a couple of dowel pins, slide the drum rod in place, and have a trial fitting—just so you can see how all the components come together (Fig 13-9).

## MAKING THE PENDULUM

**1** Have a look at the working drawing (Fig 13-1), and see that the pendulum is made up of two component parts: the disk or whorl, and the long arm. Note how the arm is shaped so that most of the weight occurs at the disk end.

**2** Take your chosen length of 1" × 1" square section wood and turn it down to a smooth, round section.

**3** N ow take the skew chisel and start turning the spindle to shape. With the spigot and large-diameter end at the headstock end of the lathe, first turn the heavy, round-nosed shape and establish the diameter of the spigot, and then make repeated "downhill" passes to turn the long, slender taper to shape (Fig 13-10).

**4** To turn the disk weight, take your chosen 5" × 5" square slab of wood and then fix the center point by drawing crossed diagonals, scribe out a 4¹/₂"-diameter circle, and cut out the blank on the scroll saw.

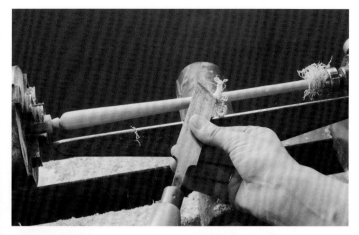

**FIGURE 13-10**

**Remove the waste with a long, slow, shaving cut.**

**FIGURE 13-11**

**The pendulum weight and the arm. Fit the two together so the grain runs across the width of the disk.**

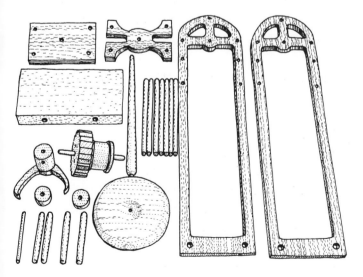

**FIGURE 13-12**

**Set out all the component parts, and check them over for possible problems.**

**5** Having mounted the wood on the screw chuck and fitted the whole works on the lathe, take the gouge and swiftly turn down the wood to a smooth pill, or disk.

**6** Make sure the wood is still secure, and then turn the edges to a nicely rounded profile and rub down the face and edge to a smooth finish.

**7** With what is now the back of the pendulum disk, cleanly and crisply turned, remove and refit the workpiece on the screw chuck so the other face is presented, and follow the turning procedures as already described. Note that we have given the front of the pendulum a more adventurous profile—a nicely plumped-out front with a dimple at center (Fig 13-11).

**8** Finally, when you have what you consider is a strong shape—with all faces and edges being well finished—remove the workpiece from the lathe, and drill a ¼"-diameter spigot hole at top-edge center.

## ASSEMBLY AND FINISHING

**1** When you have completed all the component parts that make up the project (Fig 13-12), have a trial run and then do the gluing when all the problems have been sorted out.

**2** Start by pegging the frames at either side of the base slab, as in our original tryout stage (Fig 13-4).

**3** Drill and peg the long spacer cylinder to the front face of the anchor, and test it out for fit and function (Fig 13-13).

**FIGURE 13-13**

**Make sure the toothed wheel and the anchor escapement are carefully, correctly aligned. Check against the working drawing.**

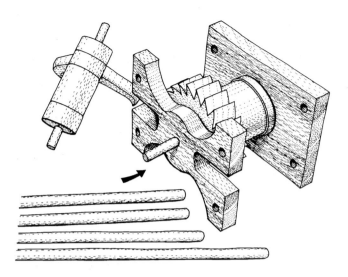

**FIGURE 13-14**

**Gather all the parts that make up the escapement, and make sure they fit and come together nicely.**

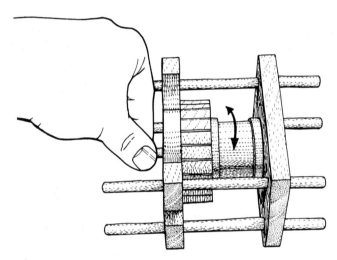

**FIGURE 13-15**

**Set and support the toothed wheel and the drum between the cradle plates, and recheck that the pivot is still free running.**

**4** Take the two secondary "cradle" plates and the toothed, wheel-and-drum unit, fit the pivot rod, drill the rod holes, and generally make sure it's all going to come together (Fig 13-14).

**5** Set the wheel and drum in place—on the pivot rod and in the cradle—and make sure the anchor escapement is smooth and easy on its pivot (Fig 13-15).

**6** Having completed the whole escapement unit, take your knife and a fold of fine-grade sandpaper and generally fit and fiddle until all the bearing surfaces move with the minimum of friction (Fig 13-16). Note that the

spacer cylinders are used to ensure that the anchor escapement sits over the pallet wheel. You might find you need extra spacers or you need to set the spacers in a different sequence on the pivot rod (Fig 13-17).

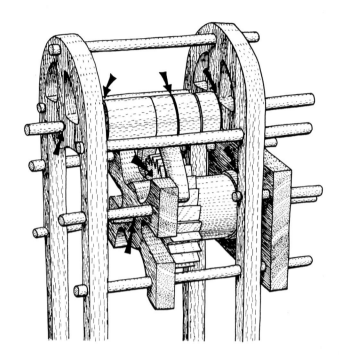

**FIGURE 13-16**

**The bearing faces, meaning the moving faces that rub together, need to be absolutely smooth.**

**FIGURE 13-17**

**Set the cradle on its support rods, and adjust the distance between the front slab and the front of the toothed wheel.**

**FIGURE 13-18**

**Make sure the frames are square and not twisted or skewed.**

**FIGURE 13-19**

**Ease the movement until the anchor and the toothed wheel move in harmony.**

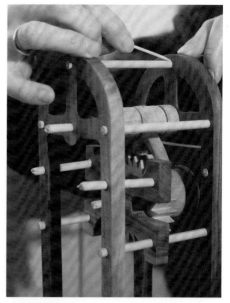

**FIGURE 13-20**

**Use the round toothpicks as temporary holding wedges.**

**7** Now make sure the recoil, or movement, is running smoothly (Fig 13-18).

**8** The movement of the anchor escapement in relation to the teeth on the wheel is critical, so spend time making fine adjustments (Fig 13-19).

**9** You might find it necessary to use the fine-point rounded toothpicks as temporary wedge pins. Set the frames the required distance apart and push the toothpicks in to hold (Fig 13-20).

**10** Once you have all the component parts well placed now that the whole machine is up and running, take a fine-toothed saw—or you might use a knife—and mark the length of the fixing rods (Fig 13-21). Allow about $1/16$" extra at each end of the rods so they stand slightly proud of the frame.

**11** Have a trial fitting of the pendulum, and cut the arm to length. The pendulum needs to clear the base by about $1/4$". Now is the time to search out a suitable weight and a length of fine, strong cord.

**12** When you have had a trial run fitting, cut the various rods and pivots to length, and generally sorted everything out, then disassemble the machine and rebuild using a small amount of PVA adhesive. Finally, burnish the machine with teak oil, fit the cord and the drum weight, and it's time to try your clock.

**FIGURE 13-21**

**Mark the rod lengths with saw cuts.**

## PROBLEM SOLVING

• If you decide to use a different wood, make sure it is strong across the grain. In the context of this project, it's most important you avoid woods that are likely to shrink.

• The mechanism can only run for a short time, as the weight has a limited fall, or drop. That said, you could modify the design and have a long fall by having the machine hanging on the wall—like a pendulum clock.

# Flywheel and Governor Machine

## PROJECT BACKGROUND

When I was a kid, I loved fairgrounds and circuses. I was absolutely fascinated by the whirling, twirling balls that could be seen on the traction engines and stationary generators that were used to power the various rides. The governor contraptions looked for all the world like little spinning men holding heavy weights out at arm's length.

The mesmerizing thing was that as the speed of the engine picked up, the little men turned faster and faster, with arms higher and higher, until the weights—usually bright, shiny balls—were being spun around at shoulder height.

In dictionary terms, "a governor is an automatic device designed to regulate the speed of a steam or gasoline engine or other prime mover." As the speed picks up and the spindle spins faster, the centrifugal force of the flyweights being thrown up and out causes the engine to slow down to its assigned speed.

With our little machine, when the cord is swiftly pulled and released, the flywheel is set in motion, with the effect that the two weights fly up and out and cause the flywheel to slow down (right).

## PROJECT OVERVIEW

This project requires turning on the lathe (Fig 14-1). You will see that apart from the two spindle-shaft collars, the two linkup arms and the shop-bought dowels, just about everything else is turned on the lathe.

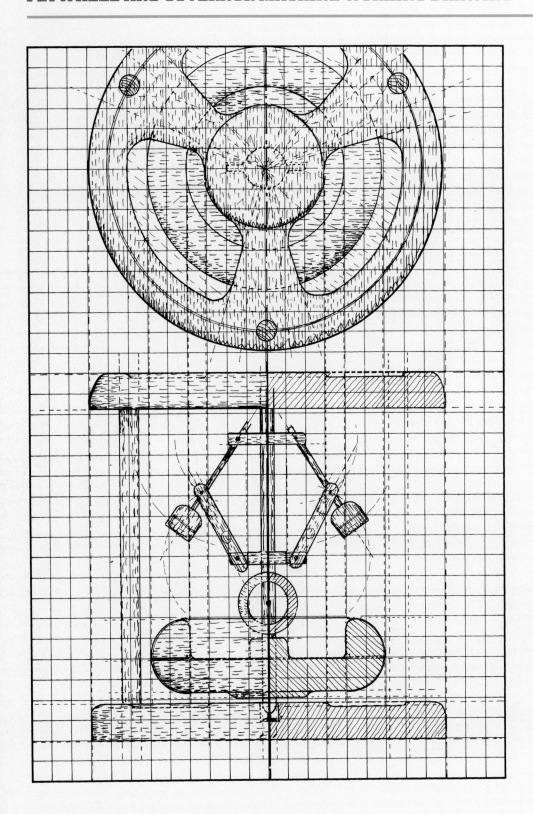

**FIGURE 14-1**
At a grid scale of two squares to 1", the machine stands about 9" high and $8^1/_2$" to 9" in diameter.

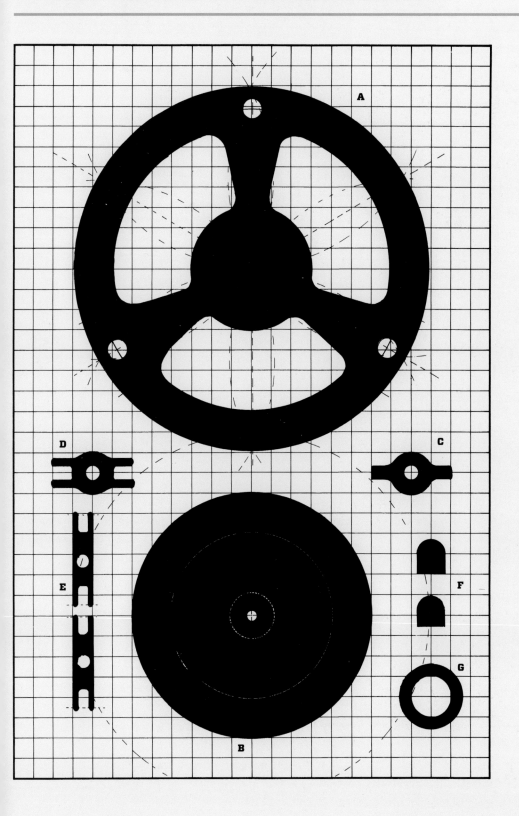

**FIGURE 14-2**

**The scale is two grid squares to 1".**

**A** Disks (2).

**B** Flywheel.

**C** Male collar.

**D** Female collar.

**E** Linkup arms.

**F** Weights.

**G** Pullcord ring.

## CUTTING LIST

| | | |
|---|---|---|
| A | Disks (2) | 2—1 × 10 × 10 tulip |
| B | Flywheel | 2 × 7 × 7 sycamore or beech |
| C | Male collar | $^3/_8$ × 1$^1/_4$ × 2$^1/_4$ plum |
| D | Female collar | $^3/_8$ × 1$^1/_4$ × 2$^1/_4$ plum |
| E | Linkup arms | 2—$^3/_8$ × 1 × 2$^1/_2$ plum |
| F | Weights | 2 × 2 beech |
| G | Pullcord ring | 2 × 2 beech |
| | Central shaft | white dowel |
| | Support columns (3) | dark wood dowel |

**FIGURE 14-3**

**Lower the moat area so the rim and the center stand in relief by about $^1/_8$".**

## CHOOSING YOUR WOOD

As always, when you are choosing wood for turning on the lathe, you need to ask yourself at least three questions. Is the wood easy to turn? Is the wood strong enough for its task? Is the wood suitable in terms of weight, color and texture? Keep these things in mind when choosing wood for the different parts of this project.

## MAKING THE TOP AND BASE DISKS

**1** Notice when looking at the working drawing (Fig 14-1) and the templates (Fig 14-2) that the two turned disks have more or less the same cross-section profile. They are about 9" in diameter, with a raised rim and center at about $^7/_8$" thick and a lowered moat between the rim and center at about $^1/_8$" deep. Don't struggle too hard to turn two identical disks because, after all, the greater part of the base disk is hidden from view.

**2** Begin by taking one of the slabs and fix the center point by drawing crossed diagonals. This done, scribe out a 9"-diameter circle, and cut out the blank on the scroll saw.

**3** Screw fix the 9" blank on the large faceplate so the screws are near the center, mount the whole works on the outboard end of the lathe, and turn down the wood to a smooth-faced, round-edged disk.

**4** When you have turned a good disk, take the dividers and mark the three guideline circles that make up the design. Working from the center, you need a 1$^1/_2$" radius for the central plateau area, a 3$^1/_2$" radius to set the width of the moat, and a 4" radius to fix the position of the line on which the three pillars are to be placed.

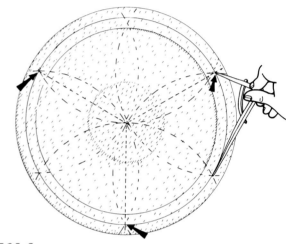

**FIGURE 14-4**

**Set the dividers to the radius of the guideline circle, and step off six equidistant points. Use every other point for the pole holes.**

**5** Having checked that the lines are correctly placed, lower the moat area by about $^1/_8$". The raised areas should run in a smooth curve into the moat (Fig 14-3). Mark the center point of the disk.

**6** With the first disk made and off the lathe, rerun the whole procedure to make a second disk.

**7** With the two disks being more or less the same size, run a $^1/_{16}$"-diameter hole through the center point, and fit the disks together with a nail or pin so they are placed one on top of another—like a turntable. Make sure the top disk is uppermost.

**8** Having first looked at the working drawing (Fig 14-1) and templates (Fig 14-2) and seen how the three posts are set equidistant around the circle, set your dividers so the radius matches the distance from the center point through to the outer-circle guideline, and then pace off around the guideline to make six equal stepoffs. Mark every other step-off so the circle is divided into three equal cake-wedge slices (Fig 14-4). This done, use the pencil, ruler and compasses to mark all the other lines that make up the design.

**9** With all the guidelines in place, remove the top disk and run the three postholes through with the ½"-diameter bit. While you are at it, run a single pilot hole through each of the enclosed windows of waste that make up the design.

**10** Set the top disk back on the base disk and use the three postholes you've already drilled to run holes through the bottom disk. The procedure is: drill one of the holes on through the bottom disk, fix the position of the hole by pegging it with a dowel, and then complete the other two holes (Fig 14-5).

**11** Having drilled the three postholes through both disks, put the base disk to one side, remove the pin, and shade in on the top disk the windows of waste that need to be cut away (Fig 14-6).

**12** Move to the scroll saw and fret out the windows of waste. To cut out the enclosed windows, the order of work is:
• Unhitch the scroll saw blade.
• Pass the blade through the pilot hole.
• Refit and retension the blade.
• Cut out the window.
• When you have fretted out one window, reverse the procedure to remove the blade, and move on to the next window to be cut out.

**13** After cutting out all three windows, go over the piece lightly with the sandpaper. Now drill two ³/₈"-diameter, ½"-deep holes—one down into the center of the base slab and the other up into the center of the underside of the top slab.

## TURNING THE FLYWHEEL

**1** After looking at the working drawing cross sections (Fig 14-1 bottom right), study the overall shape and profile of the flywheel. Note that although the form is very much like a bowl—it has a rim at the circumference, a slight foot or step-up on the base, and a lowered or sunken area—it also has the addition of a raised dias, or hub, at inside center.

**FIGURE 14-5**

Tap a dowel through the first hole to hold everything in place, and then drill out the other two holes.

**FIGURE 14-6**

Mark the shape of the three spokes and the shape of the windows, and shade in the areas that need to be cut away.

**2** When you have familiarized yourself with the form, take the 2"-thick slab of wood and follow the marking and cutting procedures as already described. Aim to finish up with a disk blank at about 6½" in diameter.

**3** In sequential order, mount the blank on the screw chuck and then mount the chuck on the lathe so the whole works is safe and secure.

**4** Position the tool rest over the bed of the lathe, and set to work turning down the blank to size. The best procedures for setting out a turning of this character are to first run the parting tool straight into the wood to establish the diameter, then true up the face of the disk with the large gouge, and then use the dividers to mark the guidelines. And, of course, along the way, you are swiftly turning off the large areas of waste, so you have to make repeated checks with the calipers. For example, you need to check the overall diameter, the depth from front to back, and so on.

**5** Having turned down the blank to a diameter of about 6", marked the 2"-thick edge with a center line, and used the dividers to mark the width of the rim and the diameter of the central hub, use the parting tool to rough out the inside-bowl area. Being sure your tools are razor sharp, run the parting tool straight into the wood to establish the depth and width of the lowered area, and then systematically clear the waste with repeated side-by-side thrusts (Fig 14-7).

**FIGURE 14-7**

**Use the parting tool to clear the bulk of the waste.**

**6** With the bulk of the waste out of the way, use the tools of your choice to bring the blank to shape. I used the skew chisel and the round-nosed gouge for shaping the curved shoulders and the parting tool for tidying up the back of the turning.

**7** Use the wire to burn in the decorative scorch line around the tirelike rim (Fig 14-8) and the sandpaper to bring the turning to a supersmooth finish. If your lathe has a change of direction option, it's best to rub down in both directions of spin.

**8** Finally, run a $^3/_8$"-diameter hole through the center of the hub.

## TURNING THE FLYWEIGHTS AND PULLCORD RING

**1** The flyweights' shape is not too important, as long as they are not so large they clunk into the support posts when they are set in motion. You can use different wood types for these parts.

**2** Mount the 2" × 2" square section wood between the chuck and the tailstock, and swiftly turn it down to the largest possible diameter. Take the parting tool and the calipers and reduce a 3" length at the tailstock end to a diameter of between $^3/_4$" and $^7/_8$".

**3** Use the dividers to set out the step-offs that make up the design. Working from the tailstock end, allow about $^1/_2$" for the tailstock waste, $^3/_8$" each for the two halves of the first weight, $^3/_8$" for the between-weight waste, two more $^3/_8$" step-offs for the second weight, and another $^1/_2$" for waste.

**4** Use the parting tool to sink the waste. Run the tool straight in so you are left with a central core at about

**FIGURE 14-8**

**Hold the cutting wire so you can swiftly let go of the stick handles if the wire snags.**

**FIGURE 14-9**

**Use the toe of the skew chisel to cut in the midlines.**

**FIGURE 14-10**

**The best way of achieving a well-matched pair of forms is to work them as a mirror-image profile.**

$^1/_2$" diameter. Use the toe of the skew chisel to cut in the decorative midlines (Fig 14-9).

**5** Now use the skew chisel to turn off the round shoulders at the top of the weights. Being mindful that the two turnings need to be identical, it's best to turn off the shapes little by little so they are looking at each other and are mirror imaged. If you take a slice off the left-hand shoulder and then a little off the right-hand shoulder and so on, backward and forward, you are more likely to achieve two well-matched turnings.

**6** Having turned off the round shoulders on both turnings (Fig 14-10), use the fine-grade sandpaper to rub down the whole workpiece to a smooth finish, and then part off with a fine-toothed saw.

**7** One piece at a time, mount the little turnings in the four-jaw chuck so they are gripped by their stalks of waste, and use the skew chisel to turn down the shouldered end to a smooth, rounded finish (Fig 14-11).

**8** While the workpiece is still held in the four-jaw chuck, set the drill chuck in the tailstock end of the lathe, and drill the turning through with a $1/4$"-diameter bit (Fig 14-12). Lastly, take the turning off the lathe, and rub down the flat end to a smooth finish. Rerun this procedure for the other turning.

**9** Having turned off the two flyweights, remount the other end of the turned cylinder in the lathe—or you might be using another length of wood—and set to work turning off the pull cord ring.

**10** With the wood turned down to a diameter of $1^1/_2$", set the dividers to $1/_2$" and mark all the step-offs that make up the design. The best procedure is to set out four $1/_2$" step-offs, one at each end for waste and two at the center for the ring.

**11** When the guide cuts are in place, take the skew chisel and swiftly bring the wood to shape. Simply lower the waste at each end, cut in the decorative midline, and then round over the shoulders.

**12** When you are satisfied with the basic ring shape, fit the drill chuck in the tailstock mandrel, set a 1"-diameter Forstner bit in the drill, and run a hole all the way through the turning (Fig 14-13). Be careful not to force the pace or damage the bit or the turning. The easiest method is to advance the bit a little, then withdraw, then wind back some more, until you reach the desired depth. Warning: if you try to force the bit through in one thrust, you are likely to burn the drill or split the wood. This done, back the drill bit out of the way, sand down the turning to a smooth finish and then part off. Drill a $1/_2$"-diameter hole through the ring—in one side and out the other.

## MAKING THE COLLAR RINGS AND LINKUP ARMS

**1** There are two collars on the central shaft: a fixed female collar at the top and a sliding male collar at

**FIGURE 14-11**

Secure the weight in the jaws of the chuck, and alternately use the skew chisel and sandpaper to achieve a smooth, round-topped finish.

**FIGURE 14-12**

Run the hole through with the $1/4$"-diameter drill bit. Having the bit held in the tailstock drill chuck ensures that the hole is perfectly placed.

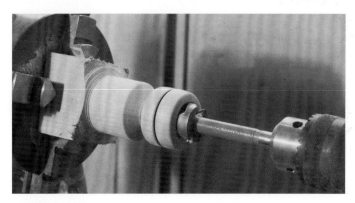

**FIGURE 14-13**

If you cut the neck of waste at a smaller core diameter than the diameter of the through-hole, the ring should come away clean as you complete the hole.

the bottom. The female collar is designed in such a way that its mortiselike flanges receive the end of a dowel, while the male collar is designed so its tenon fits into the female flange at the end of the linkup arm. Note that the two collars are more or less identical.

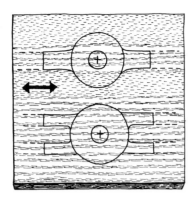

**FIGURE 14-14**

**Use the pencil, ruler and dividers/compasses to mark the shape of the two collars. Note the direction of the grain.**

**2** When you have a clear understanding of how the two collars function, use the pencil, ruler and compasses to mark them on your chosen piece of hard, close-grained, knot-free $^3/_8$"-thick wood (Fig 14-14). Note that the designs need to be marked so the flanges are aligned with the run of the grain.

**3** Still using the pencil, ruler and compasses, and still working on the $^3/_8$"-thick wood, mark the shape of the two identical linkup arms.

**4** Move to the drill press and run the collars through with a $^3/_8$"-diameter hole at the center.

**5** Move to the scroll saw, and fret out the profiles. As you are cutting out the flanges, make sure they are a loose fit one within another.

**6** When you have completed the four cutouts, sand the various flanges and extensions so they are nicely smoothed and rounded (Fig 14-15).

**7** When you have completed the four cutouts, go back to the drill press and drill $^1/_{16}$"-diameter holes at all the pivot points (Fig 14-16). Lastly, drill a single fixing hole through the top collar so it runs across the shaft hole, and then run as many weight-reducing holes through the linkup arms as necessary.

## ASSEMBLY AND FINISHING

**1** When you have completed all the component parts (Fig 14-17)—the base and top disks, flywheel, three poles, two linkup arms, two flyweights, two collars, two $^1/_4$" rods that make up the upper arms and pull cord ring—set them on the work surface and check for potential problems. Then comes the fun stage of the first fitting.

**FIGURE 14-15**

**Use the rotary tool to bring all the corners and edges to a nicely rounded finish.**

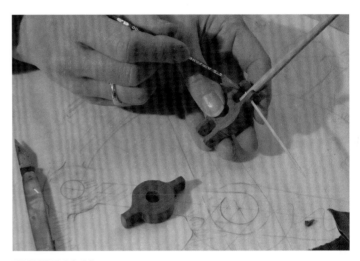

**FIGURE 14-16**

**See to it that the depth of the joint is adequate.**

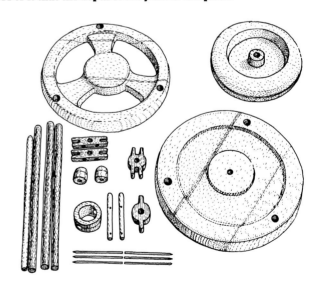

**FIGURE 14-17**

**Spread all the component parts out on the work surface, and check them against your working drawing and templates.**

**2** Having first looked at the working drawing (Fig 14-1 bottom center) and seen how the main shaft is pivoted on a little pin-and-tack bearing, tap a brass pin or nail into the bottom of the main shaft, and push a brass thumbtack into the base hole.

**3** With the base slab flat on the bench, tap the three poles in place, slide the main shaft through the flywheel, and set the bottom end of the shaft in the center-of-base bearing hole (Fig 14-18). The shaft should be a tight push fit through the wheel, with the bottom of the end protruding about $^3/_8$" or so from the underside.

**4** When you have eased the bottom of the shaft with a scrap of fine-grade sandpaper so it's a smooth fit in the bearing hole, slide the pull cord ring and the two collars in position (Fig 14-19). See to it that the ring and the male collar are a loose, easy-sliding fit.

**5** With the ring and the two collars in place, rub down six round toothpicks and then tackle one joint at a time. It's all simple enough, as long as you bear in mind that the joints need to be smooth and easy, with the pivot pins being a tight fit through the two outermost holes and a loose fit through the innermost hole. Continue one joint at a time, easing, adjusting and pencil labeling so you can repeat the correct arrangement the second time around (Fig 14-20).

**6** When all the joints are loose and easy, and when you have established the full extent of the rise and fall of the arms, slide the flyweights in place, and mark their position with pencil registration marks (Fig 14-21).

**7** With the trial fitting complete and the holes marked and drilled, disassemble the machine and rerun the sequence, this time gluing all the dowel and pin joints.

**8** Finally, rub down any rough dowel/pin ends, drill the pull string hole, give the whole works a generous wipe with the teak oil, cut a pull string, and… wonderful— the machine is ready for action.

### PROBLEM SOLVING

- When attaching the base and top blanks to the large faceplate, don't place the screws too near the edge rim.
- Use a strong, thin cord for the pull string.

**FIGURE 14-18**

Ease the bearing hole and the end of the shaft so the whole component spins like a top.

**FIGURE 14-19**

Slide the ring and the collars in place on the shaft. The top collar needs to be a tight fit.

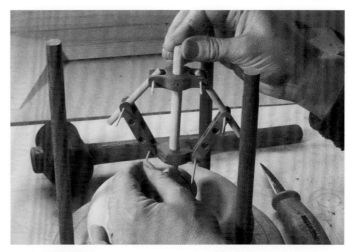

**FIGURE 14-20**

Make constant checks to ensure that every joint is a good fit.

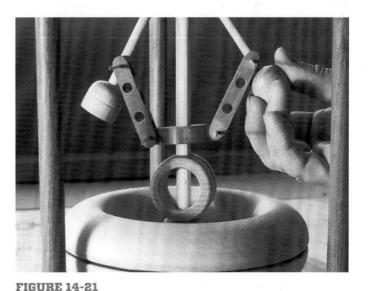

**FIGURE 14-21**

Make sure the flyweights don't in any way restrict the movement of the arms or the circumference of swing.

# Cam Machine

## PROJECT BACKGROUND

It's not simply that the movement is extra difficult or the design is ultracomplex or the techniques are more complicated than the other projects; it's all of these and then some!

As the encyclopedia so rightly says, "a cam is a part of a machine, or mechanism, used for transforming rotary or oscillating motion by direct sliding or rolling contact into any prescribed motion of a second part known as a follower." Or, to put it another way, a cam is a rotating cylinder or plate with an irregular profile attached to a revolving shaft to give a reciprocating motion to a part in contact with it.

Cams are to be found primarily in machinery where automatic control and timing are part of the operation. In simple terms, when a cam revolves on its shaft, another mechanism, called a follower, stays in close physical contact with the cam profile, with the effect that its movement reflects that of the cam. For example, if we have a true wheel on a shaft, and if we have one end of a seesaw pressing down on the wheel rim, it's plain to see that the turning movement of the wheel will have little or no effect on the seesaw. But, then again, if the wheel has a bulge or a stud set into its rim, then every time the revolving bump or peg comes into contact with the seesaw, the seesaw will jolt up and down. The predictable jolt-jolt-jolt action is the mechanical happening that turns the wheel-and-seesaw apparatus into a cam and follower.

Our machine is a disk cam with rollers. The working action is simple and direct: As the crank handle is turned, the two plate cams are set in motion and the wheels follow the cams, with the effect that the frame and the shafts bob up and down (right).

## PROJECT OVERVIEW

Although there is no denying this project is a challenge, the challenging aspect has more to do with being able to "see" the machine in your mind's eye, and successfully putting the parts together so the machine works, than with being able to perform overly complex or complicated woodworking techniques.

It's important to note that the success or failure of the machine depends almost entirely on the two cam plates being accurately cut and placed. The cams have to be spot on.

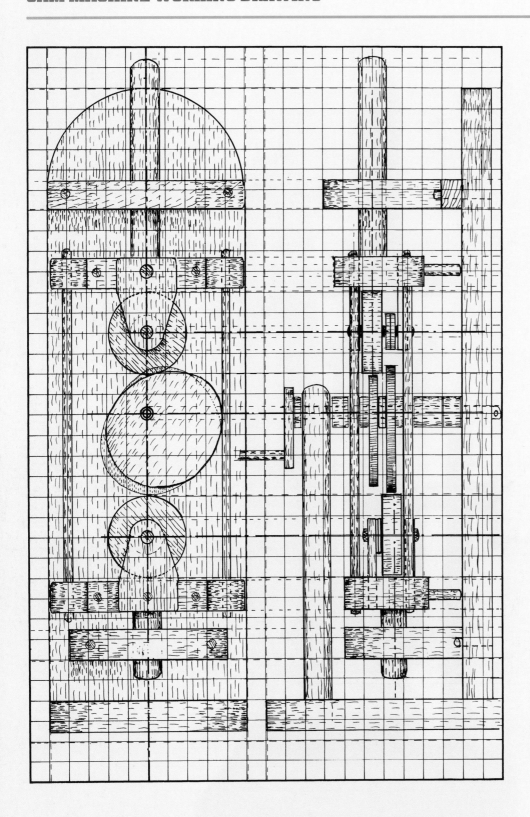

**FIGURE 15-1**

At a grid scale of two squares to 1", the machine stands about $15\frac{1}{2}$" high and 5" wide.

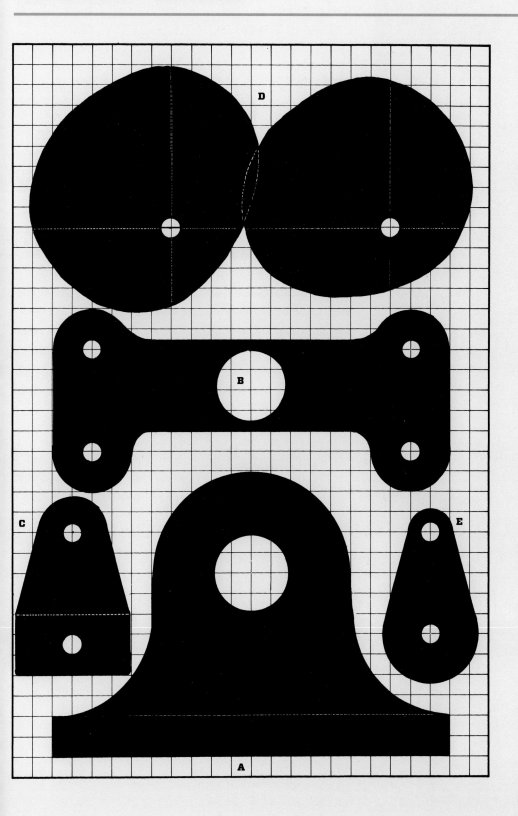

**FIGURE 15-2**

**The scale is four grid squares to 1".**

**A** Brackets.

**B** Chassis plates.

**C** Wheel plates (4).

**D** Cams.

**E** Crank.

## CUTTING LIST

| | | |
|---|---|---|
| A | Brackets | 2—³/₄ × 3¹/₂ × 5 pitch pine |
| B | Chassis plates | 2—³/₄ × 2¹/₄ × 5 tulip |
| C | Wheel plates (4) | ³/₁₆ × 1¹/₂ × 20 oak |
| D | Cams | 2—¹/₄ × 3¹/₄ × 3¹/₄ mahogany |
| E | Crank | ¹/₄ × 1¹/₄ × 2¹/₄ plum |
| | Backboard | ³/₄ × 5 × 16 oak |
| | Base | ³/₄ × 5 × 8 oak |
| | Pegs, rods, shafts and pins | ³/₄" white wood dowel |
| | Follow wheels | 2¹/₄ × 2¹/₄ × 6 plum |

## CHOOSING YOUR WOOD

As this machine needs be made with a high degree of accuracy, it's all the more important your chosen wood be hard, straight grained, easy to work, and free from knots, warps and splits. The wood needs to be stable and predictable. With these factors uppermost in our mind, we decided at the outset to use European oak for the base, backboard, and wheel plates; plum for the two follower wheels; and a nice piece of mahogany for the two cam plates; and carefully selected white wood dowel for all the pegs, rods, shafts and pins.

## MAKING THE BASE, BACK AND BRACKETS

**1** When you have studied the working drawing (Fig 15-1), the templates (Fig 15-2), and all the hands-on photographs, use the pencil, ruler, compasses and square to mark the shape and profile of the base, back slabs and two brackets. Make sure the grain runs along the length of the back and base slabs and from front to back through the brackets.

**2** With the shapes carefully drawn, then comes the task of fretting them out. No problem with the back and base slabs—all you do is run the line of cut around the drawn line and the job is done—but the brackets are a little more complicated. The easiest procedure for cutting the two brackets is to pin the two slabs of wood together, bore them through with the ⁷/₈" to ³/₄"-diameter bit, slide a length of suitable dowel in your chosen hole size, and fret them out on the scroll saw.

**3** After cutting out the two brackets (Fig 15-3), pencil label one "top" and the other "bottom." Take the "bottom" bracket, draw in the line as shown (Fig 15-2 bottom), and slice off the strip with the saw (Fig 15-4).

**FIGURE 15-3**

**To ensure a good profile and accurate hole alignment, pin the two slabs together, and have a length of dowel running through the two holes. You will need to keep a tight hold when the blade exits at the end of the cut when the two pinned areas of waste have been more or less cut away.**

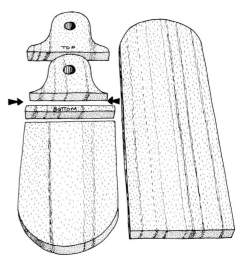

**FIGURE 15-4**

**The four large component parts—the base, backboard and two brackets—showing a slice cut away from the bottom bracket.**

**4** If all is well, when you place the brackets in position on the backboard, the shaft holes should be misaligned or offset by the thickness of the strip of waste you've just cut away. When you are pleased that all is correct, sand down all four cutouts—the base, back and two brackets—to a smooth, round-edged finish.

## MAKING THE FOLLOWER WHEEL BOGEYS

**1** If you look at the working drawing (Fig 15-1), templates (Fig 15-2) and photographs, you will see that the two wheels that follow the cam, called follower wheels, are each held and contained in a frame, or bogey, that is made up primarily from a long, bone-shaped chassis and two shield-shaped wheel plates. You will further see that although each bogey is made up of an identical chassis cutout, the top wheel chassis is arranged so that it is offset from the bottom wheel chassis. The big end bulges on the top chassis face the backboard, while the big bulges on the bottom chassis face front.

**2** Take the wood you have selected for the two bogey chassis plates, pin and drill them as already described for the brackets, and then fret them out on the scroll saw (Fig 15-5).

**3** With the two identical chassis plates crisply cut out and finished, set them flat on the surface so the big bulge ends are looking toward each other, and pencil label them for swift identification. If you look to the two cutouts shown (Fig 15-6), best label the one in the foreground "top" and the other one "bottom."

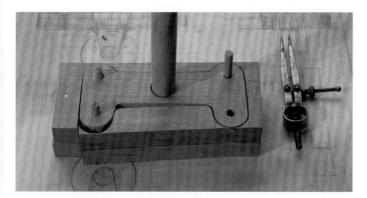

**FIGURE 15-5**
**Having the holes drilled and all the dowels set in place—all prior to cutting—is the best way of making sure you finish up with two identical cutouts.**

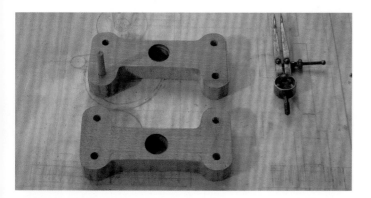

**FIGURE 15-6**
**Set the two cutouts flat so they are reversed and you know what goes where and how.**

**4** Now take the wood pieces you have set aside for the wheel plates and stack, pin, drill and dowel them in much the same way as already described so you have a single eight-layer stack.

**5** Take the eight-layer stack—with the design drawn on the top layer and the dowels in place—and run them through on the scroll saw so you have eight identical cutouts. Divide the cutouts into two stacks of four, and cut a strip from one stack (Fig 15-7).

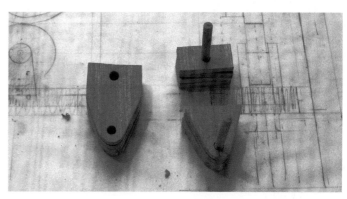

**FIGURE 15-7**
**Group the wheel plates in two stacks of four, set the dowels in place through one stack, and run that stack through on the scroll saw.**

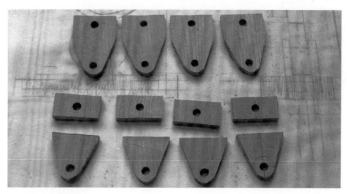

**FIGURE 15-8**
**Pair up the cutouts for best fit, and put the waste strips to one side. One pair of plates at a time, smear glue on mating faces, make sure the holes are well aligned, and put the plates to one side until the glue is dry.**

**6** You should now have four complete shield shapes, each with two holes; four strips, each with a single hole; and four triangle shapes, each with a single hole (Fig 15-8). Set the four strips aside (two of these are used at a later stage), pair the one-hole plates up with the two-hole plates so bottom holes are aligned, and glue them together as shown (Fig 15-8).

**FIGURE 15-9**

**Having turned down the wood to a well-finished cylinder and stepped off the thickness of the wheels and the areas of part-off waste, clear the bulk of the waste with the parting tool.**

## MAKING THE FOLLOWER WHEELS AND DOWEL-SLICE WASHERS

**1** Look at the working drawing (Fig 15-1) .

**2** Mount a piece of $2^1/4$" × $2^1/4$" plum on the lathe.

**3** With the wood in place on the lathe, take your gouge and turn down the wood to the largest possible diameter. Now take the skew chisel and the calipers and carefully skim the wood to a 2" cylinder. Be precise.

**4** Starting at the tailstock end, use the ruler and dividers to mark the cylinder with the step-offs: a small amount for tailstock waste, $1/2$" for the first wheel, $3/8$" for parting waste, $1/2$" for the second wheel, $3/8$" for parting waste, and the remainder for another project.

**5** Take the parting tool and sink the waste to a depth of about $3/4$", so you are left with a central core at about $1/2$" (Fig 15-9).

**6** On the lathe, drill a $1/4$"-diameter hole through the length of the project (Fig 15-10). It's a straight-forward procedure, as long as you advance and withdraw the drill in a series of small steps. Run the drill in to a depth of about $1/4$", then draw it back to clear the waste, then sink the hole another $1/4$", then withdraw and clear the waste, and so on until the hole is complete.

**Figure 15-10**

**Run the axle holes through with the $1/4$" drill bit.**

**7** Once you are satisfied with the finished dimensions of the wheels, use the parting tool to part off the wheels.

**8** Sand down the part-off faces of the wheel to a smooth finish.

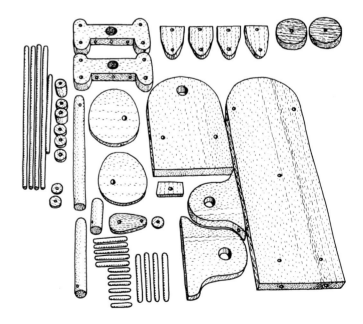

**FIGURE 15-11**

**Set out all the component parts, rub them down to a good finish, and spend time making sure you haven't made any mess-ups. Cut all the rods, dowels and pegs to size.**

**9** Now take the large-diameter dowel you set aside for the washer, drill it through with a ¼"-diameter hole, and slice it off like salami so you have a selection of varying sized washers.

## ASSEMBLY AND FINISHING

**1** The best procedure is to first dry build with the tight-push pegs, pencil label the whole works with registration marks, and then, when you are sure all is correct, begin gluing and pegging it together (Fig 15-11).

**2** Familiarize yourself with how the project fits together. Mark out the base, back and two brackets. This done, having first drilled the dowel-fixing holes, dry fit the parts in position, and drive the dowel pegs home.

**3** Take the chassis plates, shaft stubs, wheel plates and wheels—all smoothly sanded down and pencil marked—and peg them together. Don't forget to have the wooden washer to one side of the wheel so the wheel is offset in the chassis (Fig 15-12). If you look to the working drawing (Fig 15-1), you will see that with the top wheel, the washer is at the back so the wheel is pushed forward, while with the bottom wheel, the washer is set at the front so the wheel is pushed toward the backboard.

**4** Once the wheels and the washers are in place, set the wheel plates firmly in position, and hold the unit secure with the dowel and axle pegs (Fig 15-13). If you've got it right, the push-fit pegs should just about hold everything in place. While you are working on the chassis bogeys, set the distance dowels through the width of the chassis and set them so they relate to the brackets and the backboard. If you look at the working drawing (Fig 15-1), the template drawing (Fig 15-2) and the various photographs, you will see that the function of the distance dowels is to hold the chassis plate a set distance away from the backboard, while at the same time stopping the wheel frame from twisting.

**5** With the two bogey carriages complete, slide them in place in the brackets, and set the drive shaft support post in place at the front of the baseboard (Fig 15-15).

**6** Move the support post and set the four frame dowels in place so the two bogeys are linked, spaced and aligned (Fig 15-16). With the frame dowels fitted, ease the distance dowels so the whole follower frame slides smoothly up and down in the bracket holes (Fig 15-14).

**FIGURE 15-12**

**Fit the wheel plate on the side of the chassis, slide the axle rod in place, and set the distance washer on the axle.**

**FIGURE 15-13**

**Set the wheel plates firmly in position, and hold the unit secure with the dowel pegs and axle. Then pencil label the pieces.**

**FIGURE 15-14**

**The distance rods need to be a tight push fit through the width of the chassis and set so the whole bogey is able to freely slide up and down in the bracket hole.**

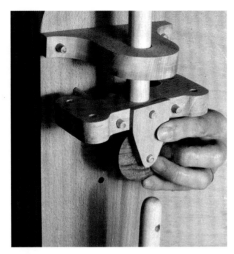

**FIGURE 15-15**

**Set the shaft support pole in place in readiness for the final fitting.**

**FIGURE 15-16**

**Slide the four frame dowels in place.**

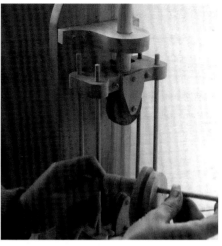

**FIGURE 15-17**

**With the cam plates on the drive shaft, test the movement with washers.**

**7** To fit the cams, slide the two cam plates in place on the drive shaft dowel so they are held apart with a suitably thick washer—I use one of the slices cut from the wheel plates. Set the dowel-slice washers at front and back of the cam plates (Fig 15-17), and set the whole component part in place so it is pivoted between the backboard and the support post. And, of course, if you need more or fewer washers, thinner slices or whatever, now is the time to prepare them.

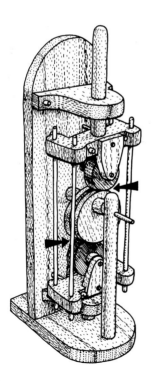

**FIGURE 15-18**

**Add washer slices until each plate is aligned with its follower wheel. You'll need to spend some time sanding and adjusting for best fit.**

**8** When you have played around with the arrangement of dowel-slice washers until the two cams are aligned with the follower wheels, and when you have popped the dowel peg through the two cams so they are linked and held together, spend time adjusting the two wheel bogeys on their four frame shafts so the follower wheels are in contact with the edges of the cams (Fig 15-18). Although you do have to do your best to achieve a good fit and finish to the whole machine, I think you also have to accept compromises. For example, if the wheel pivots are slightly askew, you might have to ease one or other of the parts with the sandpaper.

**9** When you have achieved a smooth working action with the frame being neatly lifted up and down by the cams, and when you have labeled the whole machine with as many registration marks as you think necessary, now is the time to glue it up.

**10** Finish the project with a rubbing of teak oil.

### PROBLEM SOLVING

• This is one of those wonderfully flexible machines that is open to all sorts of exciting design changes and modifications. For example, you could use it to drive one of the other projects, you could make it bigger or smaller, you could have the chassis bogeys running on tracks, you could have more cams and more follower wheels, you could redesign the frame so that it is held horizontally, and so on.

# Steam Crank Slider Mechanism

## PROJECT BACKGROUND

The steam crank slider mechanism is one of those joyous archetypal machines that sets me to thinking about steam trains and heavy industry. I'm sure you know what I mean, the good old bad days, a time before this, before plastics and computers, when just about everything to do with industry and plant was massively built in cast iron—lots of steam, grease, oil and noise!

This is a great machine to watch in action. When the handle is turned—either way—the crank moves backwards and forwards, and the piston is set to moving on its guide block.

## PROJECT OVERVIEW

Have a look at the project picture (right), the working drawing (Figure 16-2A) and the templates (Figure 16-2B), and see how the stanchion and the guide block are fitted to the base board so that the piston block is nicely in line with the crank. See also how the crank rod is fixed inside the piston block, so as to allow for the movement of both components.

Although the design is pretty straightforward—not too many precise measurements—you do have to be mindful that the relationship between the length of the rod and the length of the piston guide slot is critical. That said, if you do have doubts as to how the various slots and pins work one to another, then it's always a good idea to sort out potential problems by making a paper, pin and cardboard prototype.

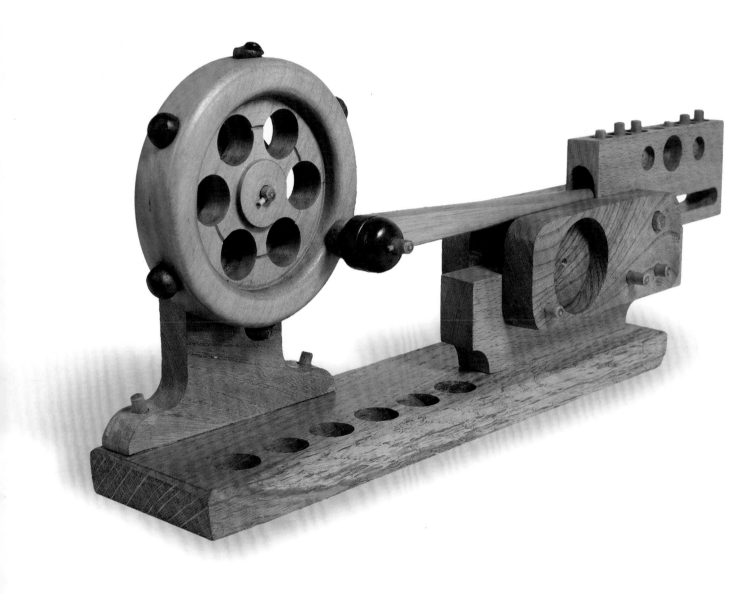

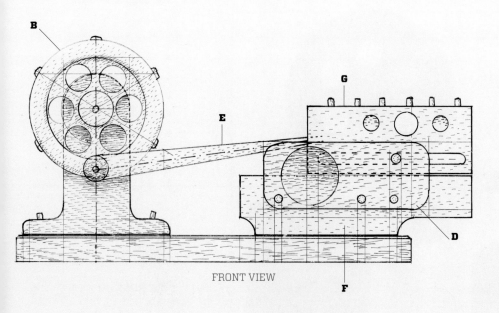

FRONT VIEW

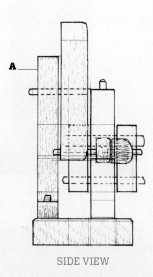

SIDE VIEW

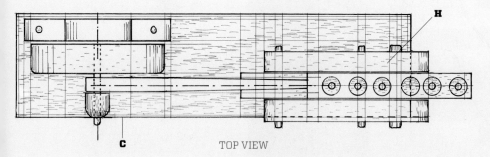

TOP VIEW

## FIGURE 16-2A

**A** Round-topped stanchion.

**B** Flywheel.

**C** Base board.

**D** Guide plate.

**E** Crank rod.

**F** Guide block.

**G** Piston block.

**H** Guide plate.

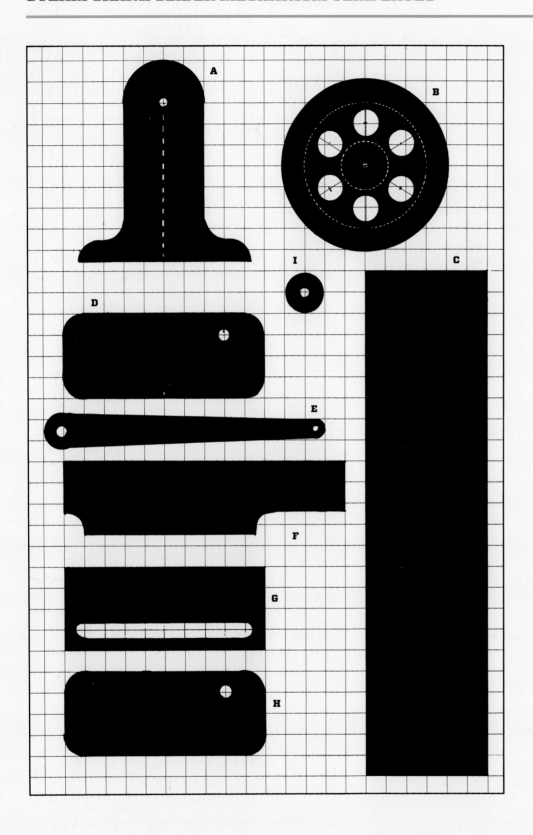

**FIGURE 16-2B**

**The scale is two grid squares to 1".**

**A** Round-topped stanchion.

**B** Flywheel.

**C** Base board.

**D** Guide plate.

**E** Crank rod.

**F** Guide block.

**G** Piston block.

**H** Guide plate.

**I** Spacer ring.

## CUTTING LIST

| | | |
|---|---|---|
| A | Round-topped stanchion | $3/4 \times 5 \times 5^{1}/_{2}$ |
| B | Flywheel | $1 \times 5 \times 5$ |
| C | Base board | $1 \times 4 \times 13$ |
| D | Guide plate | $3/4 \times 2^{1}/_{2} \times 5^{1}/_{2}$ |
| E | Crank rod | $3/4 \times 3/4 \times 7$ |
| F | Guide block | $1 \times 2 \times 8$ |
| G | Piston block | $1 \times 2^{1}/_{2} \times 5^{1}/_{2}$ |
| H | Guide plate | $3/4 \times 2^{1}/_{2} \times 5^{1}/_{2}$ |
| I | Spacer ring | $1/2 \times 1 \times 1$ |

**FIGURE 16-3**

**Use a shooting board and a smoothing plane to skim the edges to a crisp true finish. Reduce the friction by burnishing the cheeks of the plane with a white candle.**

## CHOOSING YOUR WOOD

This is one of those projects where just about anything goes—if you want to use pine throughout, or offcuts, then fine. That said, it is important that both the flywheel and the crank rod be made from easy-to-turn wood—something like lime, beech or maple. It's no good trying to turn knotty oak!

We chose to use English brown oak for the base slab, stanchion and drive plates, beech for the guide block and the piston block, and lime for the wheel and the rod.

## MAKING THE BASE SLAB

**1** Take the piece of wood that you have chosen for the base slab, and use a rule and square to draw it out to size at 3" × 12".

**2** Cut the wood to size, and use a shooting board and smoothing plane to bring the slab to a good crisp finish (Figure 16-3).

**3** Bevel the edges with a block plane. Pencil label the underside.

## MAKING THE STANCHION

**1** Use a pencil rule and compass to draw the stanchion to size on the workout paper—make changes to the profile if you have a mind to—and then use the same procedure to set the image out on your chosen piece of wood.

**2** Fix the position of the pivot point and run it through with a bit to match the diameter of your dowel rod.

**3** Use a scroll saw to fret out the form. Work at an easy pace, so that the line of cut is clean and fractionally to the waste side of the drawn line (Figure 16-4).

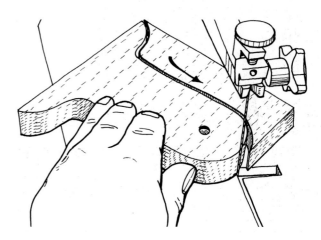

**FIGURE 16-4**

**Work at a steady pace, all the while being ready to move the wood so that the blade is presented with the line of cut.**

## MAKING THE PISTON BLOCK AND SLIDING BLOCK

**1** Cut the piston block to shape and size, and draw in the position of the guide rod slot.

**2** While there are any number of ways of clearing the slot waste—you can use a drill and/or a coping saw and such like—I found that the easiest way, in this context, was to use a router bit in the pillar drill. Drill two holes right through the piece—one at each end of the slot—and then run the router bit backward and forward from hole to hole until you are through (Figure 16-5).

**FIGURE 16-5**

**Run the workpiece backward and forward, while at the same time gently lowering the bit.**

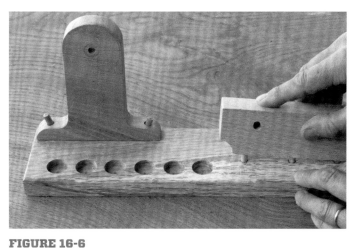

**FIGURE 16-6**

**Fix the components on the base board with dry dowel. Note that the line of decorative drill sinkings was achieved with a Forstner bit.**

**3** Cut the piston guide block to size and shape—meaning the block on which the piston block sits—and dry fix it in place on the base slab with dowels (Figure 16-6). Fix the stanchion pillar in like manner.

**4** Cut the two piston guide plates to size.

**5** Having first turned the piston rod to shape and rubbed it down on opposite sides, drill a hole into the end of the piston block and use a loose-fit pin to fix the thin end of the rod in the hole.

**6** Modify the shape of the piston hole until the rod is able to move up and down without hindrance (Figure 16-7).

**7** Finally, sit the piston block on the guide block, set the two plates one on either side, and run a dowel through the plates so that the piston is contained (Figure 16-8).

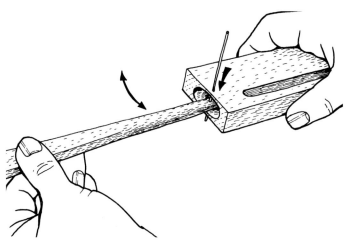

**FIGURE 16-7**

**The pin needs to be a tight fit through the block and a loose easy fit through the end of the rod, so that the movement is free.**

**FIGURE 16-8**

**Adjust the fit of the plates and the length of the slot so that the extent of the run relates to the diameter of the flywheel.**

**FIGURE 16-9**

**Use the dividers to check off measurements and to step-off around the circumference. Note the rounded finish to the top face of the rim.**

**FIGURE 16-10**

**Use a pillar drill and a Forstner bit to run the holes through the thickness. Note how the turned line helps set the position of the center points.**

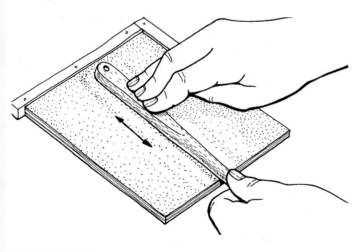

**FIGURE 16-11**

**Rub the turning down at the broad end—until there are two distinct flats, with the distance across the flats being equal to the diameter of the turning at the thin end.**

## MAKING THE FLYWHEEL

**1** Take your piece of sawn wood at 1" thick and 5" × 5" square, and check it over for problems—avoid anything that looks to be split or knotty. If you have doubts, then look for another piece.

**2** Draw crossed diagonals across the 5" × 5" slab to fix the position of the center point. Scribe a circle at 4½" diameter, and cut the blank disk out on the scroll saw.

**3** Mount the disk on the lathe and turn it down to a finished diameter of 4¼" at about ⅞" thick.

**4** Use a parting tool and the skew chisel to turn off the profiles that go to make up the design. Aim for a rim at about ½" wide, with the central boss being about 1" diameter, with the face of the boss being about ⅜" lower than the face of the rim (Figure 16-9).

**5** Rub the disk to a smooth finish and remove from the lathe.

**6** Having first used a compass to divide the circumference of the wheel into six equal segments, draw lines across the circle so as to create a six-spoke form, and then use the bit size of your choice to run six holes through the wheel (Figure 16-10).

## FITTING THE CONNECTING ROD

**1** When you are happy with the shape and finish of the wheel, and when you have drilled the holes for the central pivot and the handle, take the piston rod and continue sanding the two "flats" down to a smooth finish.

**2** The best way forward is to rub the faces down on a lapping board—meaning a sheet of abrasive paper that has been mounted grit-face-up on a sheet of plywood (Figure 16-11). Continue until the distance across the resultant flats is equal to the diameter of the rod at the thin end.

**3** Finally, have a trial fitting of the rod on the flywheel. If all is well, the wheel should be able to rotate with the flat face of the rod being in close but smooth contact—no twisting.

**FIGURE 16-12**

**Try out the movement. If all is well, the flat face of the rod will run smooth against the wheel rim.**

## ASSEMBLY AND FINISHING

**1** When you have achieved all the component parts that make up the design, then comes the testing task of getting it all together. You should have eight primary parts in all: the base slab, the stanchion pillar, the flywheel, the piston block, the guide block, the piston, and two guide plates, plus any other bits and bobs that you have the time and energy to make along the way (Figure 16-13).

**2** Check the components over, and then use the finest grade of abrasive paper to rub them down to a good finish. Give all the surfaces—barring the mating faces that are to be glued—a swift rub down with a small amount of teak oil.

**3** When you are happy with the finish, start by gluing and pegging the stanchion and the guide block to the base board.

**4** Glue the dowel in the center of the flywheel, and glue and dowel the guide plates one at either side of a guide block, so that the piston block is nicely contained (Figure 16-14).

**5** Set the piston rod in place on the handle dowel, and enter the tapered end into the piston block. Then fit with a glued pin, so that the wooden pin is a tight fit in the block and a loose fit through the rod (Figure 16-15).

**6** Test out the movement by slowly turning the flywheel. If all is well, the piston should be at the limit of its run when the rod is fully extended at the quarter-past-the-hour position (Figure 16-16).

**7** When you are happy with the movement, then comes the enjoyable task of fitting all the little embellishments that jolly up the design—the turned bead, all the little dowel stubs at the top of the piston, and the half-beads around the circumference of the flywheel.

**8** Finally, having first of all waited for the glue to set, give all the surfaces another swift rub down, wipe on another coat of teak oil, and then you can set the wheel turning.

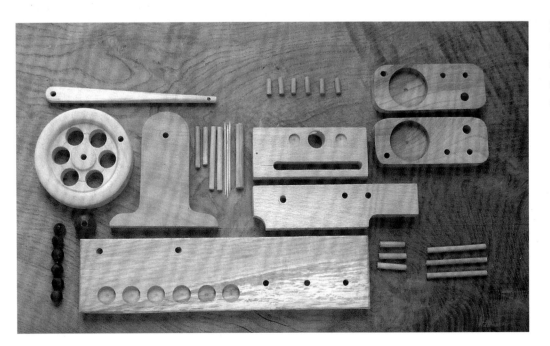

**FIGURE 16-13**

**Check all the component parts out for fit and finish. Make sure mating faces are flush and true.**

**FIGURE 16-14**

Fit one guide plate on the guide block, set the piston in place and push the slot dowel in position. You might well need to ease the slot so that the movement is free.

**FIGURE 16-15**

Push the wooden pin through the piston block and on through the hole at the end of the rod.

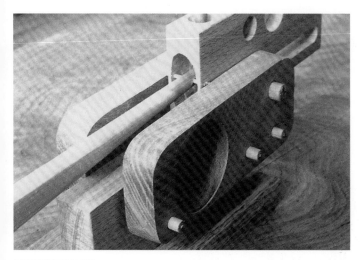

**FIGURE 16-16**

If it hangs up when the handle is at the quarter-past-the-hour position, then chances are the end of the slot will need to be extended.

**FIGURE 16-17**

When you are happy with the fit, rub the ends of the through-pin down to a flush finish.

## PROBLEM SOLVING

• If you like the overall idea of the project, but want to make something altogether more grand—say much bigger—no problem, as long as you make sure that the diameter of the flywheel, the length of the rod, and the length of the piston block slot are compatible.

• While I like the project as it stands, Gill reckons that it would be altogether more exciting if we had a set of four flywheels and four pistons, with all the pistons set so that they push one after another. She thinks that it would be more in keeping with the heavy engineering tradition. It sounds so easy!

• If you like the notion of the project but aren't so keen on woodturning, you could get away with cutting the wheel out on the scroll saw and using a ready made length of dowel for the piston rod.

• If the piston block sticks between the guide plates, then try burnishing the sides of the piston with a small amount of beeswax.

• If the rod is too long to allow the piston block to get to the end of its run, then either shorten the length of the rod or lengthen the guide slot.

• If you're a beginner to woodturning, you can take it from me that one of the best extras is the four-jaw chuck. As you can see, it allows you to hold disk blanks securely, without the need for screws.

# Differential Pulley Block

## PROJECT BACKGROUND

Vhen we lived by a boatyard, I used to watch in amazement at the launchings. Having spent six months building a wooden fishing trawler that was truly as big as a house—about 60' long with oaken ribs as thick as a man's body, 20' high from keel to deck, all built on top of a massive iron carriage—the builders would use a series of pulleys and levers to inch the finished boat out of the building shed and into the water. They made it look so easy! They would hook one end of the pulley to the carriage, and the other end to one of the huge iron rings set into the quay side. Then they would pump away at the ratchet handle, and it was beautiful to watch. Four middle-aged men little-by-little inching the big boat from the shed and onto the launching ramp. All of it done with pulleys and levers.

## PROJECT OVERVIEW

Look at the project picture to the right, the working drawing (Figure 17-2A) and the design templates (Figure 17-2B), and you'll see that the essence of this project is making multiples. There are lots of turned pulleys, wheels, groups of identical plates, sets of holder bars, and so on. If you like making repeats, then you are going to enjoy this project.

The ratchet is a bit tricky because it must be laid out accurately with a compass. Look at the design templates (Figure 17-2B) and note how the wheel design is achieved by scribing radius arcs around the circumference of the circle to divide it up into six equal parts.

This project is designed to be hung on the wall like a picture or a piece of sculpture. The holes in the backboard are used as hanging points.

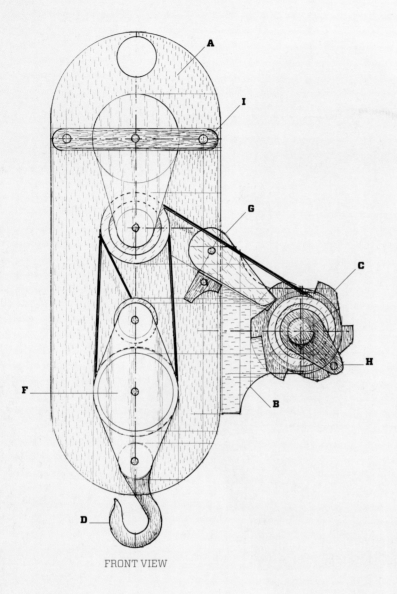

FRONT VIEW

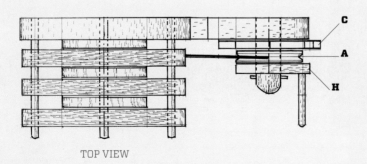

TOP VIEW

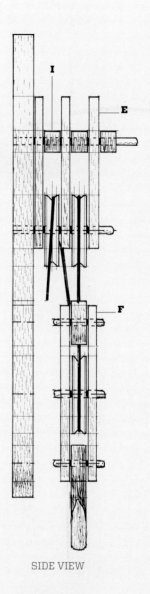

SIDE VIEW

## FIGURE 17-2A

**With this project, feel free to experiment with different sizes and thicknesses of wood.**

**A**  Backboard.

**B**  Ratchet outrigger.

**C**  Ratchet wheel.

**D**  Hook.

**E**  Top gang pulley plate.

**F**  Swinging gang pulley plate.

**G**  Ratchet stop plate.

**H**  Handle crank.

**I**  Holder bar.

**J**  Distance disk.

**K**  Pulley wheel.

# DIFFERENTIAL PULLEY BLOCK TEMPLATES

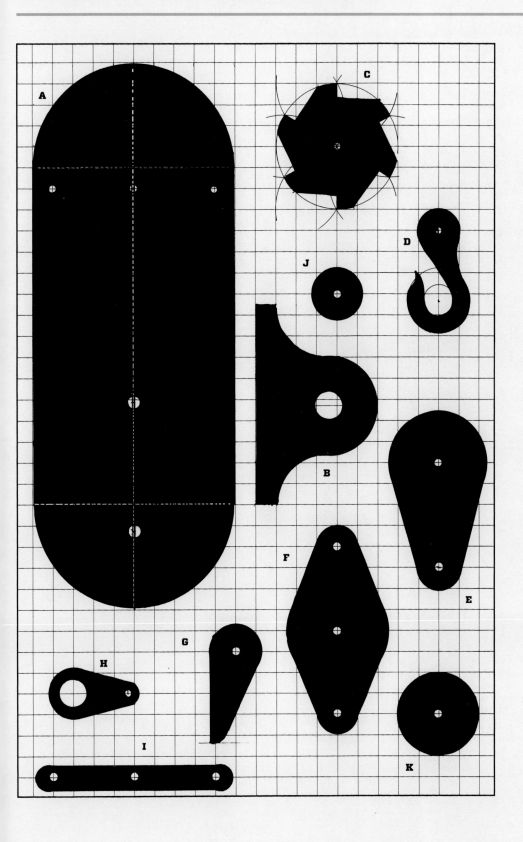

**FIGURE 17-2B**

**The scale is two grid squares to 1".**

**A** Backboard.

**B** Ratchet outrigger.

**C** Ratchet wheel.

**D** Hook.

**E** Top gang pulley plate.

**F** Swinging gang pulley plate.

**G** Ratchet stop plate.

**H** Handle crank.

**I** Holder bar.

**J** Distance disk.

**K** Pulley wheel.

## CUTTING LIST

| A | Backboard | $3/4 \times 5^{1}/2 \times 13^{1}/3$ oak |
|---|---|---|
| B | Ratchet outrigger | $3/4 \times 4 \times 5^{1}/2$ tulip |
| C | Ratchet wheel | $3/8 \times 3^{1}/2 \times 3^{1}/2$ plum |
| D | Hook | $1/2 \times 2 \times 3^{1}/2$ plum |
| E | Top gang pulley plate | $3/8 \times 3 \times 4^{3}/4$ cedar |
| F | Swinging gang pulley plate | $3/8 \times 2^{3}/4 \times 5^{1}/2$ cedar |
| G | Ratchet stop plate | $3/8 \times 1^{1}/2 \times 3$ plum |
| H | Handle crank | $3/8 \times 1^{3}/8 \times 2^{3}/8$ plum |
| I | Holder bar | $1/2 \times 1/2 \times 5$ mahogany |
| J | Distance disk | $3/8 \times 1^{1}/2 \times 1^{1}/2$ plum |
| K | Pulley wheel | A quantity of tulip, $2^{3}/4$" square |

## CHOOSING YOUR WOOD

While it's certainly true to say that I always choose my wood with one eye on the decorative appeal, in this instance certain pieces are primarily chosen for their strength and workability. For example, for the plates I chose cedar because it is strong along the run of the grain. For the pulleys I chose tulip, because it is both strong and easy to turn. Most important, I chose English plum for the hook, because the hook has to be strong in all directions. Plum is extremely difficult to carve, but the grain is tight and strong, making it perfect for the hook, and it looks really good against the bland oak backboard.

## MAKING THE BACK BOARD AND SIDE RIGGER

**1** Check your chosen pieces of wood for problems like knots and splits. Plane all pieces to a finished thickness of $3/8$".

**2** Study the working drawings carefully; then use a pencil, rule and compass to draw out the two forms for the round-ended backboard and the outrigger.

**3** Cut these pieces to shape on the scroll saw, then drill the primary holes that make up the design (see Figure 17-2B).

**4** When you are happy with the forms, draw in the necessary alignment marks so you know how the outrigger is to be fixed. Then sand them to a smooth finish.

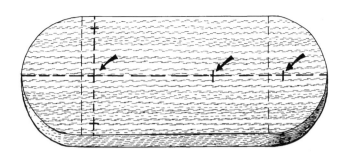

**FIGURE 17-3**

Set the design out with care, with all center lines in place, so you can establish the precise position of the various pivot points.

## MAKING THE PULLEY PLATES

**1** First study the drawings (Figures 17-2A and B), noting how there are five plates in all. Three are pear-shaped for the top fixed gang, and two are for the swinging gang.

**2** Make sure your wood is absolutely free from splits, and plane it down to a finished thickness.

**3** Again study the drawings, noting how the designs are made up of circles—two for the pear-shaped top plates and three for the bottom plates. Use a compass to draw the designs directly onto the wood.

**4** Drill the pivot points with a drill bit that matches your dowel size. Then cut out the shapes on the scroll saw (Figure 17-4).

## MAKING THE RATCHET WHEEL

**1** Take the wood for the ratchet wheel and plane it down to $1/4$".

**2** Set a compass to a radius of $1^{1}/2$" and mark a 3"-diameter circle on the wood. Then step the radius off around the circumference to divide it into six equal parts. (Note: the circle's radius will be slightly too short to give you six equal segments, so plan on doing some fine-tuning.)

**3** Mark straight lines from the six marks on the circumference to the center point. Measure $1/2$" back from the center along each line and make another mark. This allows for the width of the ratchet spurs, cogs and such. There's no problem if your design differs somewhat from mine, as long as the six spurs or cogs on your wheel are all the same shape and size.

**FIGURE 17-4**

**If you're new to the scroll saw, you might not know that the rate of cut is governed by the speed at which you advance the workpiece. To have more control when cutting tight curves, simply slow down feeding the wood into the blade.**

**4** When you're satisfied with the shape, drill a ³/₄" hole for the pivot and a small hole for the fixing peg.

**5** Cut the form out on the scroll saw (Figure 17-5).

## MAKING THE HOOK

**1** Now comes the good fun of whittling the hook to shape. It's fun because it's also a challenge. Whittling a dense wood like plum is always tough going. The only tricky part is you have to keep changing the direction of the cut as you work around the curves. If you find yourself cutting directly into end grain, turn the hook around and cut from another direction (Figure 17-6).

**2** When you have whittled the hook to shape, wrap a fold of sandpaper around a dowel to help you sand the curves. Sand until it's smooth.

**FIGURE 17-5**

**First cut out the disk, then clear each of the six pieces of waste with two straight cuts.**

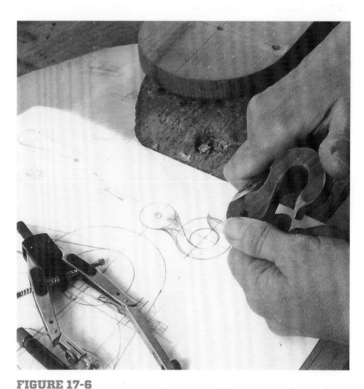

**FIGURE 17-6**

**Work with a controlled paring cut, all the while making sure that you are cutting with the grain.**

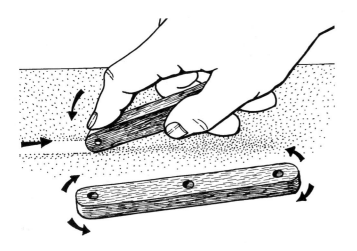

**FIGURE 17-7**

**Roll the sawn ends on the shooting board to make a rounded profile.**

**FIGURE 17-8**

**Draw back the tailstock, very carefully skim the leading face of the first wheel to a smooth finish, then wind the tailstock back up so that the wood is supported. Now part the first wheel off. Repeat these steps for each wheel.**

**FIGURE 17-9**

**Secure the wheel in the chuck, and use the parting tool to cut the characteristic pulley form.**

## MAKING THE HOLDER BARS

**1** Study the working drawings (Figures 17-2A and B) once again. Notice how you need three holder bars.

**2** Plane your wood to a finished thickness of $5/16$", then cut out the three identical bars. Strap them together with masking tape, and drill them with a bit that matches your dowel size.

**3** Finally, tidy the curved ends of the three bars with sandpaper (Figure 17-7).

## MAKING THE PULLEY WHEELS

**1** Take your length of $2^3/4$" square wood, check it for splits and knots—it can't have any—and mount it securely on the lathe.

**2** Turn the wood down to a 2"-diameter cylinder. Use the skew chisel to give it a good, smooth finish.

**3** Study the working drawings, noting the cross-section profile of the pulleys. They should be $3/8$" thick with a "V" shape at the center. Take your dividers and mark the cylinder with all the step-offs of this design. Allow $3/8$" for each wheel, $1/4$" for the parting waste, $1/16$" for the rim at each side of the wheel, and $1/4$" for the "V". Repeat the dimensions—$1/4$", $1/16$", $1/4$"—in sequence along the length of the wood. You need five wheels in all: three pulley wheels, one wheel for the ratchet unit, and a fifth wheel for luck in case you make a mistake somewhere along the line.

**4** With all the step-offs in place, take the parting tool and remove the waste between each wheel to a depth of about $1/2$", leaving a central core about 1" in diameter.

**5** Remembering that each $3/8$"-wide wheel has three step-offs ($1/16$", $1/4$" and $1/16$") and in that order, use the corner of the parting tool to cut the middle ($1/4$") "V" section. Run the "V" down to a depth of about $3/16$".

**6** After cutting the "V" on all the wheels, take the parting tool and, working from the tailstock end, skim the face of the first wheel to a fair finish (Figure 17-8). Then part off the wheel. Repeat for each wheel.

**7** When you've finished giving all five pulley wheels a V-groove and one fair face, place them one at a time in the four-jaw lathe chuck and remove the waste until the rim and the central boss stand slightly above the center section (Figure 17-9).

## ASSEMBLY AND FINISHING

**1** When all the parts have been built—the backing board, outrigger arm, three pear-shaped plates, two diamond-shaped plates, three main pulley wheels, the ratchet pulley, a cogged ratchet wheel, stop lever, winding crank, hook, three holding bars and all the other small pieces (Figure 17-10)—then comes the time to put it all together.

**2** Check all the parts for problems—splits, rough areas, warping and such. Sand all pieces smooth. Being very careful not to get any on the faces that are to be glued, apply teak oil to the pieces.

**3** Start assembly by fitting and gluing the top gang of pulley wheels in place on the backboard. The best approach is to fit the plates and the holding bars, and then attach the two pulley wheels (Figure 17-11).

**4** Peg and glue the outrigger to the side of the backboard. Set the ratchet stop in place on the board, fit the little block that limits the stop, and then glue the ratchet dowel in place (Figure 17-12).

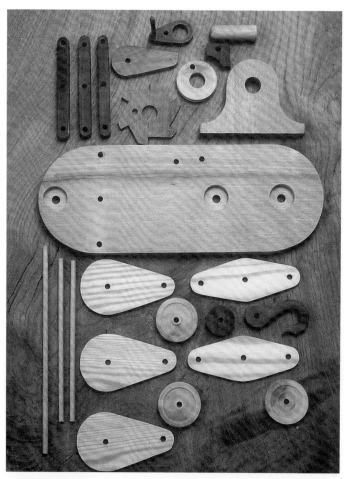

**FIGURE 17-10**

**When you've made all the parts, sand them smooth, clean away the dust and then apply a small amount of teak or Danish oil. Keep the oil off the faces that will be glued.**

**FIGURE 17-11**

**Be careful when gluing the dowel. Only glue the plate holes, so the wheels are free to move.**

**FIGURE 17-12**

**The little dark block under the ratchet stop is a limiter. It keeps the stop from dropping down.**

**5** The fitting order for the ratchet unit on the dowel is: cogged ratchet, pulley wheel, crank, hold peg and handle dowel. A small peg through the dowel holds everything in place (Figure 17-13).

**6** The swinging gang—the unit with the single pulley wheel and hook—is wonderfully easy to fit. All you do is sandwich the hook, pulley and spacer wheel between the two plates, then glue the dowel pivots in place. Keep the glue at the end of the dowels so the three components at the center of the sandwich are free to move (Figure 17-14).

**FIGURE 17-13**
**Smear glue on all mating faces of the ratchet unit—the ratchet, pulley wheel, crank and the little holding dowel. You want the three components to move as one.**

**FIGURE 17-14**
**All three components need to be free moving within the plates.**

**FIGURE 17-15**
**When you're happy with the cord, drill a small hole into the ratchet pulley and the distance disk. Then attach the cord ends with glue and pegs.**

**7** To install the drive cord, follow this road map: start at the top spacer wheel on the swinging gang, go over and around the front pulley on the top unit, then down to the pulley on the swinging unit, back up to the back pulley on the top unit, and then finally round to the pulley on the ratchet unit. Fix the ends of the cord by gluing them into pegged, drilled holes (Figure 17-15).

## PROBLEM SOLVING

• Depending on your choice of drive cord, you may need to make the V-section grooves on the pulley wheels slightly deeper.
• We relied on a four-jaw chuck to make these parts. If you don't have one, you'll need to either purchase one or work in a way that suits your lathe setup.
• In retrospect, Gill reckons that this project would have been more successful if we had made everything much smaller. You might want to build this at half the listed size.
• When you come to fitting the ratchet wheel, you may find it necessary to use pencil, paper and a piece of cardboard to determine the precise position of the stop and block.

# The Excentric Squirrel Fan

## PROJECT BACKGROUND

The excentric squirrel fan is a mechanism designed to draw in and compress large volumes of air using centrifugal force. If you want to ventilate a ship, factory or mine shaft, or push warm air from one room to another, then this is the fan to use. In use, the air is sucked in through small vents at the sides, compressed during its progress through the spiral and then forced out from the outlet mouth, with each wing of the fan acting as a valve. As to why it's called an "excentric squirrel" fan, I can't say for sure, other than this is the term and the spelling that was used by a certain Sir John Robinson, in 1850 or thereabouts, when he designed a revolutionary new warming and ventilating arrangement for his house in Edinburgh, Scotland. The spelling for "excentric" is weird but correct.

## PROJECT OVERVIEW

Have a look at the project picture (right), the working drawings (Figure 18-2A) and the templates (Figure 18-2B). The fan is made up from a backing board, a frame plate and a base board, with the three components sharing the same profile. This was achieved by sandwiching three boards and then cutting them out all of a piece—with the resultant waste being used for a good number of the other components. The movement is achieved by means of a drive belt that runs from one wheel to another, with the motive force being supplied by the crank handle. The good fun thing with this project is not so much the smooth movement of the fan, but rather in the making. I say this because, to my mind, there is something particularly pleasuresome about the procedure of cutting and fitting the fan wings so that they are a tight close fit within the frame plate.

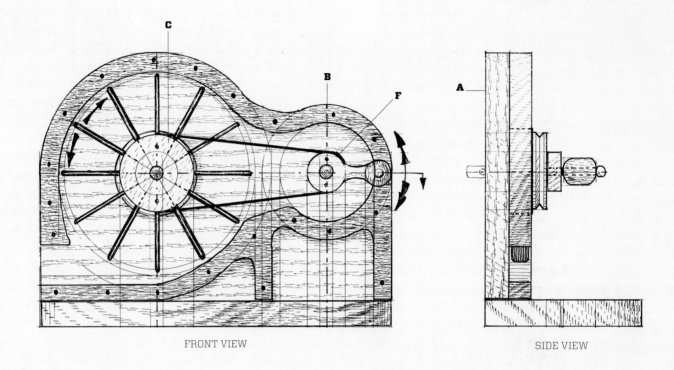

FRONT VIEW

SIDE VIEW

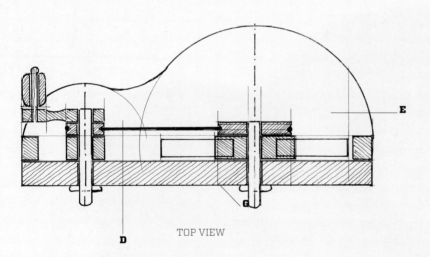

TOP VIEW

D

**FIGURE 18-2A**

**A**  Backing board.

**B**  Frame plate.

**C**  Fan hub.

**D**  Hub belt wheel.

**E**  Small belt wheel.

**F**  Crank handle.

**G**  Base board.

**FIGURE 18-2B**

**The scale is two grid squares to 1".**

**A** Backing board.

**8** Frame plate.

**C** Fan hub.

**D** Hub belt wheel.

**E** Small belt wheel.

**F** Crank handle.

## CUTTING LIST

Note: the sizes of the small parts aren't listed because they are cut from the waste necessarily left over after cutting the primary components.

| A | Backing board | 1 × 7 × 10 tulip |
|---|---|---|
| B | Frame plate | 1 × 7 × 10 plum |
| C | Fan hub | Cut from waste plum |
| D | Hub belt wheel | $1^{1}/_{2} \times 2^{1}/_{2} \times 2^{1}/_{2}$ cherry |
| E | Small belt wheel | Cut from waste |
| F | Crank handle | $^{1}/_{2} \times 1^{1}/_{4} \times 2^{1}/_{2}$ cherry |
| G | Base board | 1 × 7 × 10 tulip |

**FIGURE 18-3**

**Cut out the form so that you have three identical profiles.**

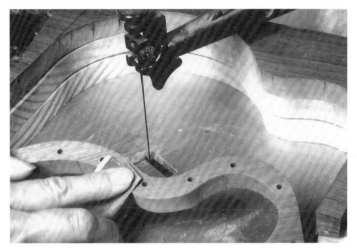

**FIGURE 18-4**

**The top profile is further worked on the scroll saw, so that you are left with the frame. Don't cut across the large areas of waste because you will need them for the other component parts.**

## CHOOSING YOUR WOOD

Though the choice of wood is pretty straightforward in terms of technique—no complex procedures that require specific wood types—you do still have to spend time making sure that there is a good contrast from one component part to another. After thinking long and hard about the various possible combinations and permutations, I decided to have the backboard and the base board cut from the same wood, with the frame plate and most of the other component parts being cut from wood of a contrasting color. At the end of it all—after searching through my wood pile and generally counting costs and looking at sizes—I went for tulip for the backing board and the base, plum for the frame plate and the hub wheel, and odds and ends for the rest. Note how the project starts with three boards being sandwiched and cut all of a piece. It's worth saying here that I never buy new endangered wood—like mahogany—I either use wood salvaged from the sea or from some long gone item of broken furniture, or I do without and use a renewable species. My wood came from the sea—probably the seat plank from a yacht.

## MAKING THE BASE, BACK AND FRAME BOARDS

**1** Having first studied the working drawings and the templates (Figures 18-2A and B), take your chosen wood for the base, back and frame, and plane the three boards to a finished thickness of $^{5}/_{8}$".

**2** Set the three boards together in a sandwich—in the order from bottom to top, base, back and frame—and tap small panel pins through the corners of waste.

**3** Draw the design of the frame out on the top board.

**4** When you are clear in your own mind as to the order of things, move to the scroll saw and carefully fret out the outer profile. At this stage, you should finish up with three identical profiles (Figure 18-3)—same shape on both the under and top sides.

**5** Take the frame profile and work on the scroll saw until you have achieved the characteristic form.

**6** Sit the frame plate on the backing board, drill the pattern of fixing holes, and then—being very careful not to split the wood along the fragile short grain—use a fold of sandpaper to clean up.

## MAKING THE FAN WHEEL

**1** Take the wood that you have chosen to use for the fan hub and then use the compass fixed at a radius of a little under 1$^1$/$_{16}$" to draw out a circle with a diameter of 2$^1$/$_8$". Draw an inner circle at about 1" diameter.

**2** Run a hole through the center of the drawn out circle to match up with the diameter of your chosen pivot dowel.

**3** With the compass still set at the radius measurement, first step off around the circumference so that you have six equal divisions, and then halve the divisions so as to divide the circumference into twelve equal parts, like the face of a clock.

**4** Draw lines from the circumference intersections to the center—just like the spokes of a wheel—and then move to the band saw and run straight saw cuts along the spoke lines, stopping short at the line of the inner circle.

**5** Lastly, move to the scroll saw and cut around the outer circle so that you finish up with the hub wheel (Figure 18-5).

**6** Take the wood for the wing flats and plane it down to a thickness of about $^1$/$_{16}$". Cut the wood into twelve identical lengths at a little under $^1$/$_2$" wide and 1$^7$/$_8$" long.

**7** One piece at a time, take a small sharp knife and shave away the thickness at one end, until it is a tight push fit in the band saw cut (Figure 18-6).

## MAKING THE BELT WHEELS

**1** Having first used a plane to thickness your chosen wood to $^3$/$_8$", then use the compass to set out the two circles—1$^7$/$_8$" diameter for the large wheel, and $^3$/$_4$" for the small one.

**2** Cut the two circles out on the scroll saw.

**3** One blank at a time, take the knife and the riffler file and cut and work the V-groove (Figure 18-7). Run three pencil lines around the thickness of the wood so that you have four bands—two equal outer bands at $^1$/$_8$" and two inner side-by-side bands at $^1$/$_{16}$". Run a stopcut down between the two $^1$/$_{16}$" bands, and cut into the stop-cut to make the V-section. Do this on both wheels.

**FIGURE 18-5**

**First cut the slots and then cut out the circle. This way of working allows you to correctly align the band saw cuts well before they enter the circle.**

**FIGURE 18-6**

**Shave the wood on both sides so that each wing is a tight push fit. If you are using a hefty saw blade or thin veneers, then you could maybe miss out on the shaving stage.**

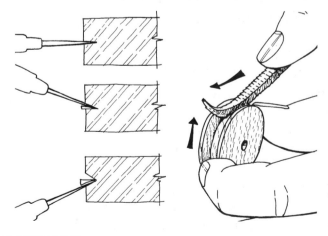

**FIGURE 18-7**

**Use a knife to cut the V-groove, then run the riffler file over and round—always working with the run of the grain.**

**FIGURE 18-8**

Work with a tight paring stroke—as if you were paring a small apple.

## MAKING THE CRANK HANDLE

**1** Plane the chosen wood to a thickness of about $^3/_8$".

**2** Run a center line down the width of the wood so that it is aligned with the direction of the grain. Then use the compass, rule and pencil to set out the design.

**3** With a drill bit to match the diameter of your dowel, run holes through the two pivot points. Then fret the profile out on the scroll saw.

**4** Use the penknife to whittle the arm of the crank to a round section finish. Work from end to center so as to avoid running the blade into end grain (Figure 18-8) .

**5** Having made the knob—I turned mine, but you could just as well use a found bead—take a little scrap of easy-to-carve wood and make a little pivot pin to run through the knob (Figure 18-9). Work the whittling with a knife and fine-grade sandpaper, until it is a tight fit in the crank and a loose fit through the knob, with the swelling at the end of the pivot acting as stop.

## ASSEMBLY AND FINISHING

**1** Take all the component parts and check them over for possible problems—pay particular attention to the fan hub. See how I trimmed back the width of my base board by about 2", so that it looks more balanced. When you are happy that all is correct, then comes the time to a have a trial run putting together.

**FIGURE 18-9**

Sand the peg to a round section so that it's a loose fit through the knob and a tight fit in the crank hole.

**FIGURE 18-10**

The frame plate might well warp when it has been cut. If this happens, then you will need to ease it to fit.

**FIGURE 18-11**

Trim the wings on both sides, and set them in the slots so that they are in alignment with the radius lines.

**2** Position the face frame plate on the backing board and mark its position. Establish the precise position of the two wheel pivots, and run them through with a bit size to match your chosen dowels.

**3** Set the frame plate in position on the back and run selected fixing holes through the thickness of the backboard. Fix the frame with three or four cocktail-stick pins (Figure 18-10).

**4** Set the wing flaps in the hub slots, and make adjustments (Figure 18-11) until the total diameter of the fan makes for a tight fit within the frame plate.

**5** Place the drive belt wheel on the top face of the hub, and fix it with wooden pins (Figure 18-12).

**6** Once the fan wheel is in place, drill the rest of the holes through the base board. If your frame warped, you might need to fiddle around for best fit (Figure 18-13).

**7** Slide the spacer wheel on the drive pivot (Figure 18-14), and then fit the crank and wheel unit.

**8** Take a waxed twine and cut and knot a two-strand drive belt to fit.

**9** Finally, disassemble the components and work through the usual procedures of fine sanding, oiling, gluing and waxing.

## PROBLEM SOLVING

• One of the biggest difficulties with this project is choosing the wood for the fan wings. Not only do you need a wood that is straight grained, with a lot of strength along the run of the grain, but the wood must be relatively easy to plane. I chose ash, but you could just as well go for beech, maple or some types of pine. You could even buy ready-cut veneers and sandwich them to make the thickness.
• Be very careful when you are cutting the frame plate that you don't break the form across the short grain.
• Use wax-lined cord for the drive belt, or even one of those little track belts from a child's construction kit.
• When you are working the V-section wheels with the riffler file, you will need to change your approach to suit the run of the grain. For example, if you arrange your disk blank so that the grain runs from 6 o'clock to 12 o'clock, then you will have to work up and down from 3 o'clock and 9 o'clock.

**FIGURE 18-12**

The belt wheel is best fixed in place with a couple of pegs—the idea being that you then don't have to worry so much about the fitting at the gluing stage.

**FIGURE 18-13**

The frame might need to be repeatedly eased to fit.

**FIGURE 18-14**

It's important that the spacer stands slightly proud of the frame plate so that the crank handle is lifted fractionally clear of the frame.

# Six Valve Radial Engine

## PROJECT BACKGROUND

I have to admit that I am not an engineer. I know something about pumps and pulleys, and I'm very interested in wind power, motorcycles and all manner of old machines. But when it comes to sophisticated items like the six valve radial engine, I'm in the dark. Maybe I ought to explain.

When I see an engine, all stripped down and oily, I don't see it in terms of valves, pistons and gears, but rather as a mechanical sculpture. I don't need to know that such and such an engine comes from a 1999 Chevy or a 1961 Jaguar or whatever; my pleasure is seeing how the shapes of the pistons, valves and cranks fit together and move. To me it's pure joy to watch as one movement is converted into another. So when I first saw a working model of an early radial engine in a museum, I was excited by the sheer beauty of the mechanical motions.

## PROJECT OVERVIEW

Study the project picture (right), the working drawing (Figure 19-2A) and the templates (Figure 19-2B). More than anything else, this project is about working on the lathe. Just about everything is turned. Plus, you will need a four-jaw chuck and should be pretty confident in your wood-turning skills.

The building process is not so much tricky, or even difficult, as it is finger-knotting and time-consuming. If you have a lathe and enjoy turning, then you are going to have a lot of fun building this project.

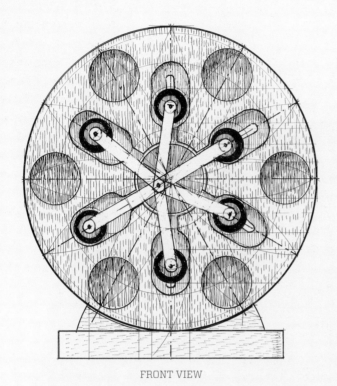

FRONT VIEW

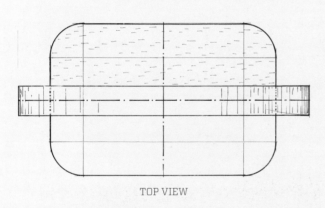

TOP VIEW

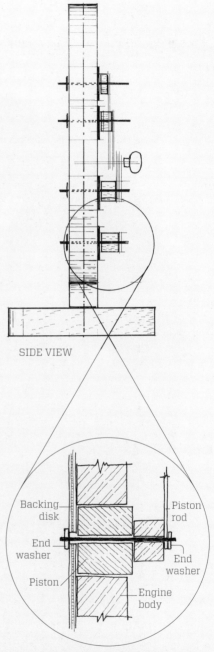

SIDE VIEW

CROSS-SECTION DETAIL SHOWING
THE PIVOTING ARRANGEMENT

**FIGURE 19-2A**

**A** Engine body.

**B** Backing dish.

**C** Crank dish.

**D** Pistons.

**E** Spacers.

**F** Base mounts.

**G** Base slab.

**H** Piston rods.

# SIX VALVE RADIAL ENGINE TEMPLATES

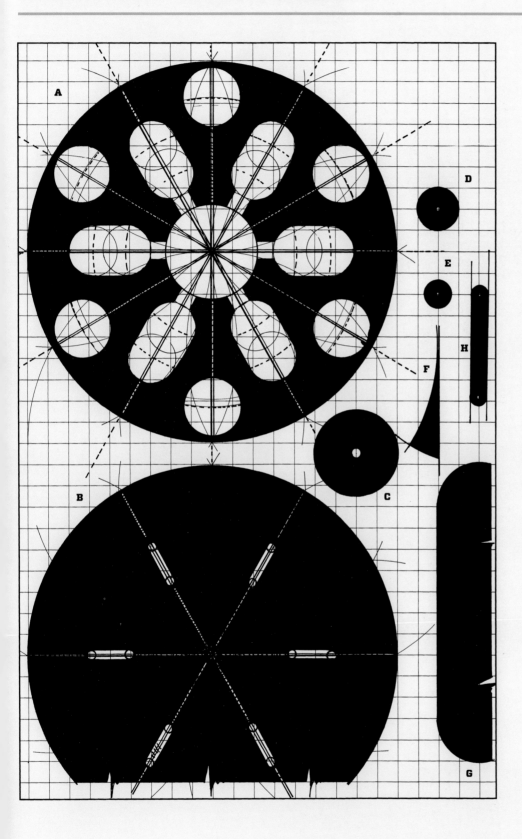

**FIGURE 19-2B**

**The scale is two grid squares to 1". Note with the engine disk how the design is based on a hex form, with the step-offs being established by making radius arcs.**

**A** Engine body.

**B** Backing disk.

**C** Crank disk.

**D** Pistons.

**E** Spacers.

**F** Base mounts.

**G** Base slab.

**H** Piston rods.

## CUTTING LIST

| | | |
|---|---|---|
| A | Engine body | 1¼ × 10 × 10 lime |
| B | Backing disk | ⅛ × 10 × 10 plywood |
| C | Crank disk | 1¼ × 2½ × 2½ cherry |
| D | Pistons | 1½ × 1½ × 1½ walnut |
| E | Spacers | ½ × 1 × 1 |
| F | Base mounts | Offcuts of beech |
| G | Base slab | 1 × 5 × 7½ beech |
| H | Piston rods | 3/32" thick plum |

**FIGURE 19-3**

**Set the wedges to the base so that the part-circumference curves fit a 9"-diameter disk.**

## CHOOSING YOUR WOOD

The choice of wood is governed almost entirely by technical need. The wood needs to be easy to turn and strong. For these reasons, I chose lime for the main engine body, thin plywood for the backing disk, beech for the base and the side mounts, a dense African walnut for the pistons and plum for the piston rods. The pieces that pose the most challenge are the piston rods. The wood for these needs to be strong even when it's cut into thin slices.

## MAKING THE BASE

**1** Take the 1"-thick slab of wood for the base and plane it down to a finished thickness of ¾".

**2** Use a square, rule and compass to lay out the design on the wood, then cut it to shape on your scroll saw.

**3** Sand it to a smooth finish.

**4** Cut the two little mount wedges to shape and size, so the top curve is a partial circle that comes from a circle with a radius of 4½" (Figure 19-3).

## MAKING THE ENGINE BODY

**1** Take your 10" × 10" slab of wood and draw crossed diagonals to find the center point. Set your dividers to a diameter of 4¾" and scribe a 9½"-diameter circle.

**2** Use a 2¼"-diameter Forstner bit to drill through the center of the blank.

**FIGURE 19-4**

**The whole procedure of turning the engine disk is made easy by the use of a four-jaw chuck. You will need to turn the jaws around so that the steps fit inside the hole at the center of the circle, so that the jaws grip when they are wound apart.**

**3** Change the jaws of your lathe chuck so they're in the expanding mode. Mount the disk on the lathe and turn it down to size: ⅞" thick and 9" in diameter (Figure 19-4).

**4** Turn the finished disk over in the chuck. Cut a guide line around the circle about ⅛" in from the edge, then lower the face of the resulting 8¾"-diameter circle to a depth of ⅛" or the thickness of the plywood you're using. The idea is to fit the plywood disk into the recess so it's contained.

**5** With your compass set at a radius of 4½", make six equal step-offs around the circumference. Then use the six points to draw in all the details of the design (see Figures 19-2A and B).

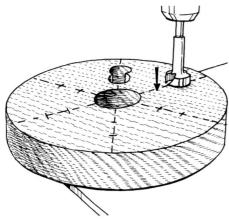

**FIGURE 19-5**
**You need to sink two holes for each piston chamber—one at each
end of the chamber.**

**FIGURE 19-6**
**Use a slightly heavier blade to saw the edges of the piston
chambers so that the sawn faces are at right angles to the face
of the disk.**

**6** Use a $1^{3}/_{16}$"-diameter Forstner bit to drill out the
piston chamber holes (Figure 19-5). Drill two holes
for each chamber.

**7** When you have marked out the design and drilled
out the ends of the piston chambers, use a scroll saw
to cut out the rest of the design (Figure 19-6). Make sure
the sawn edges are clean and crisp and at right angles to
the face of the disk.

**8** Finally, use progressively finer grades of sandpaper
to get a smooth finish. Pay particular attention to the
sides of the piston chambers (Figure 19-7).

## MAKING THE BACKING DISK

**1** On the plywood, draw a circle that matches the
turned recess, and cut it out on the scroll saw.

**2** Study the working drawing, noting how the slots on
the plywood disk relate to the movement of the
piston centers. Using a pencil, rule and compass, mark the
position of the slots. Make the slots slightly wider than the
diameter of your piston-center dowels.

**3** Cut the slots out on the scroll saw. The best way is to
drill two holes in each of the drawn slots, one at each
end. Detach the saw blade and pass it through the hole,
reattach and tension the blade, then cut out the slot
(Figure 19-8). Remember to drill a hole through for the
crank disk pivot.

**4** Finally, sand all the sawn edges to a smooth finish.
Do a trial fitting in the recess, sanding until
everything fits properly.

**FIGURE 19-7**
**Spend a good time sanding all the sawn faces to a good smooth
finish. Make sure that all the edges are slightly rounded—
especially the edges of the chamber holes.**

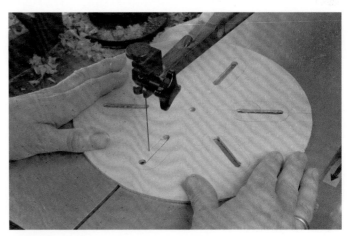

**FIGURE 19-8**
**The best way of establishing the position of the slots is to draw
the shape of the chambers through from the engine disk. If you
follow this course of action, you must put alignment marks on
both components so that you can correctly fit them back together.**

## MAKING THE PISTONS AND SPACERS

**1** With the engine body complete, take the wood you chose for the pistons and check that it's free from splits and knots.

**2** Set the square wood section in the lathe and turn it down to a cylinder with a diameter that is slightly smaller than the width of your piston chambers. For example, if your chambers are $1^3/_{16}$" wide, then make a cylinder that's 1" or $1^1/_{16}$".

**3** Using dividers make alternate step-offs $1/_4$", 1", $1/_4$", 1" and so on along the length of the wood until you have seven 1" pistons marked (six you know you need and one extra for luck).

**4** Mark the wood and the chuck so you know how it fits in the lathe. Then take it off and see how the cylinder fits in the chambers (Figure 19-9).

**5** Remount the workpiece, and turn it down to a good fit. Part off the pistons by bringing the leading face of the first piston in line to a good finish, removing the waste so the piston falls free. Wind the tailstock center in so that the wood is once again supported, face up the next piston, and so on down the line. If all is well, the pistons should be a nice fit and stand above the face of the engine body by about $3/_{32}$" (Figure 19-10).

**6** When you have made all the pistons, make the spacer disks in like manner. The only difference this time is that the disks are about $5/_8$" diameter and made so that they range in multiples of the thickness of the piston rods. That means if your piston rods are $3/_{32}$" thick, then the first disk needs to be $3/_{32}$" thick; the next one twice $3/_{32}$" (that would be $3/_{16}$"); the next three times $3/_{32}$" ($9/_{32}$"); the next four times $3/_{32}$" ($3/_8$"); and so on (Figure 19-11).

**7** Finally, part the spacers off as described for the pistons, and drill them through with holes to match your piston dowels.

## MAKING THE CRANK DISK

**1** Study the working drawing and the templates. Note the relationship between the movement of the pistons within their cylinders and how the length of the rods governs the precise position of the crank hole on the crank disk. Draw your disk to size accordingly, aiming for a tight but smooth fit.

**FIGURE 19-9**
**The piston needs to be sized so that when it is fitted it stands slightly proud of the face of the engine disk.**

**FIGURE 19-10**
**Try the piston out for size. If the fit is close and you need to adjust the chambers, then be sure to number the pistons and the chambers so that they match.**

**FIGURE 19-11**
**The spacers are vital to the smooth running of the machine, so spend time making sure that they are all correctly sized.**

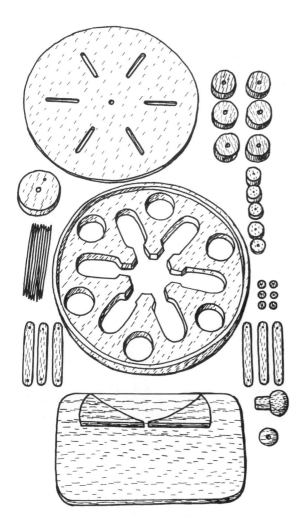

**FIGURE 19-12**

Gather all the component parts and check them over for problems. Make sure that mating surfaces are smooth to the touch and free from rough corners and edges.

**2** Plane the wood to thickness, and cut the disk out on the scroll saw.

**3** Drill two holes—one at the center for the main pivot dowel, the other one about $^{7}/_{16}$" out from center for the crank rod.

## MAKING THE RODS AND PISTON WASHERS

**1** Take your carefully selected wood—I chose plum—and plane it down to a thickness of $^{3}/_{32}$".

**2** Layout the rod dimensions on the wood. They should be about $^{3}/_{8}$" wide and the holes centered about $2^{1}/_{2}$" apart. The exact measurements should come from your specific parts.

**FIGURE 19-13**

Check the rod for size—make sure that the piston doesn't stick in its chamber—meaning when the crank pin is furthest away from the piston.

**3** Cut the rods to size on the scroll saw, then strap them together with masking tape so you have a little bunch. Drill the two holes through all the pieces at once.

**4** Use the same thickness of wood for the washers. Cut the washers to size at about $^{1}/_{2}$" diameter, then drill to suit. You need twelve washers in all: six for the front of the machine and six hidden away at the back.

**5** Thread the twelve washers on a piece of wire or toothpick and sand them until they're smooth and crisply rounded.

## ASSEMBLY AND FINISHING

**1** Group all the component parts and check them for fit and finish. It may help you to number the parts and draw in alignment marks. Wipe on a small amount of teak oil (Figure 19-12).

**2** Glue and pin the plywood disk in place in the recess at the back of the engine disk. Set the crank disk in place, and then put the six pistons into their chambers (Figure 19-13).

**3** Run the small diameter rods through the pistons, and set the spacers in place. The assembly order around the engine disk is: no spacer, thinnest spacer, next thinnest spacer and so on, with the number six spacer the thickest. Set the crank rod in place in the crank disk, and start placing the piston rods (Figures 19-14, 19-15).

**FIGURE 19-14**

**Fit the rods in sequence so that they are parallel and aligned to the face of the engine disk.**

**4** Set the turning handle in place and test the movement (Figures 19-16, 19-17). You may have to ease the holes a bit until the movement is smooth.

**5** When you've fitted the rods in an ascending spiral, mark what goes where and how.

**6** Finally, when you are sure everything is properly in place and up and running, glue the whole works together. Set the engine disk on its stand, burnish the moving parts with a small amount of beeswax to reduce friction, and the job is done.

### PROBLEM SOLVING

• If you find the movement sticking you could add a crank handle at the back of the model – a handle that links through to the central crank disc.
• If you're unsure how something works and the components relate to each other, it's a good idea to make a working model. It's easy enough to make a flat desktop model from cardboard.
• The piston rollers need to be made from a dense, heavy hardwood, ideally one that has an oily finish.
• Finding good-quality small-diameter dowels is always a problem. I tend to use a mix of cocktail sticks, barbecue sticks and kebab skewers.
• Be sure to wax moving parts before you assemble the machine, to cut down on the friction.

**FIGURE 19-15**

**If the rod looks to be a little short, then be ready to sand the chamber so that it's slightly longer.**

**FIGURE 19-16**

**Note how piston number one doesn't need a spacer.**

**FIGURE 19-17**

**Test out the full movement before you lift the whole works up, and fit the washers to the ends of the through-piston pins.**

# Wheel and Worm Gear Mechanism

## PROJECT BACKGROUND

The wheel and worm gear mechanism is a device for "cross-axis movement"—a device for changing the direction of the movement while at the same time changing the gear ratios. In this instance, the speed of the fast-turning worm gear is converted into a slow-turning wheel. If you really enjoy techno-babble, worm gears provide the simplest means of obtaining large ratios in a single pair. Such mechanisms are used when the axes for transmitting motion are not in the same plane. Just in case you're more a sculptor-woodworker than a mechanical engineer, what this means is that the screw zooms around while the wheel creeps. It's a fascinating mechanism to watch in action. It is beautiful, almost hypnotic.

## PROJECT OVERVIEW

Study the project picture (right), the working drawing (Figure 20-2A) and the templates (Figure 20-2B). For the most part, this project has to do with careful layout, precise work on the scroll saw and painstaking whittling. Note how the mechanism is made up of two primary parts: the large wheel with all the teeth, and the turned cylinder or shaft with the carved worm. In action, the crank handle turns easily in one direction while the wheel slowly turns in another. While the building steps are all pretty easy, it's fair to say that cutting the worm takes a lot of finicky patience. That said, this is one of those beautiful, juicy projects that—once the basic sawing and turning are out of the way—can be quietly worked on out on the porch or in the garden.

# WHEEL AND WORM GEAR MECHANISM WORKING DRAWING

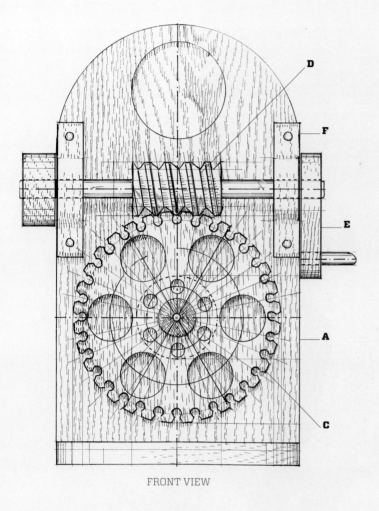

FRONT VIEW

SIDE VIEW

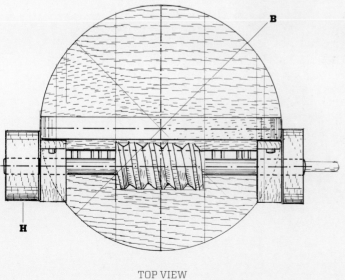

TOP VIEW

## FIGURE 20-2A

**A** Backboard.

**B** Base board.

**C** Toothed wheel.

**D** Worm drive.

**E** Crank handle.

**F** Bearing lugs.

**G** Disk spacer.

**H** Drive shaft end-stop disk.

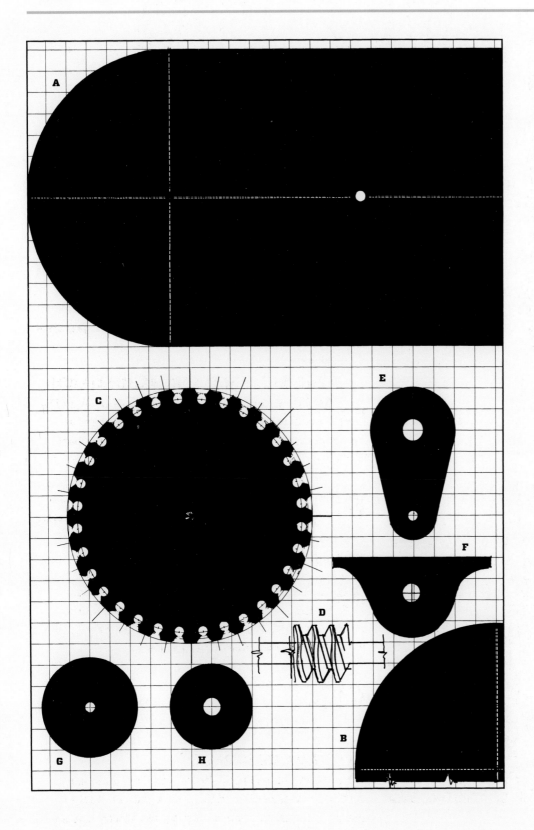

**FIGURE 20-2B**

**The scale is two grid squares to 1".**

**A** Backboard.

**B** Base board.

**C** Toothed wheel.

**D** Worm drive.

**E** Crank handle.

**F** Bearing lugs.

**G** Disk spacer.

**H** Drive shaft end-stop disk.

## CUTTING LIST

| | | |
|---|---|---|
| A | Backboard | $3/4 \times 7^1/2 \times 12^1/2$ tulip |
| B | Base board | $3/4 \times 7^1/2 \times 7^1/2$ tulip |
| C | Toothed wheel | $3/4 \times 7 \times 7$ oak |
| D | Worm drive | $2 \times 2$ lime at least 10" long |
| E | Crank handle | $3/4 \times 2^1/2 \times 4$ cherry |
| F | Bearing lugs | $3/4 \times 2 \times 4^1/2$ plum |
| G | Disk spacer | $3/8 \times 3 \times 3$ |
| H | Drive shaft end-stop disk | $1^1/4 \times 2^1/4 \times 2^1/4$ cherry |

## CHOOSING YOUR WOOD

When choosing your wood, remember: the wheel must be strong across the run of the grain so it can be sawn and pared without crumbling, and the worm must be both easy to turn and easy to carve. Taking these considerations into account, and having first dug into my mountain of scrap pieces, I opted to use oak for the wheel, tulip for the back and base boards, plum for the bearing lugs, lime for the worm and whatever happened to fall to hand for the other parts.

**FIGURE 20-3**

**Using a combination plane is a great swift and easy way of cutting the housing channel. Note the setup that allows the plane fence to run clear of the edge of the bench.**

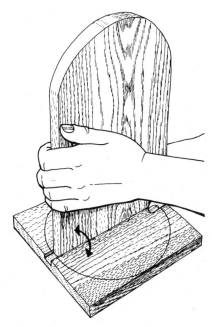

**FIGURE 20-4**

**Make sure that the boards are a good tight fit and at right angles to each other.**

## MAKING THE BACK AND BASE BOARDS

**1** Study the working drawings (Figures 20-2A and B) so you understand how the project needs to be worked and put together. Plane your wood for the back and base board down to a finished thickness of $3/4$".

**2** Use a compass to draw the 7"-diameter circle to make the base and the half-circle that goes to make the backboard. Complete the design with a rule and square. Cut the backboard out on your scroll saw.

**3** Use the tools of your choice to run the $3/4$"-wide housing channel across the base. I used an old combination plane (Figure 20-3), but you could just as well use a saw and chisel or a router.

**4** Work the channel until it takes the backboard for a nice tight push fit (Figure 20-4). When you're happy with the joint, cut the base disk out on the scroll saw.

## MAKING THE WHEEL

**1** Having planed your chosen wood to a finished thickness of $5/8$" and drawn and cut out the 6"-diameter blank, use a protractor, square and compass to lay out the design of the teeth. Lay out a $5^1/2$" circle on the 6"-diameter blank, then divide the circle into 64 equal segments. Mark the intersection of every other point. You should end up with 32 center points about $3/8$" in from the circumference of the blank.

**2** When you are satisfied with the arrangement of the teeth, use a compass to lay out the position of the various holes that make up the decorative design.

**3** Move to the drill press and drill a $1/4$"-diameter hole through every other intersection, so you have alternating holes and spaces running around the circle—a total of 32 holes and 32 spaces.

**4** Using the holes and the guidelines as an aid, draw out the shape of the teeth using a pencil and rule.

**5** When you're sure all is correct, move to the scroll saw and very carefully cut out the shape of the teeth (Figure 20-5). For me, the best procedure was to work each tooth in turn—two straight cuts in toward the center point of each hole.

**6** When you've cut out the basic profile, take a razor sharp knife (or you may prefer a chisel) and pare the teeth to a slightly rounded finish (Figure 20-6). Be watchful that you don't cut directly into end grain.

**7** Finally, put the wheel on a rod, and see how it looks from various angles and when it's turning (Figure 20-7).

## MAKING THE WORM

**1** Make sure your square section length of wood is free from splits and awkwardly placed knots. Look especially for end splits that darken as they run up the length of the grain. If you have any doubts at all, reject the wood and find another piece.

**2** Mount the wood on the lathe, and use a gouge to swiftly turn it down to a $1^5/8$"-diameter cylinder. Keeping in mind that it's important the turning be crisp and smooth, switch to the skew chisel and skim the cylinder down to a finished size of $1^1/2$".

**3** Use a rule and the point of the skew chisel to lay out the central stepped area on the cylinder. I divided the length of the wood in half and put the $2^1/2$"-long step-up at the center.

**4** Use the gouge to turn the wood at each side of the central step-up to a finished diameter of about $1/2$". You should finish with the shaft $1/2$" in diameter to each side of center, and the central area $1^1/2$" in diameter and $2^1/2$" long (Figure 20-8).

**FIGURE 20-5**
It's important that the cuts are clean and at right angles to the face of the wood. It's a good idea to fit a new blade, adjust the tension and make sure that the table is set at 90° to the blade.

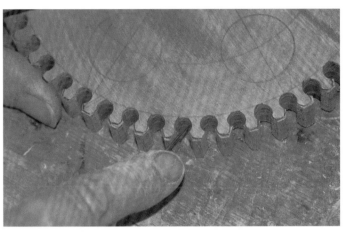

**FIGURE 20-6**
Be sure, when you are tidying up with the knife or chisel, that the workpiece is arranged so that you are cutting with the grain. It's a good idea to work on a smooth surface or a work board.

**FIGURE 20-7**
Make yourself a jig so that you can test out the movement. All you need is a vertical surface with a pivot hole—the edge of the bench, a piece of waste... anything will do.

**FIGURE 20-8**

**Though I spent some considerable time deliberating over my choice of wood, I still came across a small knot—see just right of the cylinder. Fortunately, it doesn't get in the way of things.**

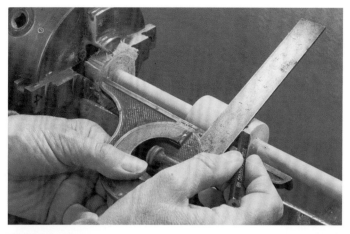

**FIGURE 20-9**

**Note the protractor square—the perfect tool for the task—picked up for pennies on a junk market.**

**5** Study the working drawings (Figure 20-2A) and the templates (Figure 20-2B), then use a combination square with a protractor head (or a similar tool) to lay out the angle of the worm (Figure 20-9). Although it looks a little complicated, the point to remember is that the windings of the worm as they wrap around the shaft must be spaced so that they fall naturally between the teeth of the wheel. If the tooth V-section centers are about 1/2" apart, then the top peaks of the worm also need to be about 1/2" apart.

**6** With the guidelines in place, take a sharp knife and run a stop-cut around the cylinder, centered between the worm peaks.

**7** Make the stop-cut to a depth of 1/8", then make slicing cuts at an angle at each side so you have a V-section furrow running around the wood (Figure 20-10). The band at the top of the worm should be about 1/8" wide.

**8** Continue in this way, repeatedly making the stop-cut deeper, slicing down at each side into the stop-cut at an angle until you've created the characteristic worm profile (Figure 20-11).

**9** Try out the wheel on a jig, turning the worm over by hand so the wheel makes a full revolution without sticking. Use fine-grade sandpaper to rub the whole worm down until it's smooth.

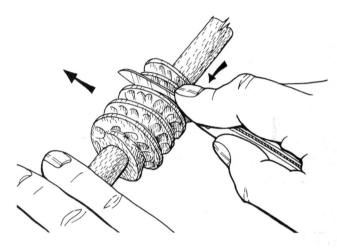

**FIGURE 20-10**

**Repeatedly run and roll the blade in the V-furrow so as to cut a stop-cut guide for subsequent cuts.**

**FIGURE 20-11**

**Remove the waste by sliding the blade down at an angle into the stop-cut. Do your best to keep the 1/8"-wide band at the top of the peak.**

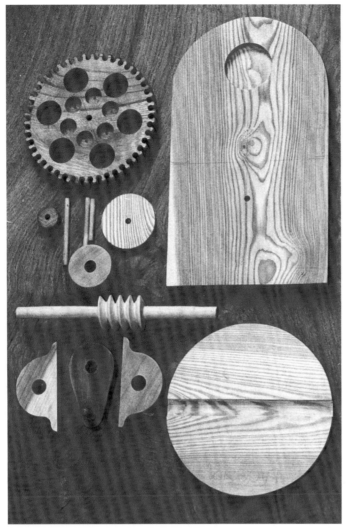

**FIGURE 20-12**

Check the components out for problems—especially the worm drive and the wheel. It's vital that all the teeth are intact—no splits or knots.

## ASSEMBLY AND FINISHING

**1** Lay out all the component parts (Figure 20-12) and check them over for potential problems. Make sure that the wheel is free from splits, with all the teeth intact, and the worm drive is as near perfect as you can make it.

**2** Don't worry at this stage about the final finishing of the other parts. It's much more important to make sure the movement is going to work properly. Set the wheel in place on the backboard (the assembly sequence is backboard, spacer disk and wheel) with the dowel pivot pushed through from the front (Figure 20-13).

**3** Set one lug bearing in place, then slide the worm drive shaft through the bearing so the worm is aligned in the teeth of the wheel. Then fit the other lug bearing (Figure 20-14).

**FIGURE 20-13**

At a later stage, the dowel can be fitted by being cross-drilled and pinned with a cocktail stick.

**FIGURE 20-14**

The little strip of waste prevents the top of the dowel from being crushed and damaged.

**4** With the worm drive centered, slide the stop disk and the crank handle onto the shaft and bring them up to the lugs. Keep in mind that it's the proper placing of these two components that determines the position of the worm and the subsequent smoothness of the movement (Figure 20-15).

**5** Set the backboard in the base channel and check it over for fit (Figure 20-16).

**6** Finally, when you're happy with the way all the components come together, disassemble the whole works, do a finish sanding of all surfaces, wipe over with teak oil (but not the surfaces being glued), glue up and polish.

**FIGURE 20-15**

**Spend some time getting the spacing right, and then draw in alignment marks.**

## PROBLEM SOLVING

• If you have any doubts as to how the design of the wheel is laid out, then work it out on paper before doing anything to the wood.

• Another way to pinpoint the position of the 64 divisions: draw the circle out on paper with a compass. Draw a line dividing the circle in half, then quarters, and so on, dividing each angle until you have 64 divisions. Then cut the circle out and use it as a template in marking the wood blank.

• The choice of wood for the worm is critical. It has got to be smooth grained and easy to carve. My first choice is European lime.

**FIGURE 20-16**

**If you have got it right, the handle can be wound in either direction.**

# Film Advancing Mechanism

## PROJECT BACKGROUND

This beautiful little mechanism perfectly illustrates the action inside some old-time movie cameras—when, as a frame is shot, a claw moves on its eccentric drive pivot and pulls the film down one notch. It's good fun to watch the machine in action. When the handle is turned, the arm moves up-round-and-in, the claw at the end of the arm engages in the notch, the notched component is dragged down, the claw disengages, and the counterbalance weight pulls the notched component back up into the ready-to-go position. Of course, if you like the notion of springs or elastic bands or whatever, then you can do away with the counterweight and change the working action accordingly And just in case you have a mind to go delving into your old film camera to see if you can find such a mechanism (so that you can push and poke it around and maybe even watch it in action), I would strongly warn against it. I did just such a thing at the start of the project, and the camera had to go to the repair shop. In my camera, the mechanism is much changed—it's minute, no bigger than the lower-left side whisker on a small gnat.

## PROJECT OVERVIEW

Have a look at the project picture (right), the working drawing (Figure 21-2A) and the templates (Figure 21-2B). See how the challenge of this project has to do not so much with making the various components (after all, most of them are easily fretted out on the scroll saw) as it does with putting the whole works together. All that said, it's important to note that the relationship between the length of the crank and the position of the various pivot centers is critical. If you make a mess-up of one or all of these details, then you can expect the action to fail. Best advice with this project is to make a card prototype flat down on a board— with thick card and thumb tacks—and fix the critical measurements before you ever get to cutting the wood. Note that the large disk at middle right acts as a distance piece or spacer to keep the clawed arm on course.

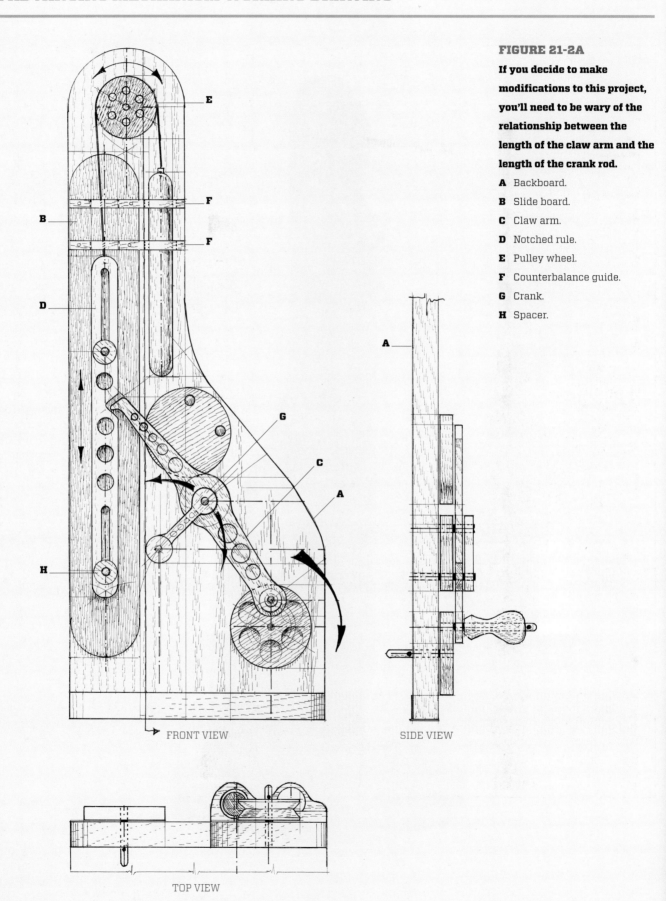

**FIGURE 21-2A**

**If you decide to make modifications to this project, you'll need to be wary of the relationship between the length of the claw arm and the length of the crank rod.**

**A** Backboard.

**B** Slide board.

**C** Claw arm.

**D** Notched rule.

**E** Pulley wheel.

**F** Counterbalance guide.

**G** Crank.

**H** Spacer.

FRONT VIEW

SIDE VIEW

TOP VIEW

# FILM ADVANCING MECHANISM TEMPLATES

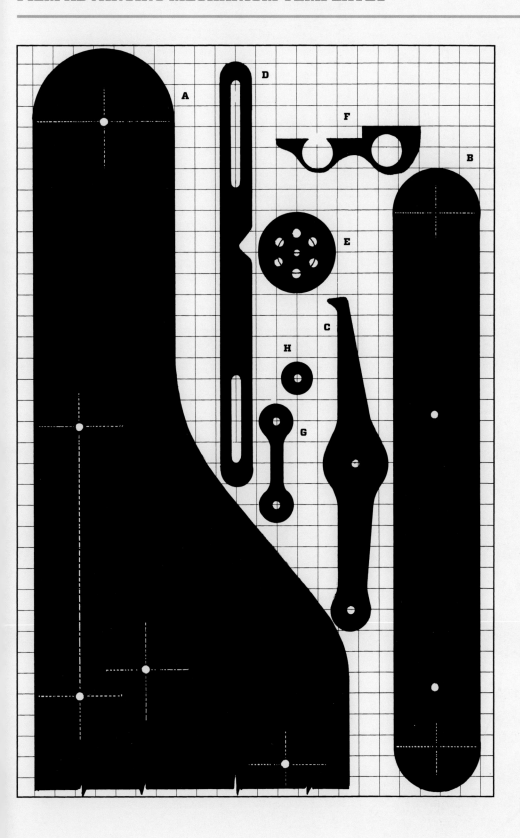

**FIGURE 21-2B**

**The scale is two grid squares to 1".**

**A** Backboard.

**8** Slide board.

**C** Claw arm.

**D** Notched rule.

**E** Pulley wheel.

**F** Counterbalance guide.

**G** Crank.

**H** Spacer.

## CUTTING LIST

| A | Backboard | 1 × 8 × 20 pitch pine |
|---|---|---|
| B | Slide board | 1/2 × 3 × 15 1/2 mahogany |
| C | Claw arm | 3/8 × 2 × 8 mahogany |
| D | Notched rule | 3/8 × 7/8 × 11 pitch pine |
| E | Pulley wheel | 3/4 × 2 × 2 walnut |
| F | Counterbalance guide | 3/8 × 1 1/2 × 4 pitch pine |
| G | Crank | 3/8 × 1 × 3 cherry |
| H | Spacer | 3/8 × 1 × 1 mahogany |

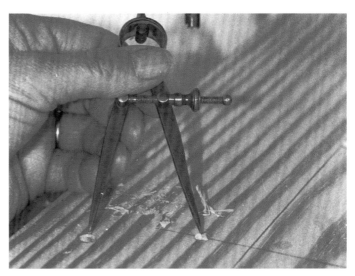

**FIGURE 21-3**

**Check the center points with a pair of dividers. It's vital that they are well placed.**

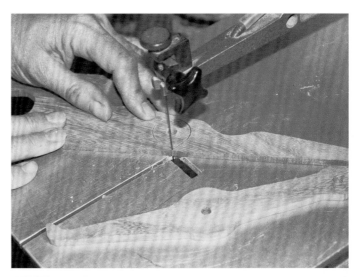

**FIGURE 21-4**

**If you go at the sawing nice and easy—with a new blade and the correct tension—you will finish up with a cut edge that is so smooth that it hardly needs to be sanded.**

## CHOOSING YOUR WOOD

Since most of the components are cut out on the scroll saw, and the mechanical movement is delicate and controlled, you can use just about any wood you like. Just make sure it's easy to saw and stable, with no warping, cracks or loose knots. I chose pine for the base, backboard, the notched slider and the balance guide; mahogany for the claw arm; a scrap of mahogany for the large wheel, and odd bits of scrap for the other parts. The counterbalance weight is made from the heaviest wood I could find, a chunk cut from an old, broken walking stick.

## MAKING THE BASE AND BACK BOARDS

**1** Study the designs, the working drawings (Figure 21-2A) and the templates (Figure 21-2B). Then plane the wood to a finished thickness of 3/4".

**2** Use a compass and rule to draw the back and base board designs on the wood. Cut the profiles out on a scroll or band saw.

**3** Make a cardboard prototype so you know the precise positions of the various critical pivot points. Transfer this information to the backboard, and drill holes that match your dowel pivots. Check and double-check the centers (Figure 21-3).

## MAKING THE CLAW ARM

**1** First study the working drawings (Figure 21-2A), noting how the position of the centers and the claw are critical—exactly 3 1/2" between centers and 3 7/8" between the crank center and the end of the claw.

**2** Plane the wood to a finished thickness of 1/4". Use a rule, compass and straight edge to lay out the design. There's no problem if you want to change the profile so long as you stay with the critical measurements just described.

**3** When you are happy with the design, drill the centers with a bit that matches your dowel pivots, and cut the form out on your scroll saw (Figure 21-4). As long as you're at the saw, cut out the spacers and the various disks.

## MAKING THE NOTCHED RULE

**1** Study the working drawings, then plane your wood to a finished thickness of ¼". Draw the design onto the best face.

**2** Run a center line down the width of the profile, and use it as a guide to mark the position of the two slots and the notch.

**3** Drill the holes through on a drill press, and cut the slots out on a scroll saw. The procedure for cutting the slots is to first drill pilot holes at the ends of both slots, detach the top end of the blade from the scroll saw and pass it through the pilot hole, reattach the blade and re-tension. Cut out the slot, then detach the blade once again (Figure 21-5). It's easy enough; the only real trick is using a new blade and adjusting the tension until the blade "pings" when strummed. Be sure to cut a little to the waste side of the drawn line.

## MAKING THE COUNTERBALANCE GUIDE BRIDGES

**1** Study the working drawings (Figure 21-2A), noting how the two guides are set together in such a way that they contain the counterbalance weight, keeping it from moving sideways and forming a channel for the cord. The outer profile of the guides can be just about any shape and size that catches your fancy, so long as the counterbalance holes fit the shape and size of your balance.

**2** Since the guides are relatively fragile, drill the holes through before cutting the profile on the scroll saw (Figure 21-6).

## DRILLING HOLES

**1** The easiest way to drill the various holes is using a drill press and Forstner bits (Figure 21-7).

**2** Use a ruler and dividers to establish the position of the various holes, mark the centers and then drill the holes through (Figure 21-8). You also need to drill some blind holes—holes that don't go all the way through the wood—so be sure to set the drill stop to the required depth.

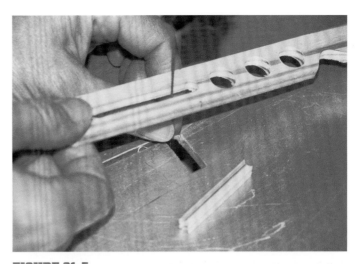

**FIGURE 21-5**

**The slot needs to be worked to fit both your chosen dowel diameter and the size of your drill bits.**

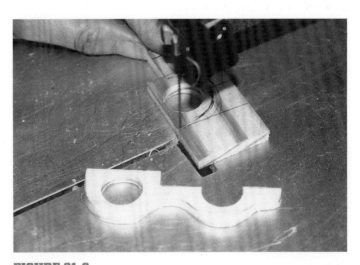

**FIGURE 21-6**

**The grain at either side of the bridge is short and fragile—go at it easy.**

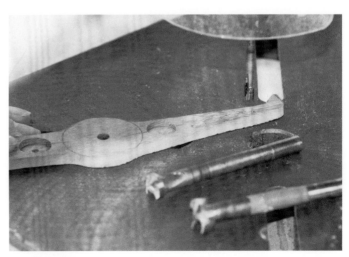

**FIGURE 21-7**

**Set the depth stop so that the blind holes are all the same depth.**

**FIGURE 21-8**

**The blind holes are purely decorative—they draw their inspiration from the forms that you see on old cast iron machines.**

**FIGURE 21-9**

**Always cut in the direction of the grain—meaning from the rim and down towards the bottom of the stop-cut.**

## MAKING THE PULLEY WHEEL

**1** Plane your wood to a finished thickness of $5/8$", then adjust your dividers to produce a $17/8$"-diameter circle. Draw the circle onto the wood and, with the compass still set at the radius measurement, strike six arcs around the circumference. Use these intersections to establish the centers of the six decorative circles.

**2** Cut the disk out on the scroll saw.

**3** Take a sharp knife, run a stop-cut around the thickness of the wood, and then, little by little, slice in at either side of the stop-cut until you have a V-section channel running around the circumference. To do this, run the blade around the disk so as to cut a stop-cut in to a depth of about $1/16$", then work around the disk making angled cuts that run into the stop-cut so that chips of waste fall away. Then tidy up the shallow "V", and make another stop-cut. Then repeat the procedure. And so you continue—cutting and slicing until you have what you consider is a good V-section groove (Figure 21-9).

**4** Drill out the seven holes that go to make the design—the central pivot hole that runs through the thickness of the wood, and the six blind holes. Plug the six holes with short stubs of dowel made from a contrasting wood—to give the wheel a rivet effect (Figure 21-10). If you cut the dowel with a sharp knife—by rolling the blade over the dowel—you will find that you finish up with stubs that are nicely rounded at the ends.

**5** It's a good idea at this stage to rub the face of the wheel down to a good finish, and then glue the stubs in place—so that they don't get mislaid (Figure 21-11).

**FIGURE 21-10**

**Use a heavy rolling action to cut the stubs. Note that the use of a level board ensures that the rolled cut runs true—to start and finish at the same place.**

**FIGURE 21-11**

**Rub the face of the wheel down to a good finish, and glue the stubs in place.**

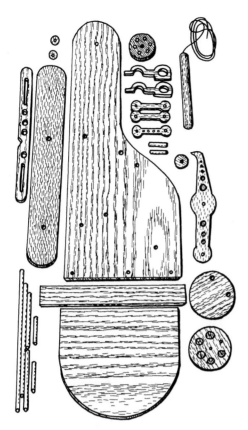

**FIGURE 21-12**

Check the component parts off against the working drawings. If you have doubts about what goes where and how, then it's a good idea at this stage to pencil label each part on its underside.

## ASSEMBLY AND FINISHING

**1** Lay out the parts and make sure they're free from splits, loose knots and warping (Figure 21-12).

**2** Now comes the exacting task of doing a dry fit assembly. Start by dry doweling the slide board to the backboard.

**3** Take the notched rule and plug the cord into a hole drilled into the top end with a small length of toothpick (Figure 21-13). Plug the other end of the cord into the counterbalance weight.

**4** Set the notched rule in place in the slide board, and fit the two stop dowels so they go through and into the backboard (Figure 21-14). These dowels have a dual function. They hold the components together and create stops that control the up-and-down movement of the notched rule.

**5** Set the various wheels in place—the pulley wheel, the handle crank wheel (Figure 21-15) and the large spacer disk.

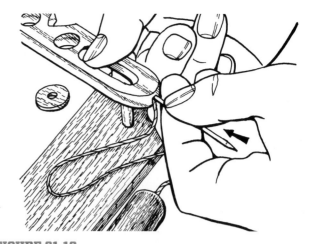

**FIGURE 21-13**

Push the cord into the hole and wedge it in place with a cocktail stick.

**FIGURE 21-14**

Fit the dowels and the washers so that there is nice smooth movement between mating parts.

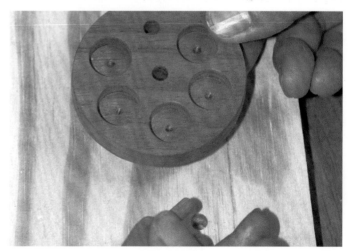

**FIGURE 21-15**

Set the crank wheel in place on its dowel. Note that when it comes to the final fixing, the dowel will need to be glued into the wheel and loose fixed through the backing board.

**FIGURE 21-16**

Fit the two bridges with wooden pins and then label them so as to avoid a mix-up.

**FIGURE 21-17**

Note that when it comes to the final fixing, the cranks need to be glued to the dowels, with the claw arm and the back end of the top dowel being a loose easy fit.

**6** Fit the two guide bridges with small lengths of toothpick. The guides need to be parallel to each other and square to the slide board, with the stepped part of the guides pressing hard up against the edge of the slide board (Figure 21-16).

**7** Proper cord movement over the pulley wheel is critical. If the V-groove is too sharp, pinching the cord, or the dowel is too tight so the wheel doesn't turn, then now is the time to fix things.

**8** When you fit the crank rods, be sure you have the slightly thicker rod on the underside. This is because the underside rod, the slide board and the large spacer disk are all the same thickness.

**9** Once the crank rods have been installed so the claw arm is nicely contained, then pivot the handle through both the lower end of the claw arm and the crank wheel. The important thing here is that the pivot dowel must be flush with the face of the wheel. This allows the claw arm to pass over the pivot without obstruction (Figure 21-17).

**10** When you test the movement, you may have to slightly trim back the tip of the claw and/or slightly modify the shape of the notch. You will almost certainly need to tweak one or all the parts to achieve a smooth movement.

**11** When you're satisfied with the movement—be picky—then disassemble the whole works. Sand all faces and edges smooth, rub oil on the parts except where glue will be applied, and then glue up.

## PROBLEM SOLVING

• The biggest problem I had was making sure the thickness of the various layers was uniform, as this is essential to smooth movement. The best way of ensuring uniformity is cutting the crank wheel, bottom crank, disk spacer and the slide board all from the same piece of wood.

• The notched rule needs to be a smooth-working fit. It's a good idea to wax the mating faces before final assembly.

• You may find the claw arm warping slightly, so the claw bends back and butts up against the edge of the slide board. The fix is to make a more stable claw arm by building it up from several laminations.

# The Universal Joint

## PROJECT BACKGROUND

This mechanism beautifully illustrates the action of the common U-joint or universal joint. You'll find these on the drive shafts of all automobiles. In engineering terms, the universal joint is used to transmit power from one shaft to another over varying angles. It's a simple solution to what was once a difficult mechanical problem, and our current wide array of vehicles wouldn't exist without them.

## PROJECT OVERVIEW

Study the project picture (right), the working drawings (Figure 22-2A) and the design template (Figure 22-2B). Note how our wooden machine replicates a universal joint from the underside of a car. Imagine the handle as the engine and the bridge stanchion as the back axle end. You'll see how, even though the engine and the axle wobble up and down independently, the universal joint still allows the two shafts to keep turning. Note how the action of the shafts as they pass through the split ball joints allows them to change in length as the angle varies.

# THE UNIVERSAL JOINT WORKING DRAWING

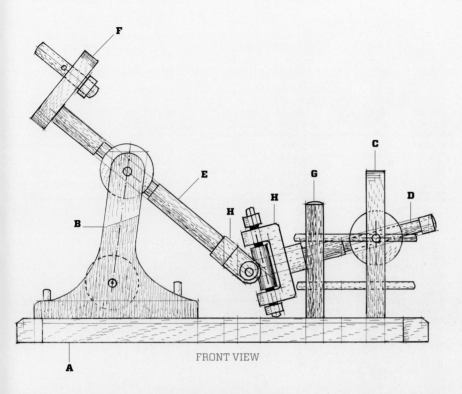

FRONT VIEW

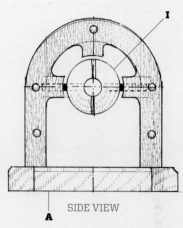

SIDE VIEW

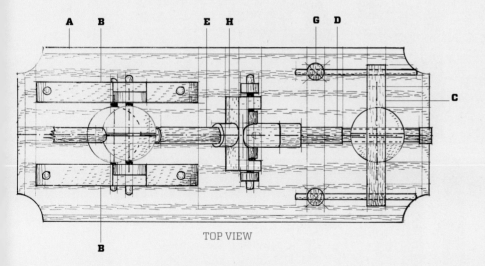

TOP VIEW

## FIGURE 22-2A

**A** Base.

**B** Leaning stanchion.

**C** Bridge stanchion.

**D** Shaft.

**E** Shaft.

**F** Crank.

**G** Posts.

**H** Knuckle fork.

**I** Ball.

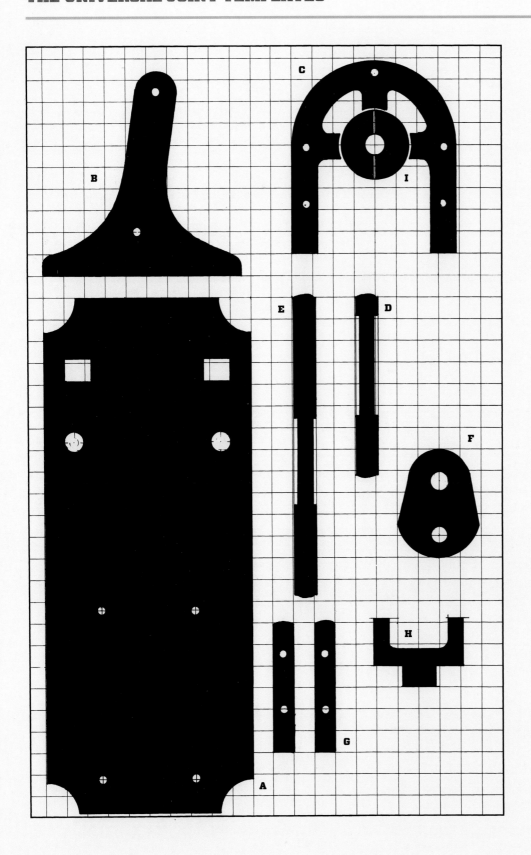

**FIGURE 22-2B**

**The scale is two grid squares to 1".**

**A** Base.

**B** Leaning stanchion.

**C** Bridge stanchion.

**D** Shaft.

**E** Shaft.

**F** Crank.

**G** Posts.

**H** Knuckle fork.

**I** Ball.

## CUTTING LIST

| | | |
|---|---|---|
| A | Base | 1 × 6 × 13 pitch pine |
| B | Leaning stanchion | ³/₄ × 6 × 6 mahogany |
| C | Bridge stanchion | ³/₄ × 5 × 5 plum |
| D | Shaft | ¹/₂" diameter mahogany |
| E | Shaft | ¹/₂" diameter mahogany |
| F | Crank | ³/₄" × 2¹/₂ × 3 cherry |
| G | Posts | ¹/₂" diameter mahogany |
| H | Knuckle fork | 1 × 2 × 2¹/₂ American oak |

**FIGURE 22-3**

**Take the squared-up partial sawn unit and run it through with the coupling pivot holes and the shaft hole—with bit sizes to suit the diameter of your chosen dowels.**

## CHOOSING YOUR WOOD

There are many factors that determine the choice of wood. The balls must be easy to turn on the lathe, the bridge needs to be strong across short grain, and the universal joint must be strong across the prongs. A search through my scrap bin produced pine for the base, American oak for the knuckle forks, a hardwood dowel for the shafts, English plum for the bridge stanchion, mahogany for the two leaning stanchions, lime for the turned balls and whatever was at hand for the secondary components.

## MAKING THE KNUCKLE FORKS

**1** Plane your wood for the two knuckle fork components down to a finished thickness of ³/₄".

**2** Study the templates (Figure 22-2B), noting the shape of the knuckle in that view, and then draw the same view out on the face of your planed wood.

**3** Partially cut the fork shape out on your scroll saw—cut just the shape at the shaft-face end. Then use a pencil and rule to mark the position of the various centers—the center on the shaft-end and the centers for the coupling pin. Establish the center of the shaft-end face by drawing crossed diagonals.

**4** Use a compass to draw in the circle at the shaft-end and the curves at the ends of the prongs. Then move to the drill press and use a ¹/₂" bit to drill the shaft hole to a depth of about ¹/₂", and a ¹/₄" bit for the coupling holes. The coupling hole should be drilled completely through the wood (Figure 22-3).

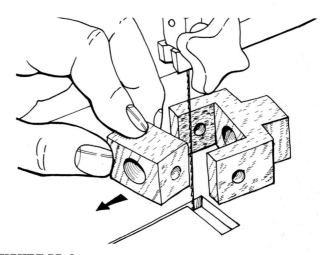

**FIGURE 22-4**

**Complete the cutting on the scroll saw.**

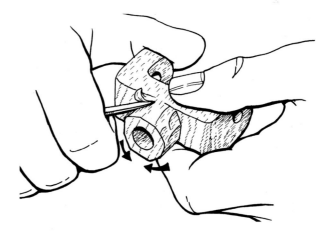

**FIGURE 22-5**

**Use a knife to whittle the curves that go to make up the design— the ends of the prongs and the shaft. Run the blade in the direction of the grain so as to avoid cutting into end grain. Whittle down to the shoulder line into the stop-cut.**

**5** When the holes are in place, finish cutting the form out on your scroll saw (Figure 22-4).

**6** Once you have the basic form, whittle out the various curves that make up the prongs of the fork and the round shape of the shaft socket. To make the shaft, make a stop-cut around the shoulders of the fork, and then, little by little, skim down the shaft and into the stop-cut until you are down to the shoulder line (Figure 22-5).

## MAKING THE CROSS-COUPLING UNION

**1** Use a knife to cut three lengths of ¹/₂" dowel for each fork. One dowel piece should fit loosely between the prongs, the other two shorter pieces at each end of the coupling pin. Roll the dowel under the knife so the cut ends are nicely formed.

**2** Using a bit size that matches the pin diameter, drill through the dowel lengths. Then check to see how the components fit together (Figure 22-6).

**3** Take the two longer dowel pieces, measure along the length to find the centers, and use a small knife to cut a little recessed "flat" on each length. Cut the flats until the two dowels mate together, forming a right-angle cross (Figure 22-7).

**4** Glue the two pieces of dowel together, creating the cross coupling. Then take the knuckle forks and push a length of ¹/₂" dowel into the shaft holes. Cut the coupling dowels either flush or leaving a bit sticking out as I did, and then do a trial fitting. If you've got it right, you should be able to hold the shafts at just about any angle and spin them with the joint happily turning to match the changing angles (Figure 22-8).

## MAKING THE STANCHIONS

**1** Look at the working drawings (Figure 22-2A) and you'll see there are three stanchions—the two leaning post stanchions at the handle end and the single bridge at the other end. With all three, the grain needs to run vertically when cut.

**2** Plane the wood to thickness of about ⁷/₁₆" for the bridge and ⁵/₈" for the stanchions.

**3** Take the two leaning post stanchion pieces and sandwich them together with pins in the waste or double-sided tape.

**FIGURE 22-6**

**Have a trial fitting with the coupling tube and the rings. Note how the little radius curves help to create an image that looks as if it has been cast—like part of a machine.**

**FIGURE 22-7**

**Cut flats so that the two units mate together at right angles. Be careful not to cut through to the pivot hole.**

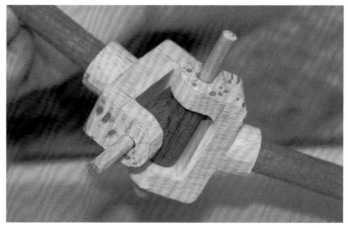

**FIGURE 22-8**

**Spin the shafts and see how the coupling rolls into action.**

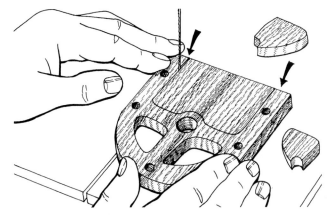

**FIGURE 22-9**

Pay particular attention to the last ½" or so of the legs that need to be tenoned into the base.

**FIGURE 22-10**

Cut the mortises to fit the legs, and then pencil label one or both so that you know what goes where. Note the way that the shaft has been necked with a stop at the end.

**4** Draw the designs of the stanchions onto all three pieces (the two leaning post pieces and the bridge stanchion). Drill the necessary holes through the bridge, then cut the profiles out on your scroll saw (Figure 22-9). Take extra care when you're cutting the legs of the bridge, keeping the cuts crisp and clean.

**5** Carefully cut away half the thickness on the top outside face of both leaning stanchions—about an inch or so.

**6** Sand the pieces smooth.

## MAKING THE BASE

**1** Plane the base slab wood to a finished thickness of about ¾".

**2** Plane one edge square, then use the square, rule, pencil and compass to lay out the design on the wood. The base will be 5" × 12", with the corner curves having a radius of ¾". Draw a center line down the length.

**3** Cut out the base. Then use a block plane to miter the edges on the top face, ends and sides. Cut the corners out on your scroll saw.

**4** Finalize the position of the components on the base—the bridge, the two leaning stanchions and the various posts—marking their location.

**5** Drill the posts and dowel peg holes. Use a small bevel-edged chisel to cut the blind mortise holes. Cut the holes little by little to a depth of about ¼", until the legs of the bridge are a tight push fit (Figure 22-10).

**FIGURE 22-11**

The bottom ball functions in much the same way as a stretcher under a chair, meaning it helps brace and distance the two stanchions.

**FIGURE 22-12**

**Run the dowels through the stanchion and on into the ball—to stop just short of the shaft.**

**FIGURE 22-13**

**Fit the crank and the handle on the end of the shaft, and check out the movement of the handle.**

## ASSEMBLY AND FINISHING

**1** Turn, drill and slice the balls in half—see other projects in this book for details on turning the balls. Take all the parts and check them over for fit, finish and potential problems. Don't worry at this stage about final finish sanding, as we're first going to do a trial assembly.

**2** Start by fitting the two leaning stanchions. Fit and peg the spacer ball between the two stanchions, then set the whole works on the center line and peg the feet of the stanchions through the base slab (Figure 22-11). Make sure that the stanchions are leaning in towards the slab.

**3** Whittle a section of the shaft so that it's a good sliding fit between the halves of the sliced pivot-ball. Then run pegs through the stanchions and into the ball so the shaft is contained and the ball pivots nicely (Figure 22-12).

**4** Set the crank plate on the end of the shaft, then cut and fit the handle from scrap wood. I used a length of dowel for the handle, with a ring pushed onto the end and a wooden peg run through to keep the whole thing in place (Figure 22-13).

**5** When you come to the bridge end, first set the bridge in place, supporting it with the two posts. The whole works must be linked with horizontal dowel rails running through the bottom holes. Contain the shaft with the two halves of the split ball, and then pivot the ball by means of two short lengths of dowel. This isn't easy because nothing has been glued together, but just do your best.

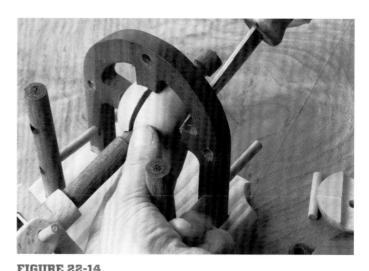

**FIGURE 22-14**

**Use the point of a knife to slide the grub dowel into place.**

**FIGURE 22-15**

**If you have got it right, the top rail will hold the grub dowel in place so that it is contained between the shaft and the rail (see Figure 22-2A top right detail).**

Use a knife point to tease the dowel stubs through the bridge hole until they're well into the ball and clear of the top rail hole (Figure 22-14).

**6** Take the two top rail dowels and run them through the bridge and into the post so that the two components are linked and the stub dowels are contained (Figure 22-15).

**7** When you are happy with the overall fit of the shaft in the ball, remove the shaft, and spend some time making sure the structure is square and stable, with all the posts and rails cut to length and tidy. If you have got it right, the whole works will be a good tight fit (Figure 22-16).

**8** You will almost certainly have to make adjustments. For example, I found I needed to lengthen and ease the sliding section of the shaft at the handle end (Figure 22-17). You should be able to squeeze the halves of the ball together, with the shaft still a nice sliding fit.

**9** Trim the coupling pins to length and hold them in place with the little dowel ring (Figure 22-18).

**10** Sand all surfaces to a smooth finish, rub teak oil on appropriate surfaces, glue the balls together so the shafts are contained, and set the balls on their pivots.

**11** Finally, give the whole works another sanding, rub on another thin coat of oil, and burnish all the surfaces with a thin application of beeswax.

## PROBLEM SOLVING

• While this project looks complicated, the only really tricky parts are fitting the cross coupling tubes and making sure the balls pivot properly. Use double-sided tape to hold the ball halves together during the trial assembly.

• To my mind, the most clever aspect of this design is the way the dowel stubs are held in place. In fact, the various parts don't need to be glued. However, success comes from the stub dowels being just the right length and a smooth push fit.

• Since the moving parts need to be smooth turning, it's a good idea to lightly wax and burnish mating faces: the slide shafts, inside the ball, and inside the crossed coupling.

• If you like the project except for the woodturning required, you could modify the design and use cubes instead of balls.

**FIGURE 22-16**
**Trim the bridge to shape, and cut a short length of dowel for the decorative detail at top center.**

**FIGURE 22-17**
**Try out various shaft angles and modify the length of the sliding necks accordingly.**

**FIGURE 22-18**
**Fit the little stop rings on the ends of the coupling pivots.**

# Camshaft Valve

## PROJECT BACKGROUND

Apart from my wife Gill, my pride and joy is an old Land Rover four-wheel-drive vehicle. It's a diesel, made in 1975, with uncomfortable seats, ungodly noisy and painted military green—a wonderful machine! It ran like a gem for the first few weeks, and then started to smoke like a bonfire! I'll spare you the mechanic's lengthy explanation, but the problem was diagnosed as a sticking valve. So there we all were, up to our armpits in grease and tools, when Gill spotted something, suddenly reached into the air intake and pulled out a squirrel's tail. Nothing else, just a slightly charred tail! The good news is the problem was solved—no sticking valves, no more smoke, and no more squirrel! My sudden immersion in engine disassembly paid off also in terms of another wooden mechanism, this one honoring those hard-working valves.

## PROJECT OVERVIEW

Study the project picture (right), the working drawings (Figure 23-2A) and the templates (Figure 23-2B). Note how this project shows the various elements of a valve-train as flat components mounted to a backboard. In action, the crank handle is turned so that the cam on the back of the handle pushes up on the rod. The rod in turn pushes up the rocker arm, which pivots like a seesaw and pushes down the valve, opening it. This action is made possible by the fact that the rocker arm is weighted with lead shot, so that while it's easy to lift, it nevertheless wants to fall back to the closed position.

The skill level for this project is low in terms of building the pieces, while the assembly aspect can be tricky, with a lot of finicky small parts that break easily. Once you have the cam in place and have added weight to the end of the rocker, then it all comes together easily.

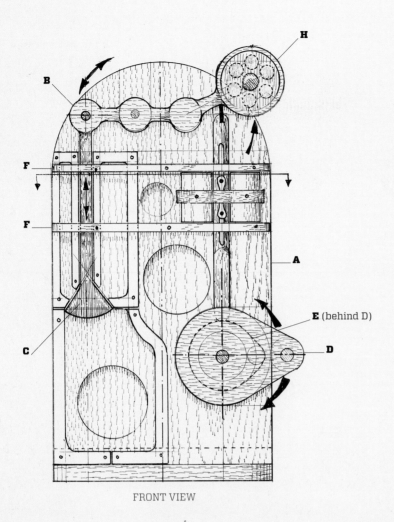

FRONT VIEW

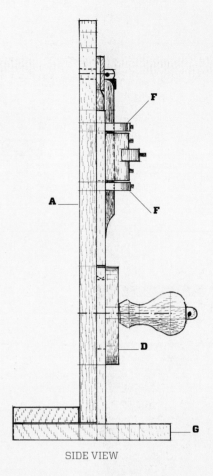

SIDE VIEW

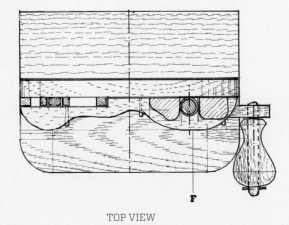

TOP VIEW

## FIGURE 23-2A

**Note how the weight is needed on the end of the rocker arm so that the arm is always falling down to make contact with the top of the push rod.**

**A** Backboard.

**B** Rocker arm.

**C** Valve.

**D** Crank handle.

**E** Cam plate.

**F** Rod and valve guide.

**G** Base board.

**H** Valve counterweight.

# CAMSHAFT VALVE TEMPLATES

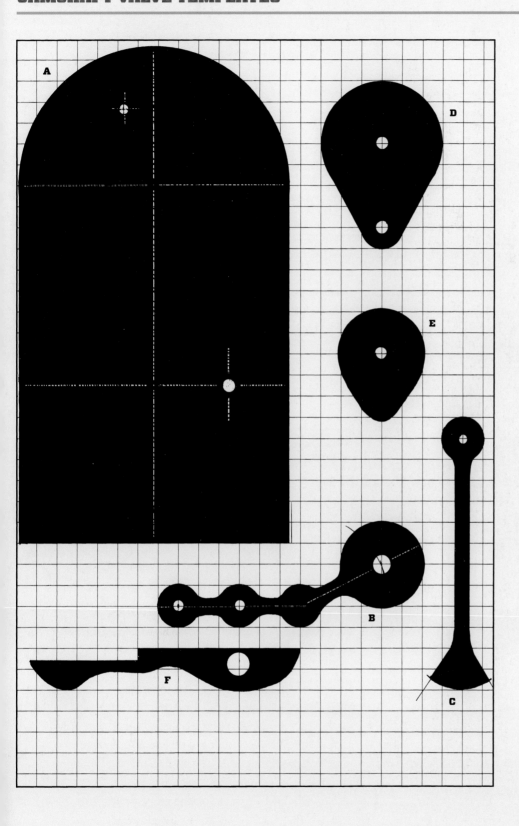

FIGURE 23-2B

**The scale is two grid squares to 1".**

**A** Backboard.

**B** Rocker arm.

**C** Valve.

**D** Crank handle.

**E** Cam plate.

**F** Rod and valve guide.

## CUTTING LIST

| A | Backboard | $3/4 \times 7 \times 13$ pitch pine |
|---|---|---|
| B | Rocker arm | $5/8 \times 4 \times 8$ pitch pine |
| C | Valve | $1/2 \times 2 \times 7$ mahogany |
| D | Crank handle | $1/2 \times 4 \times 5$ mahogany |
| E | Cam plate | $3/8 \times 2^1/2 \times 3$ mahogany |
| F | Rod and valve guide | $3/8 \times 1^1/2 \times 7$ beech |
| G | Base board | $3/4 \times 5^1/2 \times 7$ pitch pine |
| H | Valve counterweight | $1/2 \times 2^1/2 \times 2^1/2$ cherry |

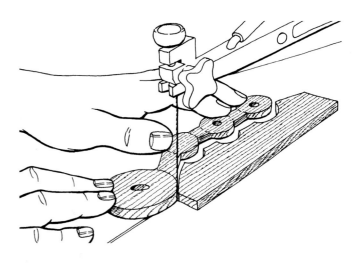

**FIGURE 23-3**

**If you use a new fine-tooth blade and make sure that it's well tensioned, then you will find that the sawn edges hardly need to be sanded. Scroll saw blades are cheap enough; there's no need to use a blade until it's toothless.**

## CHOOSING YOUR WOOD

You can use just about any wood you like. Just be sure it's free from splits and knots, is attractive to the eye, dry and relatively easy to work. We chose pine for the base and the back boards, larch for the cylinder chamber walls, mahogany for the crank, valve and rocker weight, shop-bought dowels for the push rod, and anything on hand for the bits and pieces.

## MAKING THE BACK AND BASE BOARDS

**1** Study the working drawing (Figure 23-2A), then plane the wood for these parts to a finished thickness of $1/2$".

**2** Square the wood edges with a square and plane. Draw out the design onto the wood. The $6^3/4$" circle goes on the top of the backboard, and the 1" radiuses on the front of the base board.

**3** Mark the position of all the parts and the two pivot holes—the one for the rocker arm and the one for the crank handle.

**4** Drill the holes with a bit that matches your dowels, then cut out the two boards on your scroll saw. Sand all the sawn edges to a smooth finish.

**5** With a rule and square, double-check your measurements and component positions against the working drawing, especially the position of the two pivot holes.

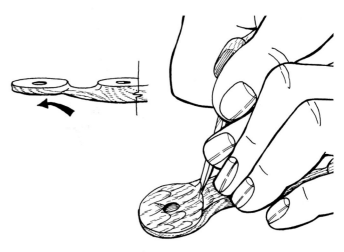

**FIGURE 23-4**

**Slice away half the thickness of the wood around the area of the pivot.**

## MAKING THE ROCKER ARM

**1** Plane your wood to a finished thickness of about $3/8$". Then study the working drawings (Figure 23-2A), noting how the design of the rocker arm is based on four circles. Three of the circles are 1" diameter, while the fourth is $2^1/8$" diameter. Note also how the three small circles are set $1^1/2$" apart on the same center line.

**2** Use rule, pencil and compass to draw out the design on the wood, then drill the holes with a bit sized to match your dowels. Cut out the profile on your scroll saw (Figure 23-3).

**3** Use a pencil to label the best face, then take a knife or chisel and pare away half the thickness of the small valve-pivot circle. Make sure that you only cut away the back face (Figure 23-4).

**4** Use a knife and sandpaper to work the neck area between the circles to a rounded shape. The original compass-drawn circles are left as flats (Figure 23-5).

## MAKING THE VALVE

**1** Plane the wood you chose for the valve down to a finished thickness of 1/4".

**2** Run a center line down the length of the grain, and mark two points 6" apart. Draw out the design on these two points so one is the rocker pivot and the other the intersection of the curve of the valve.

**3** Lay out the valve design between these two points, with the stem about 1/2" wide, and the part-circle curve of the valve based on a 1 3/8" radius.

**4** Drill a hole through the pivot point that matches your dowel, then cut the shape out on your scroll saw. Before you cut, check that the distance between the pivot center and the bottom of the curve is 6" (see Figure 23-7).

**5** Set the stem with the best face up against a suitable stop—a bench dog or shop-made bench hook—and use a chisel to pare the pivot circle down to about half its thickness (Figure 23-6).

**6** Finally, do a trial assembly of the rocker and valve. If all is well, the two half-thickness pieces should fit together so from one piece to the other the faces are flush (Figure 23-7).

## MAKING THE ROD AND VALVE GUIDES

**1** Because the guides are difficult to make and fit, start by studying the working drawings (Figure 23-2A). Note the way that the guides are cut from thin wood, with the various elements within the forms guiding and containing both the valve and the push rod. You'll see how one end of the guide bridges the walls of the chamber to contain the stem of the valve, while the other end is drilled to take the stem of the push rod. Consider also how the guides are set parallel to each other, so that they contain the guide blocks that hold the little bridge-and-plate apparatus against the top face of the rod.

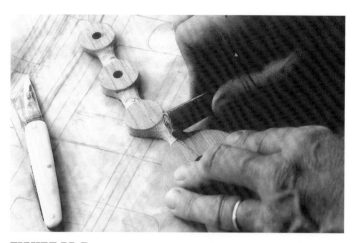

**FIGURE 23-5**

**Use a knife and sandpaper to rub the necks down to a rounded finish. Note how the circles are left untouched.**

**FIGURE 23-6**

**Hold the chisel bevel down so that the blade is always trying to rise out of the wood.**

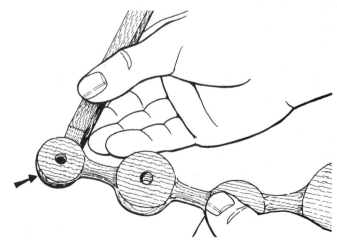

**FIGURE 23-7**

**Try the two components together, and make adjustments so they add up to the total thickness and can pivot flush.**

**2** Plane the wood to a finished thickness of ¼", and draw the design out on one piece.

**3** Sandwich the two pieces together so that the drawn design is uppermost. I used small tabs of double-sided tape to do this. Then treat the sandwiched pieces as a single unit, and drill the rod hole and cut out the profile.

**4** Ease the sandwich apart, leaving you with two identical parts. Use a knife to trim the top edge to a rounded finish (Figure 23-8).

## MAKING THE CHAMBER WALLS

**1** Once again study the working drawings (Figure 23-2A), noting how the top middle section of the chamber acts as a guide for the stem of the valve, with the stem being contained by two walls and bridged by the guide. Note also how, apart from the two guide walls and the two gates at the bottom of the valve, the chamber walls themselves can be any shape that takes your fancy.

**2** When you have decided what shape and size you want the walls to be, plane your wood down to a thickness of ¼". Trace the various designs from your working drawings, and press-transfer the traced lines through to the wood.

**3** Be careful with the thin sections as they'll be very fragile across the short grain curves. Very carefully cut the walls out on your scroll saw (Figure 23-9).

## ASSEMBLY AND FINISHING

**1** Lay out all the parts and check them over for possible problems. Don't worry at this stage about final sanding as we're going to do a trial assembly first. Just make sure that the little cut-outs aren't going to let you down—you don't want any splits or loose knots to spoil the integrity of the structure.

**2** Give all the components a quick sanding with fine-grade sandpaper, then wipe them over with a small amount of teak oil—just enough to seal the grain. Keep the oil away from areas that will be glued later.

**3** Start by using a dowel to pin the rocker arm at the top of the board. Then take the push rod (see the detail drawings for how it was slotted and pared to a flat face, with a little piece of hardwood fitted at the top) and fit it in place with the little link-and-pin component. Note how the function of the link is twofold: it allows the rod to

**FIGURE 23-8**

**Use a knife to trim the top edge to a rounded profile—like a round nosing.**

**FIGURE 23-9**

**Be careful, when you are cutting across the run of the grain, that you don't split the resultant short grain.**

**FIGURE 23-10**

**See how the little link shape needs to sit level with the flat face. Note also how the bottom end of the rod is sliced down to about half the thickness so that it's the same thickness as the cam.**

**FIGURE 23-11**

**Add as much weight as possible. It's important that the weight pulls the end of the rocker arm down against the top of the push rod.**

**FIGURE 23-12**

**The more weight the merrier—if you can find a way of casting little disks to fill the holes, then so much the better.**

slide up and down, while at the same time holding the rod in place against the backboard (Figure 23-10).

**4** Take the disk that you made for the weighted end of the rocker and cut pieces of lead to fit into the drilled pockets (Figures 23-11, 23-12). Use either lead shot or fishing sinkers—you'll find both at most large sporting goods stores. Sand the disk smooth on the pocket side, because it needs to fit flush with the rocker.

**5** Put the rocker arm, the weight disk and the short length of fixing dowel in place, and see how everything fits.

**6** Slide the rocker in place so the bits of lead are contained (Figure 23-13). Unfortunately, the decorative detailing of the pockets is hidden as I designed it here, but you can experiment with ways to display it.

**7** Fit the chamber walls in place with wooden pegs, and set the two guides across the width of the board so the valve is contained. It's important that the movement is easy. If anything sticks, then sand one or all the components until the action works properly.

**8** Slide the push rod in place and again try out the movement (Figure 23-14).

**9** Set the two little blocks in place between the horizontal guides at either side of the push rod. Then set the link down between the blocks so that the fixing sticks go down through the slot that runs up the middle of the push rod (Figure 23-15).

**FIGURE 23-13**

**Rub the mating faces down so that they fit flush together.**

**10** Set the cam on the crank pivot, then slide the crank arm in place (Figure 23-16). It's not easy to test the movement at this stage because the cam and the crank aren't yet glued together, but at least make sure that the crank is able to turn without bumping into the side of the push rod. If this is a problem, then lower the flat face at the bottom end of the rod until it's much lower than the underside of the crank.

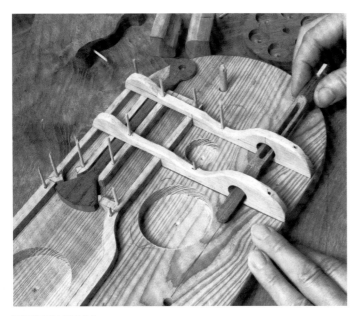

**FIGURE 23-14**

**Make adjustments so that the drilled guide holes, the push rod and the crank pivot are all perfectly aligned.**

**11** Put the handle on the crank, the little bridge in place across the push rod guide blocks, and do another dry run.

**12** When you're happy with the movement, disassemble the whole works, sand all the surfaces and edges smooth, apply teak oil again, and glue things up. When dry, give everything a light sanding, then burnish with beeswax.

## PROBLEM SOLVING

• This is one of those projects that needs to be continually tested for fit as the various parts are made. Find a way to temporarily tack parts together, such as using bits of Blue Tack, small strips of double-sided tape or tiny drops of Super Glue. The Super Glue gives the best hold, but you must be absolutely sure to only use tiny amounts—no more than a pinpoint.

• If you want to use the weighted disk but also want to have some part of the pockets showing as a decorative feature, here's a solution. Make the drilled pockets so they're a stepped hole that will trap steel ball bearings. This way the ball bearings will show through the holes on the face of the weight disk but still be held in place.

• To get a more elegant look, use better woods such as plum, lime and boxwood. The texture of these woods gives a fine finish and beautiful colors.

**FIGURE 23-15**

**Note how the two blocks both nicely distance the guides and contain the push rod.**

**FIGURE 23-16**

**See how the bottom end of the push rod has been shaved down to the thickness of the cam so that it doesn't get in the way of the crank.**

# Water Lift Pump

## PROJECT BACKGROUND

When we were first married, Gill and I lived in a farm cottage that had a well and a pump to draw our water. I was forever climbing down into the well to sort out the leather flap valve at the bottom of the pump chamber. It would get blocked with mud, stones, grit, dead frogs and all manner of things. Life with such rustic charm was never lacking in wet, muddy, cold chores.

That old lift pump was a beautifully simple piece of machinery. Basically it's just two valves working together. When the handle is lifted, the rod goes down, the valve at the bottom of the chamber closes, the valve at the bottom of the piston opens and water rushes to the top side of the piston. When the pump handle is pushed down, the rod comes up, the valve at the bottom of the chamber opens, the valve in the piston closes and water floods the bottom chamber, ready for the next pump stroke.

## PROJECT OVERVIEW

Study the project picture (right), the working drawings (Figure 24-2A) and the templates (Figure 24-2B). While the various components are relatively easy to make, the assembly is convoluted. The problem is the component parts are short grained and fragile, with lots of curved slender sections that run across the grain, plus there are lots of parts. The measurements can be modified, except for the rod and chamber lengths. If you want to alter the size of the project, use stiff paper and pins to build a prototype first.

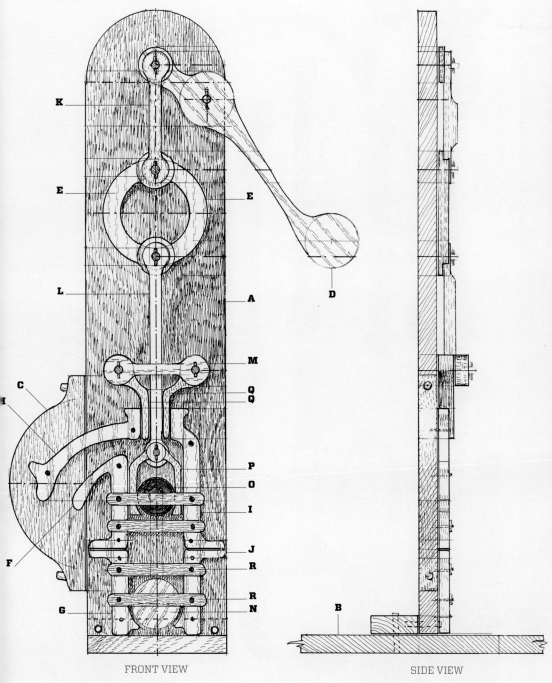

FRONT VIEW

SIDE VIEW

## FIGURE 24-2A

**The critical factors that control the action with this model are the distance between the handle pivot and the handle-rod link, and the lengths of the rods. It's a good idea to make a cardboard prototype to fix the various critical measurements before you cut them out of wood.**

**A**  Backboard.

**B**  Base board.

**C**  Side lug board.

**D**  Handle.

**E**  Joint linkage.

**F**  Chamber side, top left.

**G**  Chamber side, bottom left.

**H**  Spout.

**I**  Chamber side, top right.

**J**  Chamber side, bottom right.

**K**  Top rod.

**L**  Bottom rod.

**M**  Neck bar.

**N**  Bottom ball valve.

**O**  Top ball valve.

**P**  Piston.

**Q**  Wadding box wedge.

**R**  Chamber slats.

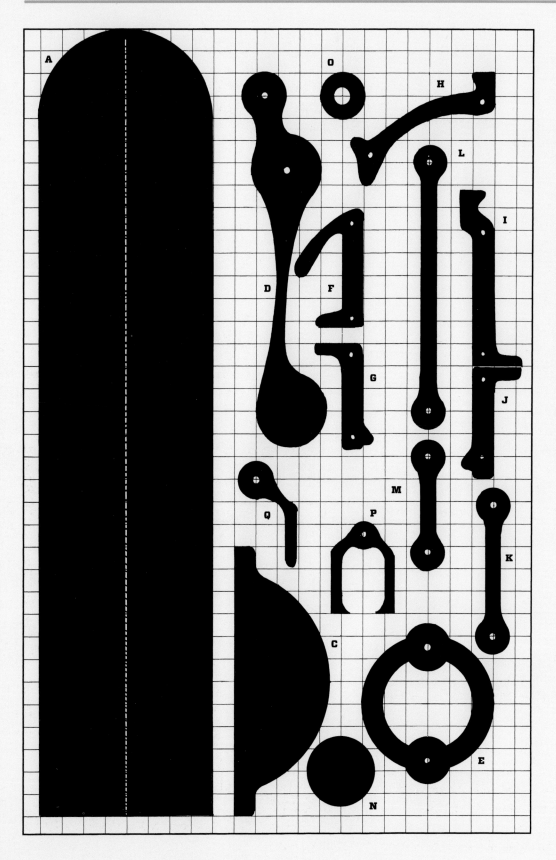

**FIGURE 24-2B**

**The scale is two grid squares to 1". Note that we have only illustrated the difficult-to-visualize components.**

**A** Backboard.

**B** Base board.

**C** Side lug board.

**D** Handle.

**E** Joint linkage.

**F** Chamber side, top left.

**G** Chamber side, bottom left.

**H** Spout.

**I** Chamber side, top right.

**J** Chamber side, bottom right.

**K** Top rod.

**L** Bottom rod.

**M** Neck bar.

**N** Bottom ball valve.

**O** Top ball valve.

**P** Piston.

**Q** Wadding box wedge.

**R** Chamber slats.

## CUTTING LIST

| | | |
|---|---|---|
| A | Backboard | $3/4 \times 4^1/_2 \times 18$ brown oak |
| B | Base board | $3/4 \times 4^1/_2 \times 12$ brown oak |
| C | Side lug board | $3/4 \times 3 \times 6^1/_2$ brown oak |
| D | Handle | $1/_2 \times 2^1/_2 \times 9$ American oak |
| E | Joint linkage | $1/_2 \times 4 \times 4$ cherry |
| F | Chamber side, top left | $1/_2 \times 2 \times 3$ pitch pine |
| G | Chamber side, bottom left | $1/_2 \times 2 \times 3$ pitch pine |
| H | Spout | $1/_2 \times 2 \times 4^1/_2$ pitch pine |
| I | Chamber side, top right | $1/_2 \times 2 \times 4^1/_2$ pitch pine |
| J | Chamber side, btm right | $1/_2 \times 2 \times 3$ pitch pine |
| K | Top rod | $1/_2 \times 1 \times 4^1/_2$ pitch pine |
| L | Bottom rod | $1/_2 \times 1 \times 7$ pitch pine |
| M | Neck bar | $1/_2 \times 1 \times 3^1/_2$ cherry |
| N | Bottom ball valve | $1/_2 \times 2 \times 2$ pitch pine |
| O | Top ball valve | $1/_2 \times 1^1/_2 \times 1^1/_2$ plum |
| P | Piston | $1/_2 \times 2 \times 3$ plum |
| Q | Wadding box wedge | $1/_2 \times 2 \times 3$ plum |
| R | Chamber slats | $1/_{16} \times 3/_8 \times 3$ plum |

## CHOOSING YOUR WOOD

You can use just about any wood you like, just make sure it's dry, easy to cut on a scroll saw and free of splits and knots. We used English brown oak for the base and back boards, American oak for the handle and scrap pieces of pine, cherry and plum for the rest. Select woods that have rich color and grain patterns from one component to the next.

## MAKING THE BACK, BASE AND LUG BOARDS

**1** Study the design (Figures 24-2A and B), noting how the base board, backboard and the small lug board are made from $3/4$"-thick wood, with the various curves drawn with a compass. The greater part of the base is set to the front of the backboard, with the two boards fixed by a glued-and-pegged batten.

**2** Plane your wood to a finished thickness of $5/_8$". It should be free of splits and knots. If you're using a tough wood like the brown oak I used, then it's also a good idea to sight along its length checking for twists.

**3** Draw the design out with a rule, square and compass, and cut the pieces out on your scroll saw.

**4** Set the backboard at right angles to the base and support it with a piece of scrap.

**5** Decide where the lug needs to be positioned, and then dry fit it in place with a couple of dowels.

## MAKING THE CHAMBER WALLS AND VALVE BALL

**1** Plane the wood to a finished thickness of about $5/_{16}$". Don't worry if it's a little oversize, as it's better to be slightly too thick than too thin, as long as the thickness is uniform.

**2** Trace the design from the working drawings, then pencil press transfer the traced lines through to the best face of your wood. Remember to position the tracings so the grain runs up through the walls of the chamber.

**3** With the design laid out, cut out the pieces on your scroll saw (Figure 24-3). While it's all pretty straightforward, be careful when you come to the curves. You don't want to go too fast or too hard and split the wood across the fragile short grain.

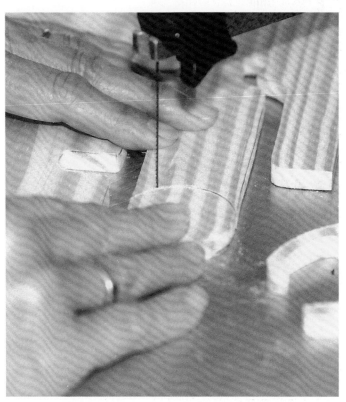

**FIGURE 24-3**

**Work with a new, properly tensioned blade. Make sure you cut slightly to the waste side of the drawn line.**

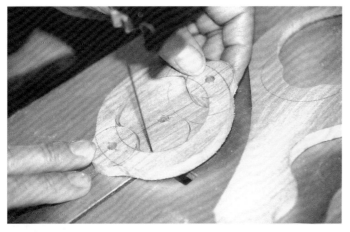

**FIGURE 24-4**

Note the little radius curves at the intersection of the drawn circles. These help to create the engineered and worked-in-steel look.

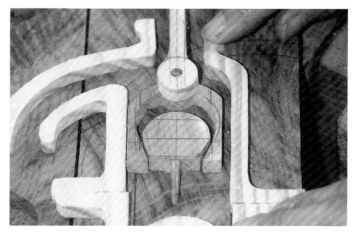

**FIGURE 24-5**

It's important that the side walls of the chamber are parallel to each other so the components within the chamber are free to move up and down.

**FIGURE 24-6**

Check and double-check the measurements to ensure accuracy. If you made a mistake, then the easiest fix is to make a new top rod.

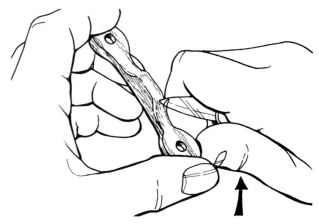

**FIGURE 24-7**

Work with a tight apple-paring stroke, with the thumb of the right hand controlling the length of the stroke. Always work with the run of the grain, from center to end—never the other way around!

## MAKING THE LINKAGE

**1** Study Figure 24-2A, noting how the linkage design is based on four circles. Two circles make up the basic hoop disk, and two smaller circles for the pivot linkage points.

**2** Plane the wood to a finished thickness of about $3/8$".

**3** Draw a center line that runs the direction of the grain. Mark a point midway along the line, and draw out two circles one within the other. One should have a radius of 1" and the other a radius of $1^1/2$". Mark the center line halfway across the width of the hoop at top and bottom, then use a compass to draw two circles with a radius of $1/2$".

**4** Draw little radiuses at the intersections of all of the circles.

**5** Drill the pivot points with a bit that matches your dowels. Then drill another hole through the waste area, and cut out the parts (Figure 24-4).

**6** Make the handle and the piston.

## MAKING THE RODS

**1** Plane the wood to size, and use a rule, square and compass to draw out the design of the two rods. Have them about $5/16$" wide along their length, with ends based on $3/4$" diameter circles.

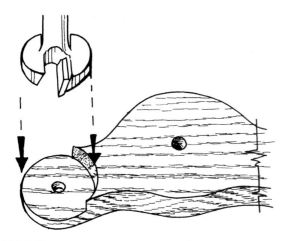

**FIGURE 24-8**

**Note how a large-diameter Forstner bit has been used to halve the thickness of the handle pivot point.**

**2** Cut out the rods on your scroll saw, drill holes through the pivot centers, then check the fit of everything (Figure 24-5).

**3** When you have fitted the two rods, the sum total length between the pivot point on the top end of the top rod and the pivot point on the bottom end of the bottom rod should be such that the piston fits on both the up and down strokes (Figure 24-6).

**4** Once satisfied with the shape and size of the rods, use a knife to whittle the ends down to about half their thicknesses so the face of the pivot circle is smooth and flush. Work with a tight paring stroke from center to end, creating a nice, clean curve from the top face down (Figure 24-7).

**5** Use a knife and fine sandpaper to give the rods and all other components a smooth finish.

## ASSEMBLY AND FINISHING

**1** Check over the parts for splits or warps (Figure 24-9). Make sure the various mating surfaces are to size so the parts can work together smoothly.

**2** Do a trial assembly. Start by pegging the chamber sides and the wadding wedges onto the backboard (Figure 24-10). Note how the wadding pins need to be long enough to take the neck bar.

**3** Set the rods and the joint linkage in place with the pivot dowels a tight fit in the linkage and a loose fit through the rods (Figure 24-11). The bottom rod should be a nice snug fit between the wedges.

**FIGURE 24-9**

**Check the components for problems. Be very careful when handling the chamber wall strips, as they are very fragile.**

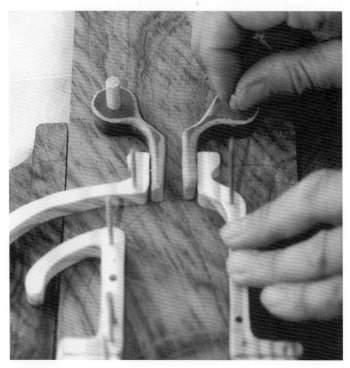

**FIGURE 24-10**

**Note how the wishbone shape of the wadding box wedges helps to create a dynamic effect by directing the eye down and towards the chamber.**

**4** Set the large disk valve in place in the chamber, the piston on the bottom end of the rod and the neck bar in place across the wadding wedges. Sand any parts that are binding until you have a good fit (Figure 24-12).

**5** Fit the valve in the piston and the slats across the chamber, then stand the whole works upright and test the movement (Figure 24-13).

**6** When you have a smooth movement, and have determined what needs to be glued and pinned, disassemble and do a final finish sanding. Apply teak oil to all surfaces except those faces being glued. Glue up, fit the small pins, and, once dry, give the whole works a coat of beeswax.

## PROBLEM SOLVING

• With a complex project like this, you're continually fitting and modifying parts. This being so, save yourself some effort and hold off on fine sanding until the very end, after everything is working properly.
• If the movement is stiff or crooked, then it could be that the handle pivot is badly placed on the backboard. If so, drill a selection of holes and test each one for the best fit.
• You could have a back-linkage function that moves the bottom ball valve up and down.
• The backboard and base can be increased to 1" thick.

**FIGURE 24-11**

**The linkage pivot dowels need to be a tight fit in the linkage circle and a loose fit in the rod. At a later stage, you will have to hold the rod and various other components in place by running a thin wood pin through the dowel.**

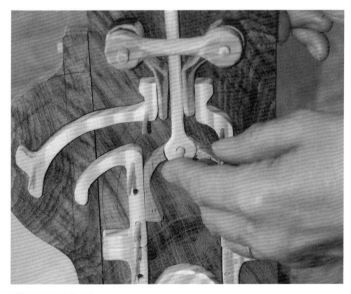

**FIGURE 24-12**

**The piston is extremely fragile, and you might need to laminate it up from veneers to give it extra strength.**

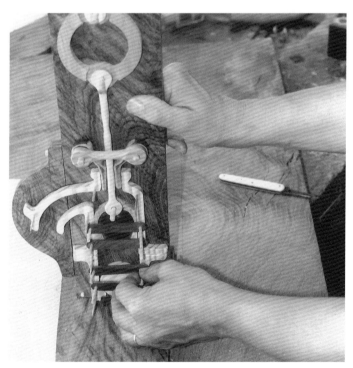

**FIGURE 24-13**

**Note how the greater length of the base needs to be at the front so the machine is stable and won't tip forwards.**

# Lever and Ratchet Mechanism

## PROJECT BACKGROUND

When we were first married, Gill and I lived in a cottage deep in the country, with no electricity and no indoor plumbing. We got by with lots of oil lamps and a well in the garden. We could have purchased a generator to provide power, but we were trying our best to be self-sufficient. The most pressing problem was always how to lift the water up from the well to the storage tank on the roof. We tried hand pumps large and small, a foot pump, a wind-powered pump with propeller blades, among other things, but none of them worked that well. The hand pumping was such hard work that I think I drank more water than I ever pumped up to the tank. Well, finally a local farmer took pity on me and showed me how to pump water up by means of a simple lever and ratchet mechanism. Summarized, you lash one end of a rope to the top branches of a tall tree and the other to the mechanism. When the wind blows, the tree sways backward and forward, the rope repeatedly snatches at the lever, the ratchet inches round and a lift pump is set into motion. While doing it this way only brings up a teacup of water at each jerk of the lever, the wind was free and did all the work. Over time, the tank would fill bit by bit, and we didn't have to spend hours each day manning the hand pump. This is not the project for you if your goal is to impress your friends with dramatic action and movement. Instead, it's a wooden representation of one of those behind-the-scenes devices that makes our lives easier by quietly going about its business.

# LEVER AND RATCHET MECHANISM WORKING DRAWING

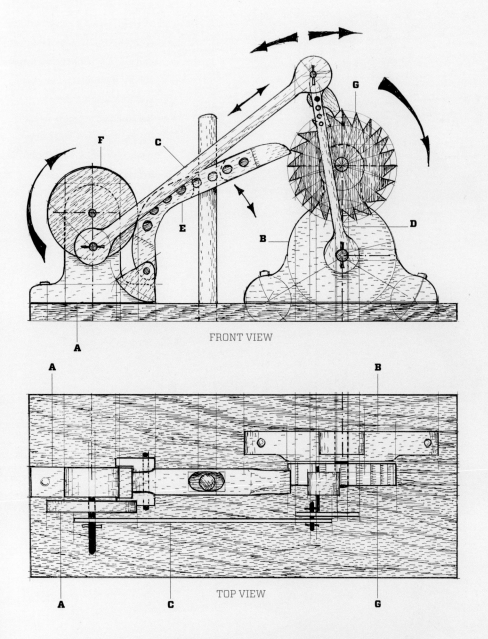

FRONT VIEW

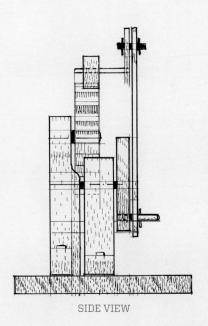

SIDE VIEW

TOP VIEW

## FIGURE 25-2A

**With this project, note how the drive wheel needs to be turned in a clockwise direction.**

**A** Drive wheel stanchion.

**B** Toothed wheel stanchion.

**C** Long crank drive rod.

**D** Short crank rod.

**E** Control arm.

**F** Drive wheel.

**G** Toothed wheel.

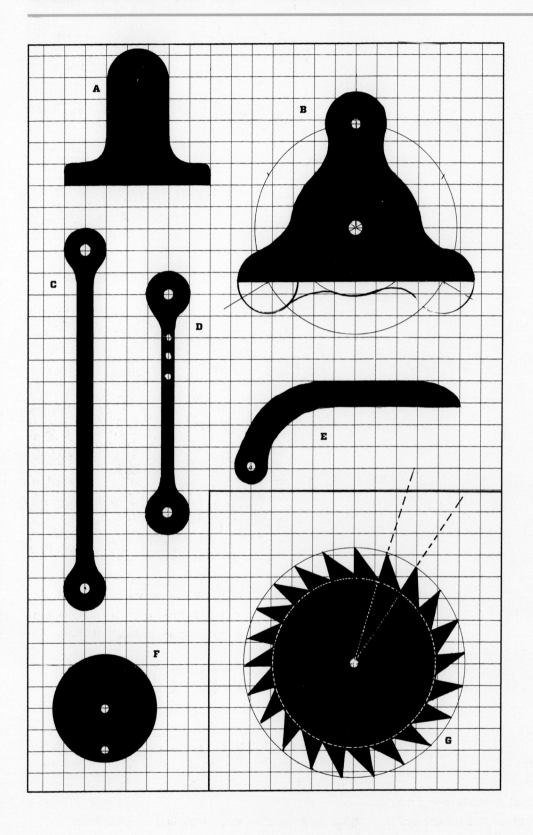

**FIGURE 25-2B**

**The templates drawn to a scale of two grid squares to 1" (top), and four grid squares to 1" (bottom right). Note how the main stanchion is drawn out by means of a compass, with the radius curves between the circles being drawn by hand. Note also how the toothed wheel is drawn out.**

**A** Drive wheel stanchion.

**B** Toothed wheel stanchion.

**C** Long crank drive rod.

**D** Short crank rod.

**E** Control arm.

**F** Drive wheel.

**G** Toothed wheel.

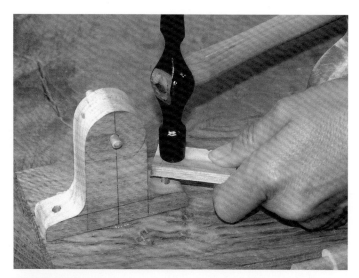

**FIGURE 25-3**
**Use a small hammer and a block to drive the dowels home.**

## PROJECT OVERVIEW

Study the project photo, the working drawing (Figure 25-2A) and the templates (Figure 25-2B). Note that all the components are fixed to the base board, with the primary moving parts pivoting on stanchions. In action, the drive wheel is turned, the long crank rod goes forward, the little finger-drag component nudges and drags, and the toothed wheel goes around. The control arm ensures that the toothed wheel only turns in the one direction.

While the individual procedures are pretty straight-forward, involving just some scroll saw work, drilling and whittling, assembling the machine is tricky. Alternatively, if you're the optimistic sort, look at the assembly as a glorious challenge.

## CHOOSING YOUR WOOD

The wonderful news is that you can use nearly any wood—lime, oak, pine, beech, sycamore, maple, cherry—just about anything you find in your scrap bin. Just be sure the toothed wheel is made from a close-grained dense wood that's strong across short grain. Remember also that you are building something that a lot of people are going to want to try out, so choose wood that will hold up to a bit of rough usage.

## MAKING THE STANCHIONS

**1** Study the working drawings (Figure 25-2A) and the templates (Figure 25-2B), so that you have a good understanding of how the project needs to be made and put together.

**FIGURE 25-4**
**Butt the workpiece hard up against a stop (I'm using a bench hook), and use a gouge to skim the waste down to a depth of about $^{1}/_{4}$". Be careful that you don't run the gouge into end grain.**

**2** Take the wood that you have chosen for the base board and plane and cut it to size—it needs to be about $^{1}/_{2}$" thick, 5" wide and 12" long.

**3** Take the 1"-thick wood for the stanchions and plane it to a finished thickness of about $^{7}/_{8}$". Draw the two images out to size, and fret them out on the scroll saw.

**4** Take the drive wheel stanchion, run the holes through—for the main pivot and the fixing dowels—and then position it on the base and fix with dry dowels (Figure 25-3). It's important that the stanchion is fair and square with the base, so spend time getting it right.

**FIGURE 25-5**

**Sand the form so that the raised circle runs in a smooth curve down to the level of the lowered waste.**

**5** Take the blank for the other stanchion, and use a compass set to a radius of 1¹/₂" to draw in the decorative casting circle.

**6** Run the four holes through with the drill—two for pivots and two for fixing.

**7** Take a small shallow-curve gouge; set the workpiece flat down on its back so that it is butted hard up against a stop with the front face uppermost. Then set to work cutting back the waste. Lower the waste little by little, with a series of shallow skimming cuts (Figure 25-4) until the casting circle is left standing proud by about ¹/₄". If you have got it right, the two side lugs and the top head will finish up at about ⁵/₈" thick.

**8** When you are happy with the overall shape of the casting feature, use graded sandpapers to rub the contours down to a good finish. Work from rough through to smooth, with the sandpapers wrapped around a length of dowel (Figure 25-5).

## MAKING THE CRANK RODS

**1** Have a look at the working drawings and templates (Figures 25-2A and B). The two crank rods are more or less the same shape—the same diameter ends and similar curves. The only real difference is that the long rod is ³/₈" wide and the small rod ¹/₄". Both rods are about ³/₁₆" thick.

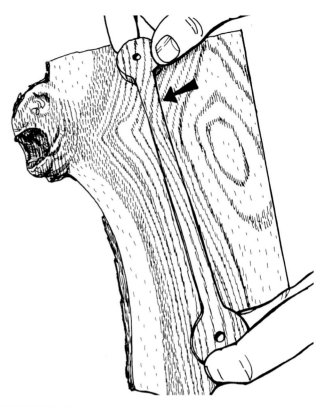

**FIGURE 25-6**

**You always need to consider the run of the grain, especially if the component parts are long and slender. All that said, I'm not entirely happy with the grain on the right-hand end of the rod—it looks a little short grained and weak.**

**2** Choose your wood with care. It doesn't matter too much if the grain is a bit wild, as long as overall it is sound and running along the length of the rod (Figure 25-6). To draw out the outer rods, start by fixing the position of the end-centers. Draw a center line, measure the end-centers on the line, and use the compass to draw the end circles. Draw parallel lines each side of the center line; draw the radius curves freehand. Drill the pivot holes, and then finally fret out the total profile.

**3** Fret out the drawn profiles on the scroll saw, and trim them up with a small knife so that all the angles are slightly rounded. They should look as if they might have been cast (Figure 25-7).

**4** Finally, take the long rod and drill a line of four little holes at one end to give you fine-tuning choice when you come to the putting-together stage.

**FIGURE 25-7**

**Cut from end to middle so that you avoid running the blade into the end grain on the edge of the disk end.**

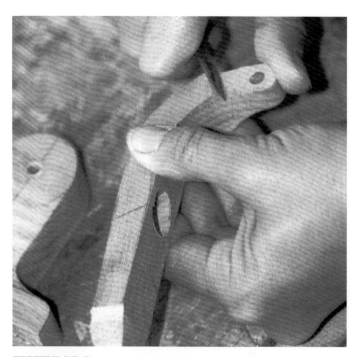

**FIGURE 25-8**

**Whittle the end of the arm so that it fits neatly between the pivot plates.**

## MAKING THE CONTROL ARM

**1** Have a look at the working drawings (Figure 25-2A), and see how the function of the arm is to sit heavily on the toothed wheel so that the back-dragging action of the finger-drag component can't pull the wheel in reverse. Note how the arm is pivoted between two plates that are fixed at either side of the stanchion feet, with the width of the arm being reduced so that it fits between the plates. See also how the arm is held in alignment by being threaded on a large dowel post that is socketed into the base slab, with the threading hole being shaped so as to allow for movement.

**2** When you have a clear picture of the shape and function of the arm, draw the image out on your chosen wood and fret it out on the scroll saw.

**3** Run the holes through to match the diameter of your chosen dowels, and then use a knife to shape up the details—the narrowing at the tip and the pivot area, and the free shape around the large posthole (Figure 25-8).

## MAKING THE TOOTHED WHEEL

**1** Use a compass to draw two circles, one within the other—the outer with a radius of 1½", and the inner with a radius of about 1¼". Use a pair of dividers to run 22 equal step-offs around the circumference of the large circle. You could use math and a protractor to set the size

of the step-offs (360° divided by 22 = 16.36°), but it's so much easier to go for a guesstimate size and to work the step-offs out by trial and error. Draw radius lines from the resultant intersections. Lastly, draw diagonals across each of the step-offs.

**2** With all the guidelines in place, use a band or scroll saw and slowly cut out the teeth (Figure 25-9).

## ASSEMBLY AND FINISHING

**1** Now comes the finger-aching task of having a dry run put together. Don't worry about fine sanding at this stage; just make sure that everything is tickety-boo and all present and correct (Figure 25-10)—no splits or warping. When you are satisfied that all is correct, wipe the surfaces (barring those that are going to be glued) with a small amount of oil.

**2** Set the two stanchions in place on the base and fix them with stubs of dowel.

**3** Fit the control arm post, slide the main pivots in place in the stanchions, and fit the drive wheel (Figure 25-11).

**FIGURE 25-9**
**Don't be tempted to rush this task. The teeth need to be cut with care, and, more than that, the band saw is potentially a very dangerous machine.**

**FIGURE 25-10**
**Give all the component parts a swift rub down—just enough to remove the worst of the sawn edges—and then give them their first wipe over with oil.**

**4** Take the control arm, pivot it between the little plates (Figure 25-12), and then fix it in position at the bottom of the drive wheel stanchion.

**5** With the control arm in place and located on the alignment post, slide the toothed wheel on its pivot, and make fine adjustments—to the pointed end of the arm and/or the size of the alignment post hole (Figure 25-13).

**6** Pivot the little finger-drag block in place in one or other of the four holes (Figure 25-14). Note that you might well need to drill another hole—it all depends on the shape of your finger-drag and the shape of the teeth on your wheel.

**FIGURE 25-11**
**Fit the large-diameter dowel rod in the center of the stanchion. Note the spacer that is used to distance the crank so that it doesn't wander from side to side.**

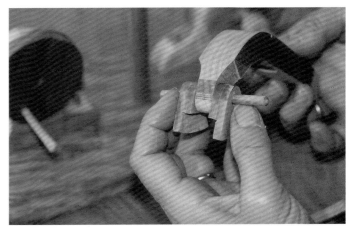

**FIGURE 25-12**
**I built each pivot plate up in two layers so that the two plates could be stepped at either side of the stanchion.**

**FIGURE 25-13**

**Fiddle around with the length of the arm and the shape of the posthole until the painted end of the arm comes nicely to rest on the toothed wheel.**

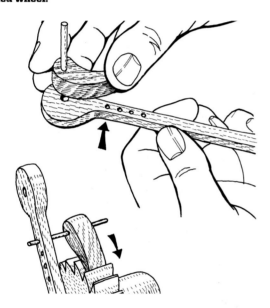

**FIGURE 25-14**

**Locate the little pivot in one of the four holes in the shaft of the rod, as indicated by the top black arrow above.**

**7** Fit the short crank rod in place, set the finger-drag in position, and then link the drive wheel and the top of the short crank with the long crank. The long dowel at bottom right gets cut back later (Figure 25-15).

**8** When you have struggled to get all the parts in place, then have a trial turn and see if the finger-drag does its thing (Figure 25-16). Be mindful that you might have to make adjustments to one or all of the moving parts.

**9** When you have achieved what you consider to be a good movement, then disassemble, and rub all the parts down to a fine finish.

**FIGURE 25-15**

**If the length of the rod is such that the finger-drag unit fails to do its stuff, then consider fitting the drag in the next hole down.**

**FIGURE 25-16**

**When you have got the movement right, you can cut the various dowels to length and fit the holding pins.**

**10** Finally, glue up, rub the whole works down with oil, let the oil dry, and wax polish. Then the machine is finished and ready for showing.

## PROBLEM SOLVING

• If you look closely at Figure 10-15, you will see that there is a drilled hole on the top end of the short crank rod, just to the left of the pivot. This is a mistake that occurred when I was trying to figure out how to fit the finger-drag component.

• If the side-to-side movements of the two crank rods are a bit slack and messy, then you might well consider sandwiching the long rod between a couple of posts.

• If you decide to use a band saw to cut the toothed wheel, then you must for safety's sake control the workpiece with a couple of push sticks—it's too small to be handheld.

# Screw Jack

## PROJECT BACKGROUND

The screw jack is a mechanism in common use for raising heavy weights through short lifts. It consists of a powerful combination of teeth and pinions enclosed in a metal frame, stock or box. If you are interested in math and have got a year or two to spend reading up, then there is a whole mountain of figures on the screw jack: the ratio between the number of teeth, the diameter of the wheel, the length of the handle, and so on. All you really need to know is that if a man or woman is able to raise about 50 pounds in weight, then they will, by means of a jack, be able to raise about twenty times this weight (about 5 tons). The jack is usually fitted out with a simple mechanism known as a pall and/or ratchet that stops the motion when it begins to run back.

## PROJECT OVERVIEW

The jack is made up of three primary parts: the small gear wheel, the large gear wheel, and the long toothed bar or rack—all pegged and pivoted on a frame. The toothed and slotted rack is held in place by means of a long plate, with the two dowels that run through the plate also controlling the height of the movement. The little pall mechanism that sits just above the large wheel is pegged into a slot in such a way that it rises, falls and jams the mechanism so that the rack is held in place. When you want to bring the rack down, you simply raise the pall, flip it over and then wind back. The success of the project has to do with cutting the teeth. If you like working with rule and compass, and if you have a scroll saw, then you are going to get a good deal of pleasure from this project.

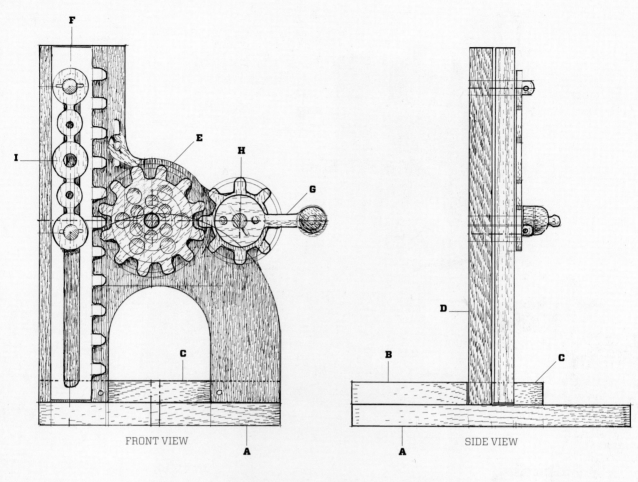

FRONT VIEW

SIDE VIEW

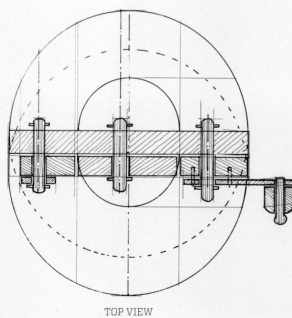

TOP VIEW

### FIGURE 26-2A

**Apart from the rack and the wheels (which need to be drawn correctly), the only other things you have to worry about are the positions of the wheel pivots to one another, and of the two wheels in relation to the rack.**

**A** Base plate.

**B** Frame support.

**C** Dais.

**D** Frame.

**E** Large gear wheel.

**F** Rack.

**G** Crank handle.

**H** Small gear wheel.

**I** Washer plate.

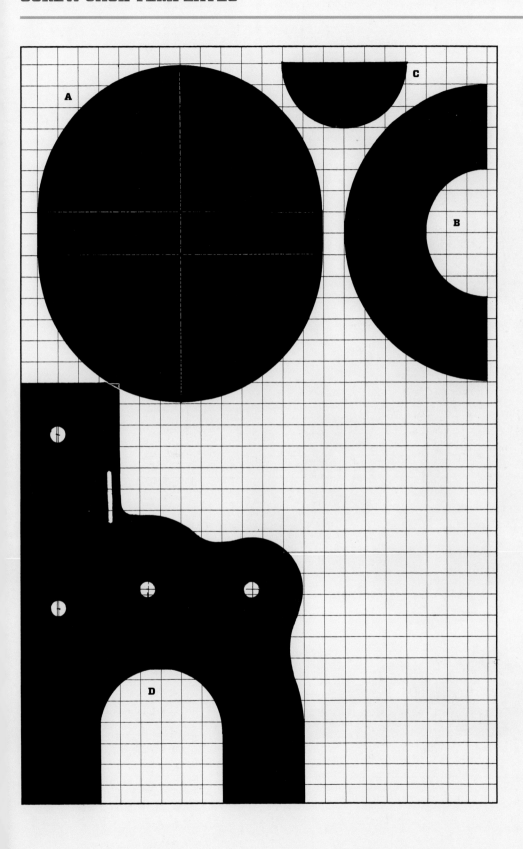

**FIGURE 26-2B**

**The scale is two grid squares to 1".**

**A** Base plate.

**B** Frame support.

**C** Dais.

**D** Frame.

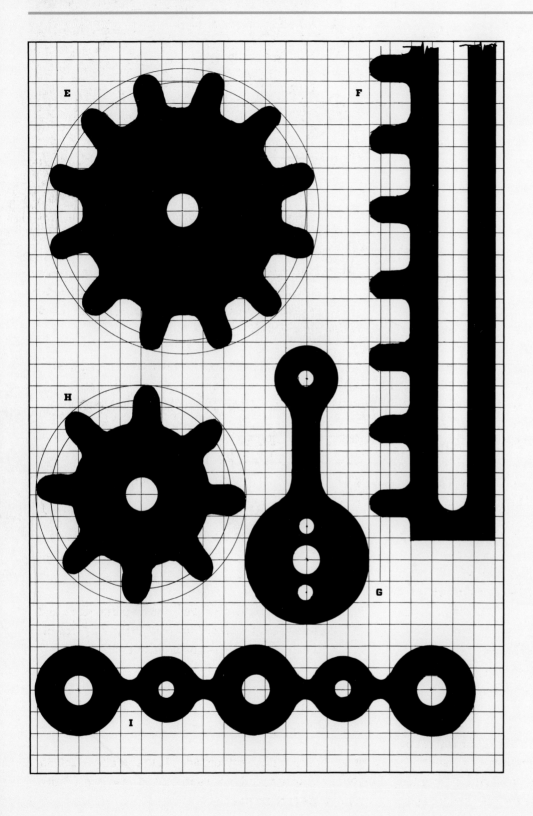

**FIGURE 26-2C**

**The scale is four grid squares to 1".**

**E**  Large gear wheel.

**F**  Rack.

**G**  Crank handle.

**H**  Small gear wheel.

**I**  Washer plate.

## CUTTING LIST

| A | Base plate | $3/4 \times 8 \times 9$ oak |
|---|---|---|
| B | Frame support | $3/4 \times 8 \times 8$ oak |
| C | Dais | Cut from frame support |
| D | Frame | $3/4 \times 8 \times 12$ cedar |
| E | Large gear wheel | $3/4 \times 3^{1}/_2 \times 3^{1}/_2$ walnut |
| F | Rack | $3/4 \times 2^{1}/_2 \times 12$ pine |
| G | Crank handle | $1/4 \times 2 \times 3^{1}/_2$ mahogany |
| H | Small gear wheel | $3/4 \times 3 \times 3$ oak |
| I | Washer plate | $1/4 \times 1^{1}/_4 \times 6$ plum |

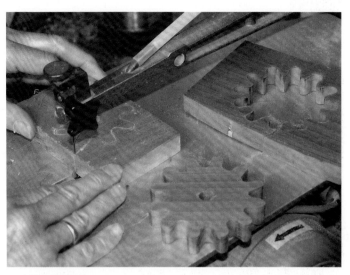

FIGURE 26-3

**Take extra care when you are fretting out the wheels. Keep the line of cut slightly to the waste side of the drawn line, and make sure that the saw table is correctly set—meaning at right angles to the run of the blade.**

## CHOOSING YOUR WOOD

This is one of those projects where you need to be pretty choosy over your wood. I say this because the success of the project hinges on the teeth being cut and worked with care—with all the teeth being nicely shaped. And of course, it's no good working with a loose-grained easy-to-cut wood that is likely to split and/or crumble. If a tooth splits off, then the project is ruined. What all this amounts to is that the wood needs to be hard and dense grained, so that it leaves the saw with the edges being hard and well defined. I used salvaged cedar for the frame, walnut for the large wheel, oak for the small wheel, straight-grained pine for the rack, oak for the base, and bits and bobs for all the rest. If you are short of wood, then it is best to save the choice bits for the toothed components—meaning the two wheels and the rack.

## MAKING THE FRAME AND BASE

**1** When you have spent a good long time studying the working drawings and designs—so that you have a clear picture in your mind as to what goes where and how—take the wood that you have chosen for the frame and the base, and plane it down to a finished thickness of about $3/4$". Not to worry if it's a wee bit thicker, as long as it's a uniform thickness overall.

**2** Notice how the frame and the base plate are in the main achieved by using a compass, and the little dais piece is no more or less than the waste cut from the frame support. This done, then use the rule, square and compass to set the lines of the design out on the best face of the wood.

**3** Fret the profile out on the scroll saw.

**4** Establish the precise position of the various pivot holes, then run them through with a bit size to match up with the diameter of your chosen dowels.

## MAKING THE GEAR WHEELS AND THE RACK

**1** Plane your wood to a finished thickness of about $3/4$" for both wheels and the rack.

**2** Use a compass to draw the two circles out on the wood—the large one with a radius of $1^{5}/_8$", the small one with a radius of $1^{1}/_4$".

**3** Trace the designs from your working drawings, and then transfer the traced imagery to the best face of the wood. Use the circles as an alignment guide.

**4** Run the three components through with drilled holes—at the center of the two wheels and at each end of the rack slot.

**5** Fit a new fine-toothed blade in the scroll saw, adjust the tension, and make sure that the saw table is at a right angle to the blade.

**6** Finally, fret out the design. Take your time and go slowly so that all the sawn faces are crisp and smooth (Figure 26-3).

**FIGURE 26-4**

Do your best to ensure that the sawn lines are smooth-running and nicely curved. If the saw feels to be hard going, then wax the table to cut down on friction, and check that the blade is in good condition and well tensioned.

## MAKING THE WASHER PLATE AND THE CRANK HANDLE

**1** Plane your chosen wood down to a thickness between $^3/_{16}$" and $^1/_4$".

**2** Draw the imagery out on the best face of the wood, run the holes through with the appropriate size bits, and then fret the profiles out on the scroll saw. Go at it very slowly, all the while doing your very best to ensure that the line of cut is crisp and smooth—no stop-start steps or ragged cuts (Figure 26-4).

**3** When you have achieved the cut-out for the crank handle, first drill the two peg-fixing holes—through the crank and the small wheel—and then take a small knife and trim the arm to a rounded finish (Figure 26-5).

## ASSEMBLY AND FINISHING

**1** When you have achieved all the component parts that go to make up the project, set them out best face uppermost, and systematically check them over for potential problems (Figure 26-6). Okay, so I always say this, but the sad fact is that projects of this type and character are often less than beautiful, or are that much less successful, simply because such and such a part is flawed or needs to be re-cut.

**2** Don't worry at this trial run stage about a fine finish; just make sure that the edges are free from splinters and jags.

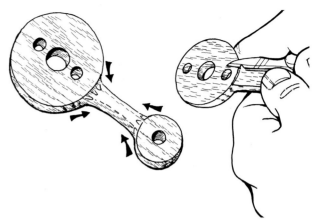

**FIGURE 26-5**

Whittle the arm to a rounded finish so that a little curve runs down from the flat face of the circle. Work from ends through to center.

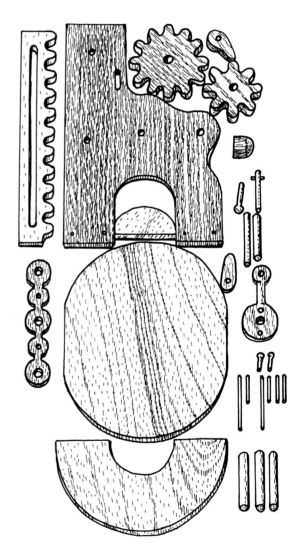

**FIGURE 26-6**

Check the components to make sure they are free from splits, and then give them a swift rub down in readiness for the dry trial run putting together.

**FIGURE 26-7**

Set the frame up on the base, and fix the large wheel in place.
Note the little fixing dowels that run through the bottom of the
frame and into the frame support.

**3** Fit the frame support to the base slab, set the large
wheel on its pivot, and fix the frame in place with
dry dowels.

**4** Make sure the frame is stable and true-firm, square
and free from wobble (Figure 26-7).

**5** Set the guide dowels in place in the frame so that
they are a tight push fit. Set the rack in place, with
its teeth nicely interlocked with the gear wheel, and turn
the wheel over to check out the movement. If need be,
adjust the dowels and/or the slot so that the rack is able to
move without hindrance (Figure 26-8).

**6** Fit the little pall foot in the slot, and fix it in place
with a backing plate so that it is loose fitting and
able to fall freely (Figure 26-9). Test it out to see if it jams
the mechanism.

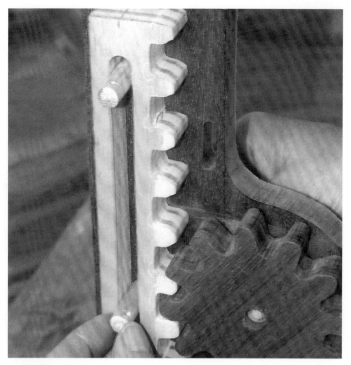

**FIGURE 26-8**

Fit the frame on its pegs and test out the movement. If necessary,
ease the movement by widening the slot and/or slightly reducing
the diameter of the dowels.

**FIGURE 26-9**

The idea is that the pall should be free to rise in its slots, with the
little backing plate ensuring that the pall is held square to the
front of the frame.

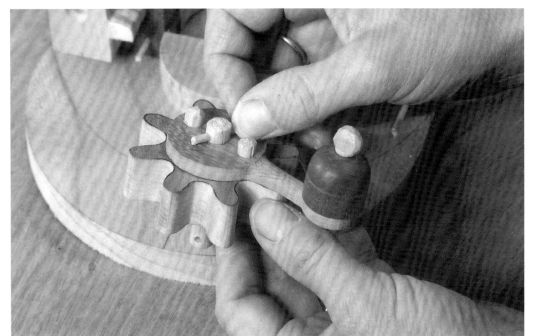

**FIGURE 26-10**
Have a small wooden pin running through the dowel pivot so that the wheel is free to move. Note the whittled end of the through-knob dowel pin.

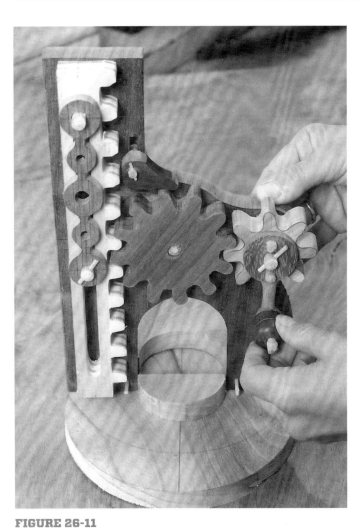

**FIGURE 26-11**
Generally ease the components until the movement is smooth.

**FIGURE 26-12**
Blind holes are best achieved with a Forstner bit. Note how the pattern of decorative holes relates to the pattern of teeth.

**7** Set the crank handle on the small wheel, and fit it in place with a couple of dowels so that the crank and the wheel become a single clenched unit (Figure 26-10). Whittle a pivot to run through the knob, so that the end of the pivot becomes a design feature.

**8** Set the small wheel in place and fix it at the back with a small wooden pin. Have a trial run and see how the movement functions (Figure 26-11). If one or other of the teeth jams, then ease it with a fold of fine-grade sandpaper.

**9** When you have achieved a good easy movement— with all the component parts running smoothly one against another—then pencil label the teeth so that you can identically refit.

**10** Disassemble the whole works, and spend time adding the decorative features like the pattern of blind holes on the front face of the large wheel (Figure 26-12).

**11** Rub all the sawn edges down to a smooth finish. Pay particular attention to the sharp corners of the teeth (Figure 26-13).

**12** Finally, give the parts a coat of teak oil; let it dry. Give the surfaces another swift sanding, glue up, burnish with beeswax polish, and the project is finished.

## PROBLEM SOLVING

• Be mindful that there are three main factors governing the smooth running movement of the teeth: the shape of the teeth, the shape of the gaps between the teeth, and the distance apart of the pivots.
• If you want to make sure that the movement is going to work the first time around, then it would be a good idea to cut a second frame board made from inexpensive wood. You can thus ensure that the pivot spacings are perfectly placed for the size of your wheels.
• If you have made a mess-up and you need to alter the position of the pivot holes, the procedure is as follows: plug and glue the holes with a dowel cut from matching wood, sand back to a smooth finish, and then drill a new hole.
• Be mindful that a good waxing is one sure-fire way of ensuring that mating components run smooth.

# The Bicycle Chain Machine

## PROJECT BACKGROUND

When I was a kid, I used to spend hours taking my bicycle apart. My big thing in life at that time was making bicycles from scrounged parts and then selling them to my school-mates. I particularly enjoyed taking the drive chain apart.

The bicycle chain is a beautiful item—lots of identical component parts, all made of steel, fitting together to make something both strong and flexible. The earliest known sketches of a bicycle (or drive) chain were made by Leonardo da Vinci. The curious thing about his sketches is that it appears he was inventing components before there was a real need—a bit like inventing the electric coffee maker before the invention of electricity!

## PROJECT OVERVIEW

Have a look at the project picture, the working drawings (Figure 27-2A) and the templates (Figure 27-2B). The machine is made up of a stand, two dowel pivots and two drive-chain wheels, with the actual

chain being made up from a large number of identical links. If you look closely at the chain, you will see that the links are first grouped in pairs, with the pairs then being linked to each other. The distance between the centers of neighboring half-circle notches—this being the tooth—is of necessity the same as the distance between the centers of the dowel pins on the drive chain. As the wheels turn, it is the half-circle notches that locate and pull on the chain.

As you might well imagine, the important thing about this project is that the notch centers and the link hole centers must be the same. Note how there are 16 notches around the circumference of each wheel, with each notch being centered on the intersection of a radial line and the circumference. See also how the 16 radial lines are equally spaced at 22.5° intervals (360 divided by 16 = 22.5). One look at the various photographs should confirm that this is one of those projects that require an electric scroll saw.

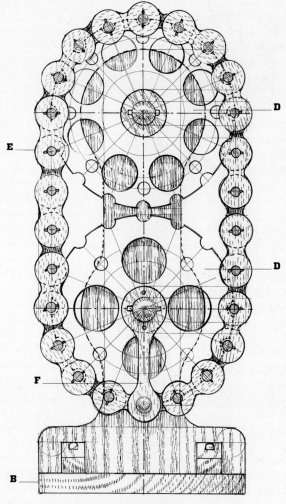

FRONT VIEW

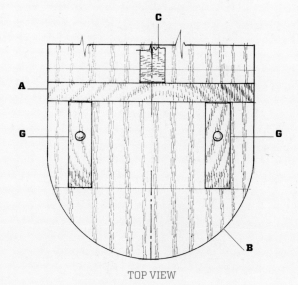

TOP VIEW

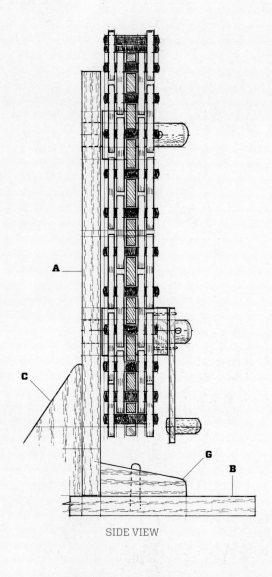

SIDE VIEW

## FIGURE 27-2A

**With this model, the critical measurements are the distance between link pivots, the length of the links, and the spacing and position of the notches on the drive wheels.**

**A** Stand.

**B** Base.

**C** Back buttress.

**D** Drive-chain wheel.

**E** Link.

**F** Crank arm.

**G** Front support.

**H** Spacers.

# THE BICYCLE CHAIN MACHINE TEMPLATES

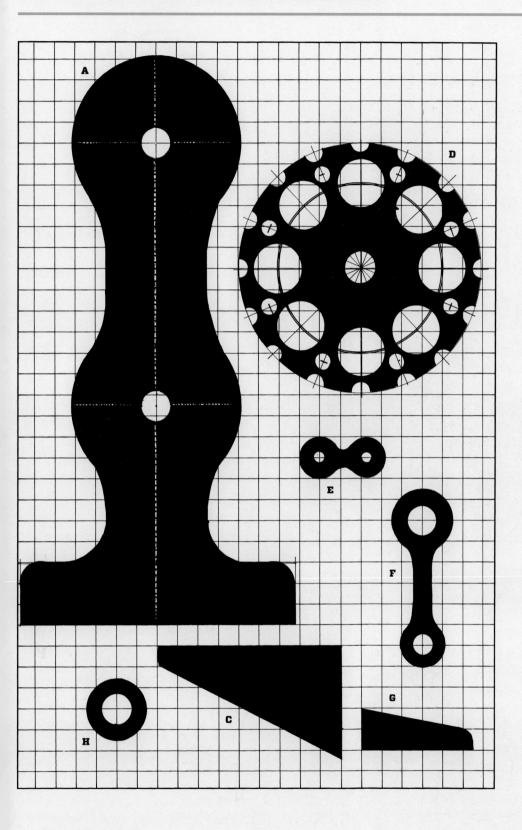

**FIGURE 27-2B**

**The scale is two grid squares to 1".**

**A** Stand.

**B** Base.

**C** Back buttress.

**D** Drive-chain wheel.

**E** Link.

**F** Crank arm.

**G** Front support.

**H** Spacers.

## CUTTING LIST

| A | Stand | $3/4 \times 7 \times 15$ pitch pine |
|---|---|---|
| B | Base | $3/4 \times 7 \times 12$ pitch pine |
| C | Back buttress | $3/4 \times 3 \times 5$ |
| D | Drive-chain wheel | $5/8 \times 7 \times 7$ brown oak |
| E | Link | $5/16 \times 1^1/2 \times 2^1/2$ cherry |
| F | Crank arm | $5/16 \times 2 \times 5$ |
| G | Front support | $3/4 \times 1^1/4 \times 3$ |
| H | Spacers | $1 \times 2 \times 2$ |

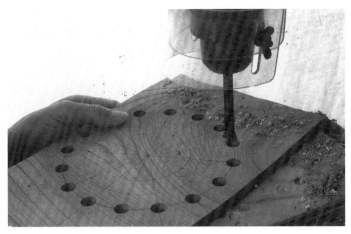

**FIGURE 27-3**

**Having drawn out the 16 radial lines so that they are perfectly placed at 22.5" intervals, then make sure that the drill bit is accurately centered on the radial-circumference intersections.**

## CHOOSING YOUR WOOD

The two main factors that determine the choice of wood used for the wheels and the chain links are strength and thickness. While the wheels and the links need to be worked from relatively thin section wood, the wood also needs to be strong. And the wood needs to be easy to work on the scroll saw.

For a mix of these reasons, I decided to use straight-grained pine for the base and the stand, English brown oak for the drive wheels, and pine and cherry for the chain links. I used two wood types for the links because the color contrast made it that much easier to put the chain together.

## MAKING THE STAND

**1** First study the working drawings (Figure 27-2A) so that you have a clear understanding of the tool and technique implications of the project. Take the wood that you have chosen for the base board, the stand back, the buttress and the two supports, and plane it to a finished thickness of $5/8$".

**2** Set the stand backboard out with a center line that runs in the direction of the grain. Draw in the various lines that go to make up the design. Note that the pivot center points are set $6^1/4$" apart.

**3** When you are satisfied with the setting out, then cut the profiles out on the scroll saw.

**4** Lastly, decide on the dowel size that you are going to use for the pivots and run them through with the appropriate size bit.

## MAKING THE DRIVE-CHAIN WHEELS

**1** Having chosen your wood and planed it to a uniform thickness of $3/16$", set your compass to a radius of 3", and draw out the two 6"-diameter circles.

**2** Use the tools of your choice to divide the circle up into 16 identical segments. You can use a protractor or a mix of a compass and the square—there are any number of options. A pretty good way is to set your compass to a guesstimate measurement, and then to repeatedly make step-offs around the circumference, making adjustments until you come up with the correct measurement. Another good way is to cut out a paper circle and then to fold it in half, and half again, and half again, until there are 16 divisions.

**3** Draw lines from the 16 step-offs through to the center of the circle, and then take a drill bit of a size to match your dowel and work around the circumference, running holes through the intersections. The important thing here is that the holes are perfectly centered on the circumference-radial intersections, and so placed that all 16 are set the same distance apart from each other (Figure 27-3).

**4** Not forgetting that you will at a later stage be drilling a pattern of decorative holes, now is the time to draw in as many guidelines as you think are necessary.

**5** Finally, when all the holes are in place, move to the scroll saw and very carefully fret out the circle (Figure 27-4).

## MAKING THE LINKS

**1** Take the wood that you have chosen for the links and plane it to a finished thickness of about $^3/_{16}$".

**2** Cut the wood down so that you have 52 little tablets at about $1^1/_8$" wide by $2^1/_2$" long.

**3** Set each tablet out with a center line that runs in the direction of the grain. Take the compass; set it to a radius of about $^1/_2$". Spike the point on the center line, and, placed as near as it can go to the end of the tablet, draw out the circle. This done, set the compass to the same measurement that you used to work around the circumference of the wheel, and then step-off from the center of the circle to a point on the center line. Draw another 1"-diameter circle at this point. If you have got it right, the distance between centers will be slightly greater than the diameter of the circles. Link the two circles up with a little freehand radius. Repeat this procedure until you have 52 or more links. I decided to make 60—my thinking being that there would be mess-ups along the way.

**4** Take a drill bit that matches the diameter of your chosen dowels and run each link through with two holes.

**5** With at least 52 links drawn and drilled, then move to the scroll saw and carefully fret them out (Figure 27-5). Don't worry too much if the profiles are askew, as long as the holes are perfectly placed.

**6** When you have achieved the 52 links, take a small sharp knife and spend time whittling the sawn edges to a rounded finish. Work with the run of the grain from the peaks down into the dips, and from the peaks and around the ends (Figure 27-6).

## ASSEMBLY AND FINISHING

**1** When you have achieved all the component parts that go to make up the design, spread them out and generally check them over for fit, finish and number. I say number because it's the easiest thing in the world, with a complex project of this character, to make a mess-up with your counting and finish up with a few links too short. And, as no doubt you know, there is nothing quite so annoying in woodwork as getting all ready for the final putting together only to find that you have got to go back to starters and cut more components.

**FIGURE 27-4**

**The line of cut must run very slightly to the waste side of the drawn line. If you fit a new blade and make sure that it is well tensioned, and if you work at an easy pace, then you will finish up with a cut line that requires the minimum of sanding.**

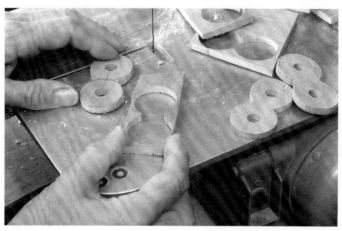

**FIGURE 27-5**

**Bridge the sharp angles between the circles with hand-drawn radius curves so that the resultant "8" shape is smooth curved and easy to cut.**

**FIGURE 27-6**

**Trim off the sharp corners so that you finish up with a form that is round-edged.**

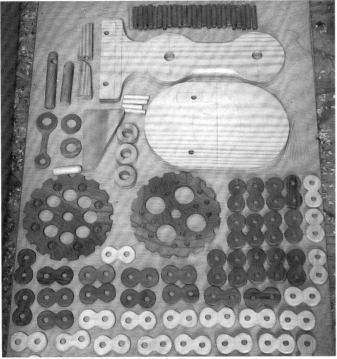

**FIGURE 27-7**

If, when you line all the component parts up side by side, you see that one or other of the links stands out as being too big, or too small, or whatever, then now is the time to throw it out and cut another one.

**2** As a trial dry run, put together—no fine sanding or glue at this stage—drill, dowel and fit the backboard to the base, the buttress to the back of the stand, and the two supports to the front.

**3** Set the two main dowel pivots in place in their holes, and slide the various spacers in place (Figure 27-8).

**4** Take the links, group them in matched pairs, and set each pair up with dowel pivots (Figure 27-9) so that the links are set together at the middle of the dowel. You need thirteen pairs in all.

**5** Set the paired links end to end in a row, and join them together with links set to the outside. You will find that the trick here is in arranging the paired links so that the dowel centers from neighboring groups are nicely matched (Figure 27-10). If necessary, use a fold of sandpaper to make the dowels slightly thinner and/or the holes slightly larger.

**6** When you have made the total chain, gently ease the links apart so that the chain fits over the edge of the drive wheels (Figure 27-11).

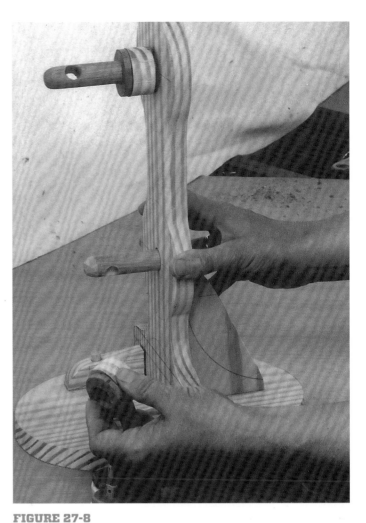

**FIGURE 27-8**

The buttress and supports ensure that the stand is true and well supported—most important with a machine of this height.

**FIGURE 27-9**

Fiddle and fuss around until the paired links are well matched, so that the dowels are parallel to each other.

**7** At this stage in the operation, you will perhaps find, as you roll the chain over the wheel, that the ends of neighboring links jam. This is because the holes are badly placed and/or the profile has been badly sawn. If this is the case, then take a scrap of sandpaper and gently sand back the shape of the links until the problem is corrected (Figure 27-12).

**8** When you have joined up the ends of the chain and generally spaced the links, gently lift the whole works up and set the two wheels on their pivots. If necessary, ease the position of the dowels for best fit (Figure 27-13).

**9** Turn the wheels slowly over by hand, and see how the individual links sit one with another. Study the way that the dowel pins come to rest in the notches and how the ends of the links relate to each other. Make adjustments accordingly (Figure 27-14).

**10** Fit the spacer and the crank handle, and try everything out for size. Of course, the handle won't actually be turning the wheel at this stage—because it's not pegged to the wheel—but you will at least be able to test out the feel of the machine. The other thing to bear in mind is that you have choices—you can fit the handle to the top pivot, as shown in this photograph, or you can fit it to the bottom, as shown in the working drawings (Figure 27-2A). As to the best position, much depends on the weight of your wood and the size of your hand. For example, if the wood is weighty and the machine top-heavy, then it would be a good idea to lower the center of gravity by having the handle on the bottom wheel. But then again, if your hands are large and the turning space is tight, then it might be a better idea to have the handle on the top wheel. It needs thinking about.

**11** When you are satisfied with the movement, slowly disassemble the whole works, carefully pencil numbering the links as you go so that you know the order of things.

**12** Sand all the components to a fine finish, oil the appropriate surfaces, and then glue up. Finally, burnish all the surfaces with wax, and the project is finished.

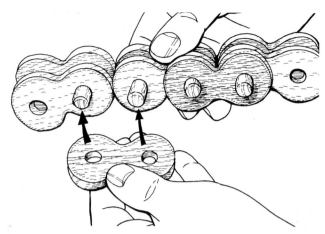

**FIGURE 27-10**

**The outer links need to be matched so that they also hold the dowels parallel to each other.**

**FIGURE 27-11**

**Part the links and slide the wheel in place.**

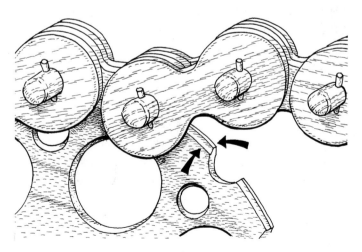

**FIGURE 27-12**

**Once the chain has been fitted, then you can, to a great extent, adjust the fit by sanding a chamfer on the edge of the wheel—on both sides, so that the teeth are slightly beveled.**

**FIGURE 27-13**

**The whole thing gets a bit weighty and difficult to handle at this stage, so be on your guard that everything doesn't spring apart. I needed to push a few pegs through some of the dowel pins.**

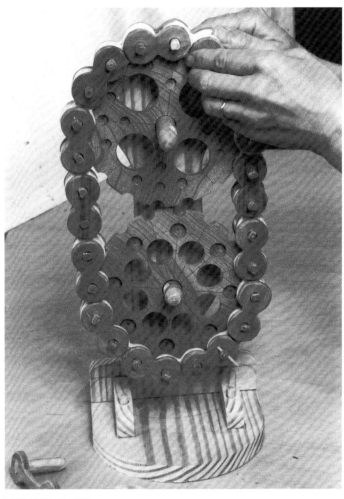

**FIGURE 27-14**

**Make sure that you ease the chain over the wheel so that there is close contact with the link dowels sitting nicely in the wheel notches.**

## PROBLEM SOLVING

• The big difficulty with this project is drawing out and cutting the links. The problem isn't that the individual procedures are particularly difficult; only the sum total of cutting each and every link to the same size and drilling perfect-every-time holes calls for a certain regimented way of working. One way out of this problem is to build a drilling jig. In action, you drill one hole, slide the link on the jig, and then drill the other hole. This way of working ensures that the holes are all set the same distance apart.

• In the light of having made this machine, I think that next time around I will go for much smaller links—say half the size. I will have the wood much thinner, the pivots smaller and the wheels with twice as many notches. I will use a wood like European box or English plum. All that said, I think that it's vital to have a go at this machine before trying for something smaller.

• If you find that the movement is loose and sloppy, then it could well be that the links and/or the wheels are badly cut, with the effect that the chain is loose. If this is the case, then you could modify the machine by designing and fitting a mechanism that moved one or other of the wheels up and down and then clamped it in place. You could have the pivot moving in a slot rather than a drilled hole, or you could make the stand so that top and bottom can be moved apart.

• If you think that the height of the stand is a bit clumsy, then you could change it about so that the two wheels are set side by side—more like a bicycle.

# The Wonderful Wilmhurst Machine

## PROJECT BACKGROUND

A Wilmhurst machine is an apparatus that is used to demonstrate and produce static electricity. We had such a machine at school. It was a bit like an H.G. Wells time machine—a huge affair with two glass disks, brass rods, metal balls, drive pulleys and crank handles, all mounted on a mahogany base. In action, the massive handle was turned, the two wheels zoomed around in different directions and two metal foil brushes stroked the wheels while they were turning, with the effect that electricity was generated and the thing began to produce a series of snappy, banging and fizzy sparks—really amazing!

## PROJECT OVERVIEW

Have a look at the working drawings (Figure 28-2A) and the templates (Figure 28-2B). The Wilmhurst machine is made up from a base with two stanchions, with all the workings being pivoted on two horizontal dowel shafts. The small pulley wheels on the top shaft are glued to the disk plates, while the large pulley wheels on the bottom shaft are glued to the shaft itself. Perhaps most importantly, one of the two pulley belts (both made of cord or elastic) is twisted into a figure eight so that it reverses the direction of spin of one disk.

# THE WONDERFUL WILMHURST MACHINE WORKING DRAWING

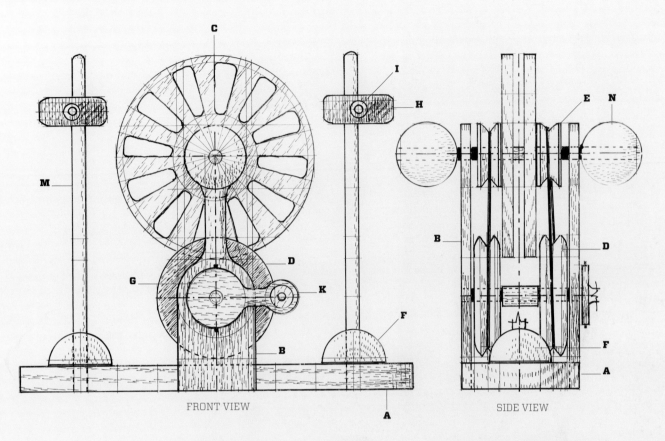

FRONT VIEW

SIDE VIEW

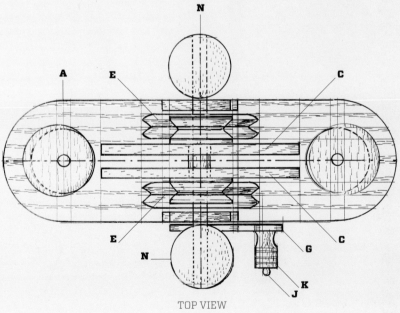

TOP VIEW

## FIGURE 28-2A

**With this project, note that the spacers (the parts set between the wheels and the pulleys) need to be sized so that the pulley wheels are aligned one above the other.**

**A** Base.

**B** Stanchion.

**C** Disk plate.

**D** Large pulley wheel.

**E** Small pulley wheel.

**F** Half balls.

**G** Crank handle.

**H** Post finial.

**I** Post pin.

**J** Drive knob pin.

**K** Knob.

**L** Drive shaft.

**M** Post.

**N** Balls.

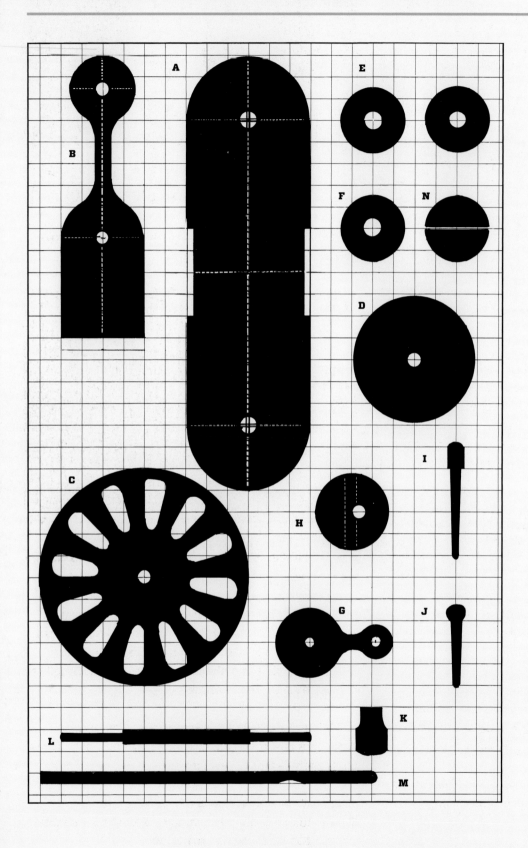

**FIGURE 28-2B**

**The scale is two grid squares to 1".**

**A** Base.

**8** Stanchion.

**C** Disk plate.

**D** Large pulley wheel.

**E** Small pulley wheel.

**F** Half balls.

**G** Crank handle.

**H** Post finial.

**I** Post pin.

**J** Drive knob pin.

**K** Knob.

**L** Drive shaft.

**M** Post.

**N** Balls.

## CUTTING LIST

| | | |
|---|---|---|
| A | Base | $3/4 \times 3^1/_2 \times 11$ pitch pine |
| B | Stanchion | $1/2 \times 2^1/_2 \times 8$ mahogany |
| C | Disk plate | $1/2 \times 6 \times 6$ brown oak |
| D | Large pulley wheel | $3/4 \times 3^1/_2 \times 3^1/_2$ cherry |
| E | Small pulley wheel | $3/4 \times 2^1/_2 \times 2^1/_2$ cherry |
| F | Half balls | From $2^1/_2$" square section beech |
| G | Crank handle | $3/8 \times 2^1/_2 \times 3^1/_2$ mahogany |
| H | Post finial | From $2^1/_2$" square section plum |
| I | Post pin | Cut from scrap |
| J | Drive knob pin | Cut from scrap |
| K | Knob | Turned from 1" square sections |
| L | Drive shaft | 4" long |
| M | Post | $8^1/_2$" long |
| N | Balls | From $2^1/_2$" square section beech |

## CHOOSING YOUR WOOD

The only real needs for the wood are that the disk plates be made from a wood that can be worked on the scroll saw, and the various balls be worked from a wood that can be turned. We used oak for the disk plates, pine for the stand, beech for the balls and stand supports, mahogany for the stanchions, a scrap of plum for the two post finials, and offcuts for the rest.

## MAKING THE BASE AND STANCHIONS

**1** Take the wood for the base slab and plane it to a finished thickness of $5/8$".

**2** Use the rule, compass and square to set out the profile, and then fret it out on the scroll saw. You should have a base at 3" wide and 10" long, with the ends being based on 3"-diameter half circles.

**3** Set the base out with four center lines—one that runs end to end to halve the width, one running across the width to halve the length, and the other two at each end to mark the diameter of the half circle.

**4** With all the guidelines in place, use a square to draw the stanchion laps in at $1/4$" deep and 2" long.

**FIGURE 28-3**

**Run the chisel with a sliding paring action so that the cut goes diagonally across the run of the grain.**

**FIGURE 28-4**

**Whittle from the drawn circles, so that the faces of the circles are left in flat relief.**

**5** Cut the laps with a saw and chisel. First, saw in at each end to establish the depth of the lap, and then use the chisel to make horizontal paring cuts (Figure 28-3). The trick is to make sure that you cut fractionally to the waste side of the drawn lines.

**6** Take the wood for the stanchions, plane it to a thickness of $1/4$", and use a rule and compass to draw out the profile for both stanchions.

**7** Fret the profiles out on the scroll saw, so that the bottom 1" is slightly oversize—about $2^1/_8$"—so that the width is too big to fit into the lap.

**8** Size the width of the stanchions until they are a tight push fit in the laps.

**9** Run the pivot points through with a bit to match the size of your dowel shafts, and use a knife to trim the neck of the stanchion down to a slightly round-edged finish. Work from end to middle so as to avoid running into the end grain curves (Figure 28-4).

## MAKING THE DISK PLATES

**1** Take your chosen wood and plane it to a finished thickness of about ⁵⁄₁₆". Sight across the wood so as to ensure that it's free from twisting, and then saw it in two so that you have a piece for each circle.

**2** Take a piece, set the compass to a radius of 2¹⁄₂", and draw out a single 5"-diameter circle. Now, still working from the same center, draw out circles with radiuses of 1" and 2¹⁄₄".

**3** Use the tools of your choice to divide the circle up into 24 equal 15° segments. I used an engineer's protractor, but you could just as well use a compass by stepping the radius off around the circumference and then quartering the resultant six divisions. You could even do it with a compass and by trial and error.

**4** When you have drawn out the circles and their 24 divisions, take a pencil and draw a corner radius in every other division so that you have 12 spokes and 12 round-cornered windows.

**5** When you have drawn the circle imagery out on one piece of wood, pin it to the other piece, with the little nails being set in the waste areas well outside the circle.

**6** Select a bit size to match the diameter of your chosen dowel, and run a hole through the center of the circle so that it runs through both pieces. Plug the hole with a short length of whittle dowel, then change the drill bit to a smaller size—say about ³⁄₁₆"—and run a hole through every other window.

**7** Finally, use the scroll saw to cut out the circle and the windows of waste (Figure 28-5).

## MAKING THE PULLEY WHEELS

**1** Look at the working drawings (Figure 28-2A); see how you need four pulley wheels in all—two at a 3" diameter, and two at a 1⁵⁄₈" diameter.

**FIGURE 28-5**

**Note the two holding pegs—one at the center of the circle, the other in the last window to be cut.**

**FIGURE 28-6**

**As you work around the wheel, you will need to be constantly changing the angle of cut to suit the run of the grain.**

**2** Plane your chosen wood down to a ⁵⁄₈" thickness, draw out the circles, drill the centers out with the appropriate bit size, and then cut the blanks out on the scroll saw.

**3** Take the disk blanks one at a time, and first run a pencil center line around the thickness, and then run lines about ¹⁄₈" in from the edges.

**4** Cut the V-section by first running a stop-cut around the center line. Slice in at an angle into the cut so that the waste falls away, and then deepen the stop-cut, and so on, until the V-section reaches the desired depth. The precise shape of the wheel is a matter of choice— I went for a slightly rounded feel (Figure 28-6), but you could just as well go for a crisp sharp-angled finish.

**FIGURE 28-7**

Though the riffler is a good tool for working hardwood, it's horrible for softwood—be warned.

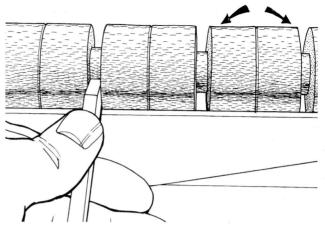

**FIGURE 28-8**

Sink the waste so that you can shape up the half ball.

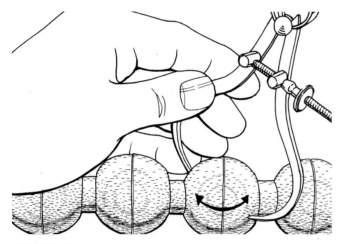

**FIGURE 28-9**

Make constant checks with the calipers to see how close you are getting to turning a perfect sphere.

**5** When you have whittled the pulleys more or less to shape, bring them to a good finish with a riffler file and the graded sandpapers (Figure 28-7).

## MAKING THE BALLS AND POST SUPPORTS

**1** Mount your square section wood on the lathe and swiftly turn it down to a smooth cylinder at about $1^5/_8$" diameter.

**2** Set the dividers to the diameter of the cylinder, and make step-offs along the cylinder—$^1/_4$" for tailstock waste, $1^5/_8$" for the first ball, $^1/_4$" for parting waste, $1^5/_8$" for the next ball, and so on along the length of the wood.

**3** Take the parting tool and sink the bands of waste in to a depth of about $^1/_2$" so that you are left with a central core at about $^5/_8$" (Figure 28-8).

**FIGURE 28-10**

The sticks ensure that your hands are clear of the blade. **DO NOT** attempt this procedure without the sticks.

**4** To make the ball shapes, use the skew chisel to shave the corners off the remaining $1^5/_8$"-diameter sections. If you work backward and forward along the wood with a little-by-little approach, you will eventually finish up with a string of balls—like beads on a necklace (Figure 28-9). Run a little line around each ball to mark the median.

**5** Part the balls off from the lathe and select the best of the bunch for the project. You need two complete balls for the end-of-shaft details, and two half balls for the base supports.

**6** Run all three balls through with $^1/_4$"-diameter holes. Take the ball that needs to be sliced in half, cut a couple of sticks to push in the ball so that you can hold it safely, and then slice it through on the band saw (Figure 28-10).

**FIGURE 28-11**

**Use a sanding board to rub the sawn faces down to a good finish. The stick saves your fingertips from damage.**

**7** Rub the two half balls down so that the sawn faces sit flat and firm so that the drilled holes are well aligned and square (Figure 28-11).

## ASSEMBLY AND FINISHING

**1** When you have made all the component parts, gather them on the bench and check them over for problems. Don't worry at this stage about a fine finish because this is a dry run put together; just make sure that the various parts are well cut and sound.

**2** Start by setting the two stanchions in place at either side of the base. Trim them to fit and set them upright so that they are at right angles to the base and parallel to each other.

**3** Slide the drive shaft through the stanchions— through the bottom hole—and fit the two large pulley wheels and the spacer. Be mindful that the shaft needs to be a loose fit through the stanchions and a tight fit through the wheels (Figure 28-12).

**4** Set the disk plate shaft in place, complete with the two disk plates and the small pulley wheels. This time around, the disks and the pulleys need to be a loose fit on the shaft, with the shaft being a loose fit through the stanchions, and the balls being a tight push fit on the ends of the shaft.

**5** The order along the length of the shaft is: ball, stanchion, pulley wheel, disk plate, spacer, disk plate, pulley, stanchion and ball.

**FIGURE 28-12**

**Cut the spacer to length so that it pushes the wheels out to within $^{1}/_{16}$" of the stanchions.**

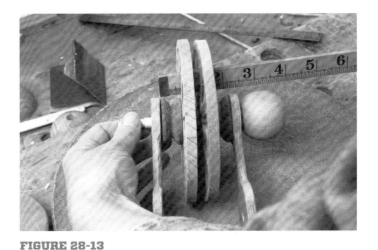

**FIGURE 28-13**

**Measure the spacing and decide if one or more of the parts needs to be modified.**

**6** Take a rule and decide whether or not one or more of the thicknesses needs to be adjusted (Figure 28-13).

**7** Consider how the position of the disk plates and the large pulley wheels is to a great extent governed by the spacers between the wheels, and then make adjustments accordingly.

**FIGURE 28-14**

**The ball ends govern the length of the shaft and the consequent placing of the components on the shaft.**

**FIGURE 28-15**

**The little peg runs through the side hole and glances off the notched posts to wedge the finial in place.**

**8** Trim the end of the shaft so as to make a spigot that is a tight fit in the ball (Figure 28-14).

**9** The finials at the top of the posts are no more than decorative details but are interesting to make. Held in place by a wedge pin, two holes are drilled through the pill shape so they intersect. The shaft is notched, the pill is slid into position, and a whittled pin is pushed in place so that it locates with the notch (Figure 28-15).

**10** The turned knob is held on the crank by means of a whittled pin. The shapes aren't too important as long as the knob is free to turn.

**11** At the end of it all, when all the parts are in place, then have a trial run to see if it's going to work. Of course, the plate disks won't turn at this stage, but you will at least be able to see if the large pulley wheels are going to do their stuff.

**12** Finally, disassemble the whole works, oil the components, rub down to a good finish, reassemble, wax, fit the drive cords and the machine is ready.

## PROBLEM SOLVING

• If you would like to give the laps a miss and go for another joint, then you could peg the stanchions to the edge of the base. If you go for this option, then you will need to modify the spacers accordingly.

• While just about everything can be modified—the size of the plates, the height of the stanchions, and all the rest—the only detail that you have to stay with is the alignment of the pulley wheels. The top and bottom wheels must be aligned so that they are set directly one pair above the other.

• If you don't have a lathe, then you could set the posts directly in the base and miss out the supports, and you could go for pins run through the ends of the drive shaft instead of having the balls.

• If you have trouble getting the drive cords to grip, then you can use waxed yarn, rubber bands or rubber belts borrowed from children's construction kits, or even the drive belts from video players.

# Index

First published in the UK in 2012 by
**Fine Folio Publishing**
6 Bourne Terrace, Bourne Hill, Wherstead,
Ipswich, Suffolk, IP2 8NG, UK

ISBN 978-0-9570969-3-6

1 3 5 7 9 10 8 6 4 2

Designer: **Glyn Bridgewater**
Illustrator: **Gill Bridgewater**
Editor: **Alison Copland**

Printed and bound by
**Voion Printing Group (International) Co., Ltd**
Unit 305-306, 3rd Floor, Yen Sheng Centre,
64 Hoi Yuen Road, Kwun Tong, KLN, Hong Kong